Accountancy in Transition

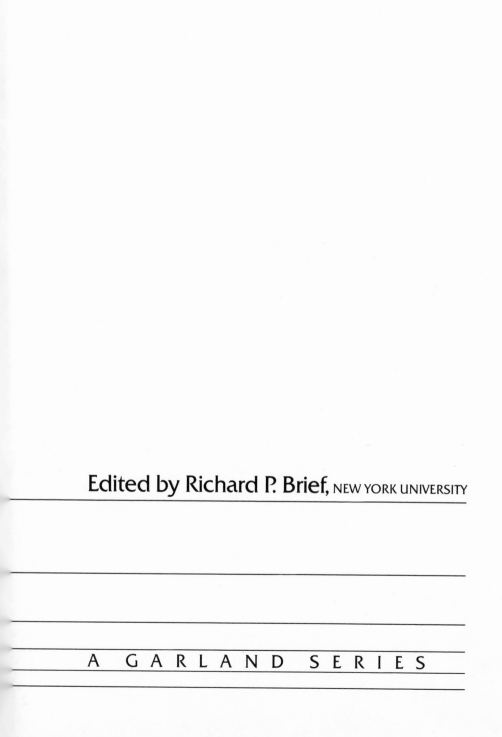

Edited by Richard P. Brief, NEW YORK UNIVERSITY

A GARLAND SERIES

Accounting Queries

Harold C. Edey

Garland Publishing, Inc.
New York & London   1982

ACKNOWLEDGMENTS

"Published Accounts as an Aid to Investment" and "Thinking in Figures" are reprinted by permission of *The Accountant.*

"Reflections on the Accounting Provisions of the Companies Act, 1948," "The True and Fair View," and "Why All-Purpose Accounts Will Not Do" are reprinted by permission of *Accountancy.*

"A Note on Reserves, Provisions and Profits," "Income and Capital in Income Taxation—Distributions by Companies," "Accounting Principles and Business Reality," and "Accounting Standards in the British Isles" are reprinted by permission of The Institute of Chartered Accountants in England and Wales.

"Accuracy and Innaccuracy in Profit Calculation" is reprinted by permission of *The Modern Law Review.*

"Company Accounting in the Nineteenth and Twentieth Centuries" is reprinted by permission of The Association of Certified Accountants.

"The Valuation of Stock in Trade for Income Tax Purposes," "Income and the Valuation of Stock-in-Trade," "Business Valuation, Goodwill and the Super-Profit Method," and "Deprival Value and Financial Accounting" are reprinted by permission of Sweet and Maxwell Ltd.

"Memorandum of Evidence to the Jenkins Committee" is reprinted by permission of Her Majesty's Stationery Office.

"Company Accounts in Britain: The Jenkins Report" is reprinted by permission of *The Accounting Review.*

"The Principles and Aims of Budgetary Control" is reprinted by permission of the Production Engineering Association of Great Britain.

"Some Aspects of Inflation and Published Accounts" is reprinted by permission of the Chief Editor of *Omega* and the Pergamon Press Ltd.

"The Nature of Profit," and "Sandilands and the Logic of Current Cost" are reprinted by permission of *Accounting and Business Research.*

"The Logic of Financial Accounting" is reprinted by permission of the University College Cardiff Press.

Library of Congress Cataloging in Publication Data

Edey, Harold C.
    Accounting queries.

    (Accountancy in transition)
    "Reprints of articles, lectures, and talks . . . from
1949 . . . to 1980"—Pref.
    1. Accounting—Addresses, essays, lectures.   I. Title.
II. Series.
HF5629.E37   1982   657   82-82487
ISBN 0-8240-5335-4

The volumes in this series are printed on acid-free, 250-year-life paper.

Printed in the United States of America

Preface

These reprints of articles, lectures and talks cover the period from 1949, when I joined the full-time staff of the London School of Economics, to 1980, when I retired from my chair. Many of the papers deal with topics and problems that have been well worked over in recent years, but they may serve to illustrate some of the matters that were concerning us at LSE in the 1950s and early 1960s, when academic accountants were much sparser on the British ground than they are today. I hope they may be of interest to people studying the development of the subject. Apart from the correction of one or two minor errors the papers are as originally published.

One cannot usefully determine accounting procedures by a vain search for the "correct" meaning of the words "profit" and "income". A useful definition of these words can be found only in the procedures used to find the numbers in question, and then only in a particular context. The choice of procedures should emerge from the answer to the question: what is our objective in this particular context? In the 1950s and 1960s this needed more emphasis than perhaps it does now.

The relevance of financial management theory to financial accounting was also then less obvious than now. The literature of business finance was in the main directed to the description of institutions and institutional arrangements. The present abundance of writings on financial decisions did not exist. For analytical guidance one went back to the economic literature of capital theory, notably to the father of modern financial analysis, Irving Fisher, and to the ideas of demand and supply analysis, particularly as applied to problems of valuation by J.C. Bonbright, as my colleague William Baxter explains in the fascinating preface to his *Collected Papers in Accounting* (New York, Arno, 1978).

Most of the thoughts in this collection of papers were planted in my mind by the thinking, writing and conversation of my LSE colleagues. The late Sir Ronald Edwards (Ronnie Edwards to us and many others), Ronald Coase, William Baxter, David Solomons and Basil Yamey all contributed largely to my appreciation of the importance of careful and precise thought and expression, and showed me where the logical foundations of accounting might lie and how they could be related to economic theory.

Lionel Robbins (now Lord Robbins), the late Sir Arnold Plant, and Frank Paish guided my reading in economics and led me to a deeper appreciation of the simple, yet powerful and often not easily grasped, platitudes of that subject. L.C.B. (Jim) Gower developed my understanding of the role and scope of company and corporation law in financial matters. Gordon Foster introduced me to an early generation of computers and computer programming, giving me an awareness of the major role these were likely to play in accountancy, and how neatly our elegant double-entry system fits into their logic. No one could exaggerate the benefit that anyone of the staff of LSE at that time could draw from the influence of Karl Popper. Membership of the LSE Senior Common Room was the best post-graduate education one could have had.

In the 1930s relatively few young people in England considered going to university. At sixteen plus I had left secondary school and gone directly into the office of what would now be considered a small (three-partner) firm of accountants. The firm was, however, quick to delegate responsibility, and I spent an enjoyable and busy five years as an articled clerk, studying by correspondence as we nearly all did then, and qualifying as a chartered accountant in 1935. When I joined my firm my supervisor, Alan P. Hughes, to whom I shall always be grateful, left me in no doubt about the importance attached to careful and systematic work and the checking of one's calculations and statements—an approach that good accountants share with careful scholars.

I then spent a year with a large firm, Deloitte, Plender, Griffiths and Co. as it then was. My supervisor there was responsible to Russell Kettle, later a member of the Cohen Committee on Company Law Amendment. Soon afterwards I moved on to the S. Pearson and Son financial group, where I was at first concerned with routine accountancy matters. Later, after a break of five and a half years of naval war service, I became what would now be called an investment analyst and began to appreciate something of the user's view of financial reports.

Meanwhile, I had enrolled as a part-time student for the BCom degree of the University of London, studying before the war at LSE, and later with the University of London Commerce Degree Bureau. The Bureau's correspondence tuition, provided by LSE faculty staff, was first class. It has left me with the conviction that there is much to be said for education by correspondence provided it is backed up by a first-class academic staff who are prepared to guide reading and comment extensively on papers and exercises submitted to them.

I graduated in 1947 and after some part-time teaching at LSE I became a full-time lecturer there in 1949, joining William Baxter and David Solomons, then respectively professor and reader in accounting. As I have indicated above, it was then that my education in accounting theory really began.

By the middle 1960s the Council of the Institute of Chartered Accountants in England and Wales, which up to that time had regarded the inclusion of accounting matters in university education with some reserve, decided that the tentative links with universities inaugurated in 1945 should be strengthened. In 1964 I was made a member of the Institute's newly-created Research Committee, and I became a member of the Education Committee the same year. In 1969 I was co-opted to the Council of the Institute, retiring from this in 1980.

I became a member of the Accounting Standards Committee when it was set up in 1970. My experience on this and as a member of the Inflation Accounting Steering Group has brought home to me that here, as in other fields of endeavour, nature imposes strong constraints upon the speed with which new ideas—and one must include in this expression ideas which may have germinated 50 years ago or more—can be absorbed by large human groups. What is important is that there should exist means by which ideas can be generated, disseminated in as clear a form as possible, and freely discussed, so that they have a chance to ripen and be ready for adoption when the impact of reality calls for them and the more lively members of the world at large are ready to consider them seriously. This is the university's job in the division of intellectual labour.

I am grateful to the editors and publishers who readily granted permission to use material which had appeared in their publications. I am indebted to Jacky Jennings who helped in the preparation of this material.

Contents

The Principles and Aims of Budgetary Control (Production Engineering Research Assoc. Symposium Papers, 1967)

The Nature of Profit (*Accounting and Business Research*, London, Winter, 1970)

The True and Fair View (*Accountancy*, London, August, 1971)

Some Aspects of Inflation and Published Accounts (*Omega*, Vol. 2, No. 6, 1974)

Deprival Value and Financial Accounting (*Debits, Credits, Finance and Profits*, London, 1974)

Accounting Standards in the British Isles (*Studies in Accounting*, London, 1977)

Why All-Purpose Accounts Will Not Do (*Accountancy*, London, October, 1978)

Sandilands and the Logic of Current Cost (*Accounting and Business Research*, London, Summer, 1979)

The Logic of Financial Reporting (Deloitte, Haskins and Sells Lecture, Cardiff, February 28, 1980)

PUBLISHED ACCOUNTS AS AN AID TO INVESTMENT

by H. C. EDEY, B.Com., A.C.A.

Lecturer in Accounting and Business Finance, London School of Economics

1. The observations in this article follow from the study during the last three years, from the point of view of the investor, of a large number of annual accounts issued by United Kingdom companies.* The term investors includes prospective purchasers of the shares or debentures of a company as well as the existing members and debenture-holders. The interests of these parties, so far as the information which they require from the published accounts is concerned, are identical, but it is useful to consider the question from the point of view of the latter class of persons since it is they who stand in direct contractual relation to the company and are therefore entitled to expect particular consideration of their requirements. This, of course, is recognised by the Companies Act, 1948, which demands certain defined standards in the presentation of accounts to members. This Act, by bringing the accounting standards of all companies closer to those of the best, has perceptibly improved both the quality and amount of information provided by accounts, and the manner in which this is presented. There remain, however, certain limitations and defects. Some of these by their nature may not be susceptible of cure by statutory prescription. Nor in many cases can the professional accounting bodies, which have already done good work in raising standards, issue recommendations aiming at the removal of these defects (assuming they are accepted as such) before the need for improvement is more generally accepted in the business world. It is all the more necessary, therefore, that there should be the fullest discussion of these issues. Apart from the note in paragraph 3 regarding the aggregation of profits from different sources, problems arising from the consolidation of profit and loss accounts and balance sheets have not been discussed. These are fairly generally appreciated though, indeed, more companies might well make a point of drawing the attention of shareholders to the limitations of consolidated accounts.

The Investor's Needs

2. Investments are made with different aims, but it does not seem that the object in view is

---

* Most of the criticisms and suggestions which follow were anticipated by Professor (then Mr.) R. S. Edwards in his series of articles entitled 'The Nature and Measurement of Income', which appeared in *The Accountant* in 1938.

likely significantly to affect the information the investor looks for in published accounts. The emphasis placed on particular points may vary as between, say, the speculative investor who hopes for rapid appreciation in the value of his investment, and the purchaser of a well-secured debenture. The actual matters themselves on which each will wish to inform himself from the accounts will probably be substantially the same. The very nature of accounting documents as historical records places a limitation on their value for a purpose which primarily involves the forecast of future trends. As pointers to current and future profitability and financial stability, published accounts are inevitably inferior to first-hand inside information about the company in question. Nevertheless, they are in most cases all that the investor has to go on and, if informatively and reliably drafted, they may be of considerable value, especially over a number of years, enabling the reader to form some opinion of the ability of the board and some idea of the company's more immediate prospects and its current financial position. It is all the more important, therefore, that the limitations of these documents should be confined to those inherent in their nature and that the greatest effort should be made to increase the value and *quanta* of that information which can be conveyed. The investor's need is to estimate the whole future return on his investment, whether in the form of revenue items or in the nature of return of capital. He will be interested in the distribution of these incomings over time and will wish to distinguish what are conventionally treated as revenue from capital items. (Ideally, these estimates should be applied to each year in the future for the whole expected life of the company. The distinction between revenue and capital items is necessary owing to the incidence of taxation and for other legal and institutional reasons.) The more informative are the accounts of past years, and particularly of the latest year, in explaining the trading results of the company, and its financial position at the year end, the more valuable will they be as a basis for these estimates. Since, by their nature, profit and loss accounts and balance sheets of all but the simplest ventures involve the expression of opinion and estimates, and the manner in which they are drawn up depends upon the conventions adopted, it is of the first importance that items affected by these same opinions and estimates should be clearly distinguished from others and that the particular conventions adopted should be made plain. The reader of the accounts is then placed in a position to interpret them in the light of his own requirements and to substitute his own opinions for those of the management where he thinks fit. For example, a profit balance shown on a company profit and loss account might be £10,000 after a charge of £500 for depreciation of fixed assets. A shareholder might feel that the board had underestimated the provision necessary in this respect and reassess the figure at £1,000, reducing the profit figure to £9,500. Unless the annual accounts provide as much information as reasonably possible to enable the reader to make such adjustments, they have not completely fulfilled their purpose.

Trading Profit

3. As the investor's primary aim is usually to estimate future profits available for distribution, the profit and loss account will be the document to which he will naturally turn first.* It is in my opinion unfortunate that the Cohen Committee did not see fit to recommend, and Parliament in the Companies Act, to adopt, the requirement that the figure of sales turnover be disclosed in the accounts. This figure would be valuable for the purpose of comparison from year to year. The short-term trend would show how the company was weathering current trading conditions and the longer-term trend would indicate (allowance being made for price changes) whether or not the trade of the company was growing. By relating the turnover to the gross profit ratio and to the more fixed items of expense, some estimate of the 'break-even' point and of the effect of varying gross profit margins would be possible. It is usual to say that the publication of such figures would 'give away information to competitors'. This does not appear to deter American companies, however, and it does not seem that a reasoned case has been made out against such a requirement. There are one or two companies that now publish this information, while it is not uncommon for the figure to be mentioned in the chairman's customary review at the annual meeting of the year's trading. In the absence of a turnover figure the investor has to make do with the balance of profit on trading

brought into the profit and loss account, this figure usually being the profit after charging all expenses except interest, most (but not all) provisions,† directors' fees, taxation and similar items. This figure has significance of the same nature as that of sales turnover but to a considerably smaller degree. As an indicator of the general trend of the company's fortunes it is probably substantially more reliable than the net profit balance struck after taxation and after making provisions the size of which must often depend greatly upon managerial estimates. (This is not to say that even the figure of trading profit is independent of estimate since such questions as stock valuation (see paragraph 4) and the profit, if any, to be taken on uncompleted contracts, must be decided before the balance can be struck.) A further problem arises in this connection when a company carries on a number of different trading activities. The item of 'trading profit' may then be a complex of profits and perhaps losses arising from the different activities, no detailed analysis being given. The same point arises in the case of a consolidation where the results of the group are dealt with in a single profit and loss account issued by the parent company. This aggregation of trading income from all sources may conceal large losses in particular sections of the enterprise or group of enterprises, so that perhaps unjustifiable continuation of unprofitable activities may be masked and the public left unaware of the danger of a growing drain of funds from the more profitable part of the business.

Stock Valuation

4. The figure of trading profit disclosed is dependent upon the valuation adopted for stock-in-trade and this to a considerable extent is a management, not an accountancy, decision. There seems at present little hope of a single consistent basis being generally accepted and it may be that the varying conditions of different trades make this undesirable. This, however, is no reason for leaving the public in ignorance of the particular basis used by any company. Variations in a company's general practice from one period to another must indeed now be reported.‡ It seems, however, that there is still left substantial discretion in the hands of the board in the matter of writing down stocks for anticipated losses in value without obligation to disclose the amounts written off. This represents an arbitrary

---

* A banker or other person about to grant short-term credit may, in the first instance, be more interested in the liquidity position shown by the balance sheet.

† As defined in the Companies Act, 1948, Eighth Schedule, 27 (1).

‡ Companies Act, 1948, Eighth Schedule, 14 (6).

element in the accounting for which it is difficult for the investor to allow. Many companies also set aside specific reserves for possible losses in stock values. These are now necessarily shown on the face of the accounts, but the basis on which they are calculated is seldom given. A greater degree of frankness on the part of boards of directors seems called for in respect of both kinds of accounting entry. Accounts should indicate the precise basis of stock valuation and where any reserve or provision is deemed necessary in respect of anticipated future losses on realisation, the basis of calculation of these losses, the amount thereof, and the extent of the reserve or provision therefor. If then the investor disagrees with the assumptions he can allow for this in his own appreciation of the company's outlook.

Exceptional Items

5. It is now obligatory* to show as a separate item in the profit and loss account any gain or expense which is of a special nature or which does not arise in the normal course of the year's trading. Thus it is now common to see a credit item in the profit and loss account described in such terms as 'profit arising out of preceding year's trading' or 'profit on realisation of investments'. The segregation from the current year's results of items which do not relate thereto is valuable. It may, however, lead to a certain difficulty in the interpretation of accounts. As it is the nature of some businesses that there will always be profits of this kind which cannot be determined until a later accounting year, it would increase the value of published accounts containing such items if it were indicated clearly how they had arisen. This is important, as where there is a reasonable expectation of such credits occurring year after year they can be regarded as an addition to the normal trading profit. Where they are exceptional and not likely to recur they should be eliminated by the reader of the accounts when he is assessing past levels of profit as a basis for estimates of future profits.

Depreciation

6. The question of depreciation and provisions for renewals is very much a subject of current debate. The well-known difficulty that depreciation on original cost may be inadequate from the point of view of replacement costs does not need elaboration. Recognition of this problem by boards of directors has not, unfortunately, brought about a general clarification of published accounts in this respect. While accountants

---

* Companies Act, 1948, Eighth Schedule, 14 (6).

remain divided one cannot, it is true, expect any consistent method of approach. In some published accounts no provision is made for higher replacement costs, in others partial provision is made, or a lump sum is allocated with no attempt at relating the amount to any reasoned estimate, while in others again what is estimated to be the full amount required is set aside. In each of these cases the narrative in the accounts may or may not indicate which course is being followed. It is also worth noting that in some cases where the replacement provision method is being used as an alternative to providing depreciation as such, the wording of the item in the accounts suggests that provision is being made, not only for replacement of existing assets, but for further extensions and improvements. This has been noticeable for instance in the accounts of some tea plantation companies. A further point arises in that whether or not full provision is being made for replacement costs the allocation over time of the total provision made may vary substantially with different boards. All this is very confusing for the investor and it seems very desirable that in whatever manner the actual charges and/or appropriations be made and whatever their amount, the following information should be given in the accounts, if necessary in the form of note or narrative:

(a) The total provision for asset replacement which the board deem necessary from year to year in order to maintain the real earning power of the business.

(b) The actual amount provided from year to year for the purpose of (a), whether in the form of depreciation or otherwise, giving references to the relevant items in the accounts.

(c) How it is proposed to make good any deficit resulting from an excess of (a) over (b).

This might be coupled with a fairly detailed analysis of the asset headings related to the estimates referred to under (a) above, with an explanatory narrative giving the board's reasons for assuming such and such a rate of wear and tear cum obsolescence. This would provide the investor with the necessary data on which to draw his own conclusions should he disagree with the board's viewpoint.

Trade Investments

7. The Companies Act, 1948, requires that income from trade investments shall be distinguished in the profit and loss account from other sources of income. Trade investments are

not defined, but may be regarded as investments in the nature of permanent holdings which are not intended to be realised of shares in companies in associated or complementary lines of business to the company which holds them. Often holdings of this nature represent a relatively minor part of the total income of the company and no special problem arises. If the holdings amount to more than 50 per cent. of the equity capital (as defined in the Act) of the company held, or if there is control of the latter's board, it becomes a subsidiary and there is then an obligation to present group accounts, which usually take the form of consolidated accounts. It is possible, however, for a large part or even the whole of the first company's income to be derived from companies in which it has very substantial holdings which are yet not sufficient to make the latter legal subsidiaries and thus throw an obligation on the board of the first company to present any form of group accounts (there is at least one very well-known example of this). Thus the shareholders may be left with virtually no information about their investment beyond the amount of the dividend which they are to receive. It seems desirable that this loophole should be closed. The presentation of consolidated accounts would normally not be feasible here and might indeed be misleading owing to the existence of majority shareholdings outside the group. The presentation of separate accounts for the major subsidiaries, or at least a summary of these, would, however, seem desirable, or, lacking these, at least the same minimum information as is prescribed in the Act in respect of subsidiaries which, for some reason, are not dealt with in group accounts.

Taxation

8. The profit as calculated for income and profits tax assessment may, and usually does, vary considerably from the net profit figure before tax shown in the profit and loss account. Proper charges to the latter, such as deferred repairs, may not be allowable expenses for taxation. Credits brought in may not be assessable to tax, or may already have borne tax in a previous period. The depreciation charge may differ substantially from the sum of initial and annual allowances deductible in computing taxation liability. A further difficulty arose from the fact that the legal liability for income-tax for any period, which in the past was the figure commonly provided for in the accounts, is normally based on the profits of an earlier period. The position in this respect has been much improved by the practice, now general, of providing in each period for the income-tax which will be computed by reference to the profits of that period. Nevertheless, the discrepancy may still be substantial, certainly sufficiently so to invalidate to a serious extent comparisons of net earnings after tax from period to period, and to make the absolute figure of net earnings in any period of considerably less value as a basis for future estimates. The simplest and most straightforward remedy for this would be the setting out, as a note or supporting schedule to the accounts, of a reconciliation of the profit shown therein with the estimated liability in the income-tax computation. So far as I know, no company has yet done this, though directors' reports and chairmen's speeches sometimes give explanations, in varying detail, of discrepancies between the net profit balance shown and the taxation charge.

'Optional Provisions'

9. There are certain types of debit to profit and loss account—usually in the 'appropriation' section—which, though sometimes not legally 'provisions' as defined in the Companies Act, 1948, are, from the investor's point of view, a necessary deduction in arriving at the profits available for distribution. An example of this type of item is the debit for staff pension or welfare funds which is found in almost every public company's accounts to-day. So far as items of this nature are of a recurring nature, likely to arise every year, they should be regarded as a reduction in the level of distributable profits and it is hard to see why they should not always appear as a charge against profits (as in many cases they do). Where the annual allocation of this nature did in fact vary with the profit earned, the narrative could say that this was so, and should then preferably give an indication of the extent to which the item was likely to vary with profits. There may also be instances where the board do not regard such items as irrevocably set aside and feel free to bring the whole or part back into general reserve if they think fit. In such cases there would appear to be no justification for making any specific appropriation in the first instance.

The Balance Sheet

10. The investor, having formed some idea of the distributable profit (however he defines this term) for the accounting period he is studying, will then turn to the balance sheet for information about the recent state of the company's finances and to ascertain the varying claims against the general assets of the company which exist in the form of general and secured creditors

and different classes of shareholders. A comparison of recent balance sheets will give some indication of the developments, favourable or unfavourable, in the liquid position, of expenditure on fixed assets, and of the growth or fall in stocks and work in progress. As already mentioned, the Companies Act, 1948, has brought a welcome improvement in the standards of information presented. Nevertheless, interpreting the normal company balance sheet still remains in part a matter of intelligent guesswork, even though the bases on which the guesses are founded are more substantial.

Capital Structure

11. Considering first the items of share and loan capital, a minor defect common to nearly all balance sheets is their failure to give full information regarding the rights of the various classes of share capital, debentures, notes, &c. This information, though obtainable elsewhere, e.g. by reference to the memorandum and articles of the company or debenture trust deeds, is yet not so obtainable without a considerable expenditure of effort. There seems no good reason why balance sheets should not give on their face or, preferably, where a lengthy explanation is required, in an annexed note, the following information:

(a) Statement of the respective rights of all classes of shares, both as to income and capital. Apart from a bare statement of the fixed rate of dividend payable on preference shares, this important information is seldom given.

(b) Details of changes in the capital structure and in issued capital in recent years, including details of 'free bonus' issues, of the price of issue of new shares issued for cash, and of any reduction in capital. This information is necessary for the intelligent comparison of profits earned from year to year in relation to the claims against such profits, but is seldom if ever given and, except for the professional investigator with books of reference and statistical services to assist him, is hard to trace.

(c) Similar information to that suggested in (a) and (b), so far as it is relevant, in respect of loan capital items, including adequate details of the terms of redemption.

(d) Where shares have been converted into stock, the units in which this is transferable.

Available Funds

12. Turning to the assets side of the balance sheet and considering first the current assets, one could hope that a more stringent and consistent separation could be made between those assets which form part of the normal working capital

fund and those representing funds held for specific investment in fixed capital.* Even more useful would be the presentation of a simplified financial budget with the accounts, outlining in broad terms the anticipated outlays during, say, the next year and the sources from which it was hoped to obtain the necessary funds. This is less radical than it might at first seem, for information of this type, though less systematically presented, is often now given in the directors' report or the chairman's speech. It would be of great value in assessing the investment status of the company's shares since, when considered in relation to the earnings shown by the profit and loss account, it would provide the basis for an estimate of the possible dividend rate, as opposed to the earnings rate. That is, it would give some kind of indication of the extent to which it would be necessary to plough back earnings into the business or, where this source of funds seemed likely to be inadequate, of the extent to which the company would have to come on the market for additional capital, whether by way of temporary advance or of the issue of permanent loan or share capital. Anyone who has followed the course of the stock markets during the last two years will appreciate the importance of this factor in the price of a company's shares or obligations.

Stock

13. This item has already been discussed in paragraph 4 and it is unnecessary to add more to what is said there.

Fixed Assets

14. So long as fixed assets are presented in the form of a few large aggregates it is doubtful whether the current mode of setting them out can be much improved upon. Being merely a record of past expenditure, the item is chiefly of value to the investor as a very rough check on the adequacy of the depreciation provision and as a guide from year to year of the sums laid out by way of capital expenditure. To become really significant, the heading would need to be supported by a detailed schedule of the various types of asset with descriptive narrative and comments on the state of repair, upkeep, estimated value, &c., of each item. There is obviously, however, a limit to the amount of information and detail which can accompany a company's annual report and accounts to shareholders and the above suggestion probably goes beyond this limit. Yet the information required to be given,

---

* *Vide* the 1948-49 accounts of the B.B.C., in which investments and cash destined to finance capital expenditure are in fact segregated.

even by the new Companies Act, is certainly in most cases inadequate to enable shareholders to extract much of value from such statements as 'Freehold and leasehold buildings, plant and machinery at cost, £x', &c. This is the kind of problem which cannot helpfully be tackled by legislation, for the clever man who wants to conceal some relevant fact will usually find his way round it, while a growing mass of statutory requirements will pile ever-growing burdens on administrative staffs and encourage them to honour these in the letter rather than in the spirit. The average company chairman should know the kind of information his shareholders would like to have but, I am afraid, often gives them only as much as he thinks is good for them, not what they need and are, after all, as proprietors of the company, entitled to have. This latter can best be described as any information which is materially relevant to the future earning power of the business, e.g. that such and such a group of fixed assets are rapidly becoming obsolescent and that it is estimated that an expenditure of £x will be necessary on such a date in order to maintain the earning power of the business. Information of this nature would link up with the summarised financial budget which it is suggested in paragraph 12 above might be presented to the members of the company with the annual accounts, and with the board's estimate of necessary depreciation provisions. (See paragraph 6 above.)

Reserves

15. A series of items found in most company balance sheets which must be particularly confusing to the lay reader are the various reserve items. It is suggested that the time has come to simplify balance sheets by reducing the 'general' reserve items to two, representing respectively revenue and capital reserves. At the same time, the real nature of these figures might be made clearer by more apt descriptions, such as 'profits available for distribution' and 'profits reinvested in the business', or some such terms. There may indeed be an argument for retaining the description of 'reserve' for specific allocations for definite purposes, such as the controversial 'reserve for future income-tax', but there seems no reason for retaining a series of items under such headings as 'general reserve', 'contingency reserve', 'profit and loss balance carried forward' and so on. These distinctions in name seldom have any significance, and it seems very doubtful whether many boards of directors, when recommending a transfer to general reserve of £x, have

any clear idea why it should be £x rather than £y. It would be all to the good that boards should feel any encouragement to examine critically their decisions to transfer to general reserves or to retain in carry-forward profits not really needed for the purposes of the company's business and which could perhaps be distributed to the shareholders. (I am excluding, of course, the factor of governmental restriction of dividends. Even here, however, it would be well if boards showed separately in their accounts the sums they *would* have recommended for distribution in the absence of dividend limitation.)

Simplification

16. It may finally be useful to consider a question which has been raised recently concerning the growing amount of detail in published accounts. It has been said that this detail may be a source of confusion to the lay reader, obscuring the wood by the trees, and preventing him from obtaining a clear view of the state of the company's affairs. This is undoubtedly a real problem, but whether it is one of the presentation of accounts seems open to dispute. It seems rather to arise from the complexity of modern business and the fact that the lay reader is accordingly bound willy-nilly to rely on the opinion of experts for an interpretation of accounts. There would seem to be no objection to the presentation of the salient figures—capital employed, turnover figures, net earnings available for dividend, amount of dividend, &c*.—in the form of a brief summary for the benefit of lay readers *provided that the limitation of these figures be made clear*. Companies are in fact beginning to supply such summaries. It seems very doubtful whether it would be possible to simplify the basic accounting information further without it becoming dangerously misleading. So far as the layout of the accounts is concerned there is little doubt that a well-designed set of accounts is of very great assistance to the more experienced reader in studying the results, and may save him a considerable amount of labour with paper and pencil. But accounting documents are of the nature of statistical records and presented barely, without explanation, i.e. in 'simple' form, they would suggest a degree of accuracy and precision which in fact they are not capable of possessing. It is in fact the theme of this article that accounts in their present 'non-simplified' form require a substantially greater degree of explanation and more supporting notes and narratives than are at present customarily given.

* *Vide* the 1948 accounts of Lever Bros. & Unilever Ltd.

nted from ACCOUNTANCY, *September and October, 1950.*

Reflections on the Accounting Provisions of the Companies Act, 1948

By H. C. EDEY, B.COM., A.C.A.

(*Lecturer in Accounting and Business Finance, London School of Economics, University of London*)

Introduction

T HAS BEEN SAID THAT " IMPROVEMENT IN ACCOUNTING
dards begins with isolated action by a few progressive
untants and companies, often stimulated by academic
cism of existing practices." [1] The Companies Act,
8, has now been in force for over two years. Since the
represents a substantial stride forward in generally
epted accounting standards, there may now be a
ptation to be complacent and to feel that enough has
n done. The Act itself, however, recognises that the
ons of good accounting practice can change, and the
rd of Trade has, under Section 454, power to amend by
tutory Instrument the accounting provisions. Some
ughts on these provisions may not, therefore, be out of
ce, and may even, one may hope, play a small part in
viding that stimulation mentioned in the above quota-
n.

In the end a shareholder can judge the success or failure
is company only by the dividends it has paid and will be
e to pay. In appraising the dividend prospects there are
 main considerations : (*a*) the company's liquidity
ition, and (*b*) its profit-earning capacity. But (*a*) and
 are interrelated in the interpretation of accounts, for
vourable view induced by the appearance of high paper
fits may require modification if it is found that those
e profits are accompanied by a serious run-down in the
uidity position. It is with these considerations in mind
t the following comments are framed.

General

Let us first spend a few lines considering the implication
the " true and fair view " which the balance sheet and
fit and loss account are now required by Section 149 of
Act to exhibit. Most of us, even if we found it difficult
define this requirement precisely, would claim to be able
distinguish between sets of accounts which did and did
 comply. If we turn to the Report of the Cohen Com-
tee, [2] most of whose recommendations on accounting
ters were, as we know, embodied in the 1947 Act, we
 it implied by the Committee that the information
vided in published accounts should be that which will
ble the shareholder to form a " true view of the financial
ition and earnings of the company in which he is
erested." [3] And in paragraph 5 of the Report the
mmittee had said : " We consider that the fullest
cticable disclosure of information concerning the
ivities of companies will lessen such opportunities [for
use] and accord with a wakening social consciousness."
ese quotations give an idea of the way in which the

Committee was thinking but they do not help us very much
in our interpretation of the Act, [4] for they still leave us up
against the problems of determining (*a*) how much information is necessary to enable shareholders to form a " true
view " and (*b*) what is " practicable." The difficulty is
that if a " true view " is to be given that will enable a shareholder to arrive at a well-based and reasoned appraisal of
the value of his investment a set of statements no less
exhaustive than those provided for the management of the
undertaking is necessary, and these at intervals of certainly
less than one year. Indeed, an ideal requirement would
also include a statement of the management's own general
attitude towards the business and an appraisal of the degree
of optimism or pessimism with which they customarily
approached their decisions. It is obvious that " a true and
fair view " cannot be interpreted in this exhaustive manner
and that a *via media* has to be found. In practice the phrase
should presumably be defined in some such terms as these,
namely, that the standards of presentation of the required
information should be those set by the current business
practice of honest men in relation to company accounts.[5]
4. Our canons of presentation must then, subject to the
specific requirements of the Act, be framed in relation to a
general unwritten professional code. Thus the Cohen
Committee, writing this time of the profit and loss account,
said : " The account should be drawn up in accordance with
accepted accountancy principles consistently maintained." [6]
A requirement in these terms was not brought into the
Act, but is recognised by implication in paragraph 14 (6)
of the 8th Schedule, which requires that any material
change in the basis of accounting shall be noted. This
requirement would, in my opinion, have been more
satisfactory had it been extended by a further provision,
namely, that the annual accounts of every company should
be accompanied by a statement in some detail of the
accounting bases adopted.[7] The kind of information to be
given by this statement is noted below ; it would have
particular reference to the bases of valuation of stock and of
fixed assets. Accounts are only a particular form of business
statistics and it is a commonplace of statistical presentation
that the basis and method of calculation of figures should be
stated. It can, indeed, be objected that statements of the
type suggested would often be lengthy and would encumber
the accounts. The difficulties cannot be denied. Never-

---

[1] " Accounting Doctrine and the 1947 English Companies Act,"
A. Fitzgerald, *The Australian Accountant*, September, 1948.
[2] Cmd. 6659.
[3] *Ibid.*, paragraph 7 (*d*).

[4] The Report would not, of course, be available as evidence of
intention in any interpretation of the Act in the Courts—at least, not
in theory.
[5] And compare the dicta in *The London & General Bank* case (1895,
2 Ch. 673), where Section 7 (6), Companies Act, 1879 (which referred to
a " full and fair balance sheet "), applied, *vide* H. B. Samuel's *Shareholders' Money*, p. 257.
[6] Cmd. 6659, paragraph 103.
[7] This is, of course, no new idea, *vide* for example Mr. G. O. May's
memorandum on the proposed American Securities Bill of 1933,
reprinted in *Twenty-five Years of Accounting Responsibility*.

theless, the information should, even if not circulated with the accounts, at least be available for inspection both at the company's office and with the Registrar of Companies.

Fixed and Current Assets

5. Let us now pass on to some of the detailed requirements of the 8th Schedule of the Act. It will be convenient and relevant to the foregoing discussion to start with paragraph 4 (2), which requires fixed assets to be distinguished from current assets in the balance sheet. This will lead us on to a discussion of other paragraphs, all of which are of relevance to the " true and fair view " concept. I shall assume here that the broad basis of the present customary classification of fixed and current assets is accepted, if only as a convenient aid to the interpretation of accounts.[8] As already noted, the liquid position of a company is of importance in relation to the price of its quoted shares and debentures, for where the margin of working capital is insufficient—and this can often be judged from the trend of current assets and liabilities over a period of years—there is a *prima facie* assumption that the past rate of stated earnings on issued capital may not be maintainable, since additional finance will in some way have to be raised. The Cohen Committee attempted to provide a definition of fixed and current assets : " The Section shall define ' fixed assets ' as assets not held for sale or for conversion into cash, and ' current assets ' as cash and assets held for conversion into cash." [9] This definition was not incorporated in the Act, and this was perhaps wise, for it can hardly be regarded as adequate ; the time element, which is surely the essence of the distinction between fixed and current, is not mentioned, and the phrase " conversion into cash " is question-begging, for in a certain sense all assets, directly or indirectly, are held for this purpose. The generally accepted distinction, and perhaps the only useful one, depends on the " turnover period," current assets being those which are either already in cash form or are expected to be converted into cash form in the ordinary course of business within a relatively short time. The value of the concept is in relation to the short-term liquidity position of the company. In assessing this position in relation to a given company it is important to know what the category of current assets does comprise. This is particularly relevant in the case of those assets whose classification is at present often doubtful ; for example, advances to subsidiaries, and investments. To avoid the problem by classifying these items as neither fixed nor current is no solution. It must be presumed that the directors know how much of the items in question are likely to be converted into cash—and therefore to be available for current financial needs—during the next twelve to eighteen months. The shareholders are entitled to know, too.[10] One is led to the conclusion that a statutory definition is desirable and the suggestion here made is that current assets should be defined as those already in cash form or expected and intended (by the directors) to be converted into cash, otherwise made available for the purposes of curre finance, within a period of not more than (say) twe months from the date of the balance sheet. It is true th this definition would exclude from current assets so items at present included (such as work in progress long-term contracts to the extent that progress payme were not expected) and would require the division of so classes of assets, such as stock, into two sections, o " current " and one " fixed " or " non-current." Howev in their budgeting the management must make some s of division on these lines for their own purposes ; additional work involved should be small, and likely anything, to improve the information of management well as of shareholders. It is not necessary to emphasise t value to shareholders of being shown, for instance, that t amount of stocks held is steadily growing and the turno period lengthening.

Current Liabilities

6. A corollary of the above definition of current ass would be statutory recognition of the generally accep convention that current liabilities are those due for payme within one year of the balance sheet date.[11] This questi is linked with the provision of paragraph 12 (1) (b) of Schedule requiring interest on debentures and *fixed loans* to be stated separately in the profit and loss account.

Overdraft Facilities

7. Another question which arises when we are thinking the current asset-current liability position is that of o standing overdraft facilities (as Mr. H. Norris, for instan has pointed out). In estimating the liquid position o company it is important to know what kind of a marg there is in the way of overdraft facilities. There seems good case for a provision requiring disclosure of overdr or loan facilities granted but undrawn upon.

Outstanding Commitments

8. An appraisal of the liquid position cannot be compl without a knowledge of (a) the capital commitme during, say, the next 12 months and (b) any extern sources of finance during the same period which are lik to be available for (a) above, or for any existing shortage working capital. Items of class (a) are, it is true, to so extent provided for in the requirement of paragraph 11 of the Schedule regarding outstanding commitments o capital nature. This requirement, however, does not se to be adequate. In the first place the phrase " wh practicable " is used. There should surely be no difficu in giving an *estimated* figure of capital requirements. H the question of practicability can arise is difficult to s except, of course, in those cases where the board does yet know its own mind in respect of the immediate futu If this is the case it would be well that shareholders show

---

[8] We may note that, as recognised by the Board of Trade, some classes of assets may fall under neither heading (for example, preliminary expenses), while the classification of others is doubtful. The first difficulty could be met by the use of such a description as " non-current assets " instead of " fixed assets " (*vide* " The Classification of Assets," A. A. Fitzgerald in *Accounting Research*, July, 1950). The second problem would, I think, be solved by the application of the definition suggested below.

[9] Cmd. 6659, p. 58.

[10] It is no answer in the case of advances to subsidiaries to say that a consolidated balance sheet is presented ; the balance sheet of holding company is still required to show a true and fair view.

[11] This prompts the reflection that it would be useful to classify liabilities (and possibly even assets ?) in relation to their life, example, current liabilities (0-1 years), short-term liabilities (1-5 years) medium-term liabilities (5-15 years) and long-term liabilities (15 y upwards).

[12] Why not also on short-term loans, as a separate item ?

ow. Moreover, it is not enough that details of actual tracts (the requirement of the Schedule) should be ovided. It is as important that shareholders should know amounts which the board intend to spend although forceable contracts have not yet been concluded. Nor serious omission) does the requirement at present cover e case where the commitments envisaged will call for vestment in additional working, rather than fixed, pital. It is also desirable that the period covered by the imate should be made clear. Indeed, here too a period 12 months might well be fixed by statute. As regards (b) ove it may be that a company has made satisfactory rangements for financing any commitments during the suing 12 months ; for example, by private placing of loan pital, or it may expect that undistributed profits will be ficient to provide the necessary finance. But it can rdly be said that a true and fair (and certainly not a *full*) w of a company's financial position is given unless formation of this kind is made public.

Reserves

From the foregoing follows logically a discussion of the action of reserve accounts. To the extent that future pital expenditure or increases in working capital are to provided out of funds already held by the company it is dent that transfers to capital reserve should be made, as making it clear that these funds are regarded (by the ectors) as part of the permanent capital of the company d are not now available for distribution, *vide* paragraph (1) (c) of the Schedule.[13] (We find an analogy in the se of South African mining companies whose continued increased) profit-earning capacity depends upon the penditure from year to year of substantial sums by way development expenditure. These sums are regarded as pital expenditure and are commonly financed out of rrent profits, equivalent amounts being appropriated m profit and loss account to capital reserve.) This plies that all ownership funds which are intended for rmanent investment in the business should be represented the balance sheet by share capital or capital reserve. e may even toy with the idea of restoring some greater asure of control of their funds to shareholders by requir- g that such transfers to capital reserve should be subject approval in general meeting, that until so approved the ads they represent should not be available for reinvest- nt in the business, and that once so approved the ovisions of the Act as to the reduction of capital should ply to them.

Any remaining free reserves, including the profit and s balance, would then fall into the two classes of (a) neral contingency reserves and (b) reserves intended for tribution to shareholders either within the near future or er by way of dividend equalisation payments. The total (a) and (b) would then indicate how much of the assets d been allocated (a) for general contingencies and (b) for idend purposes. It would be recognised accounting ictice that the appearance of a non-capital reserve in the lance sheet implied that funds to the same amount could immediately distributed in dividend, or marshalled for contingency, *without disturbing the normal business of the pany.* The word reserve would then regain some

meaning. The present " reserve " policy of a large number of companies—I would almost go so far as to say all companies—in this country is inconsistent and has little meaning. Allocations in round figures are made to this reserve or that because it makes the balance sheet look " strong." It confuses the lay shareholder and annoys the more skilled interpreter of accounts. It may be noted that a consistent and conscientious application of the above principles would answer the question that has been raised : How much of the funds locked up in current assets are permanently liquid and how much are as fixed (so long as the business continues) as those laid out for the purchase of fixed assets, being forthwith needed on conversion into cash for reinvestment in stock, etc. ? I would almost venture to suggest that a rigorous insistence on the proper classification of reserves is the most important reform needed,[14] for it is a reform which would force directors into the light and make them reveal their dividend and ploughing-back policy. It would distinguish the action of a board who abstained from raising a dividend because of the Government's " stand-still " request from that of one who would have been unable in any case to recommend an increased dividend.

Basis of Valuation of Current Assets

11. Another question which it is interesting to ask in relation to current assets arises on paragraph 4 (3) of the Schedule, which requires that the methods used to arrive at the amount of the fixed assets under each heading shall be stated. Why should not the same information be given in respect of current assets ? Since there is a wide variation in practice in the valuation of, for example, stock and work in progress, it is most desirable that shareholders should be aware of the method and basis used by their directors. (That this can be of particular significance is illustrated by the reports and accounts of film-producing companies, some of whom have given this information. The whole financial position of such a company may be dependent on the value of the stock of unfinished produc-tions, or of productions not yet fully distributed.) Where changes in the basis of valuation take place it is of course necessary to say so in accordance with paragraph 14 (6) (b) of the Schedule. But even where there are no changes in the basis it may be very material to know *which* basis is being used—for example, where the stock figure shows a steady trend, up or down, from year to year. This is a problem which would be met by the general statement of accounting bases which it is suggested (paragraph 4 above) should be compulsory.

Depreciation of Current Assets

12. Again, provisions for depreciation or diminution in value of fixed assets are required to be stated separately in the profit and loss account (8th Schedule, paragraph 12 (1) (a)) and to be disclosed in the balance sheet (8th Schedule, paragraph 5), but this does not apply in the case of current assets. Perhaps this is because it is common for any such provision to be absorbed in the general debit to trading account. One may ask, however, whether the separation of charges to trading account representing the cost price of goods sold from those representing falls in value of stocks held would not be significant. It could certainly

---

[13] In the interpretation of which there is, however, some uncertainty.

[14] Other than a statement of accounting basis.

be argued that it is in the interest of shareholders that they should know what material falls in value have taken place or are expected to take place before ultimate sale. The question is particularly relevant to-day when the high price level of many commodities has no doubt led many boards of directors to make provisions of this nature. If these provisions were disclosed and, as already suggested, if the basis of valuation of stock were clearly stated,[15] it could be left to shareholders to draw their own conclusions from the facts given. (One may note that in many companies " stock reserves " have been created. If these are properly named reserves they are really general contingency reserves and would, if the recommendation suggested in paragraph 9 above were adopted, be shown as such.)

13. It may be that the last question (and perhaps others) could be dealt with more simply under paragraph 14 (6) (a) of the 8th Schedule by extending a little, or defining more completely, the circumstances in which a transaction will be considered to be of an exceptional or non-recurrent nature. Thus it could be argued that an unusual and severe fall in raw material prices which necessitated the writing down of stocks should require separate treatment in the profit and loss account under this heading. On the whole, however, it seems better to require a more detailed analysis of all transactions rather than to rely on the *ad hoc* reporting of exceptional items, since this inevitably involves a greater exercise of personal judgment.

Depreciation of Fixed Assets

14. Let us now examine what appear to be some inconsistencies in the 8th Schedule in relation to the balance-sheet presentation of fixed assets. In stating the normal method of arriving at the amount of any fixed asset, paragraph 5 (1) (b) of the Schedule requires the deduction of the amount provided or written off for " depreciation or diminution in value." This seems to imply that " depreciation " and " diminution in value " are synonymous or similar terms. But the term depreciation in this context is generally understood (and this is backed by the opinion of eminent counsel [16]) as an amount calculated by use of the rate currently accepted as " proper " for the kind of asset concerned and does not necessarily bear any relation to the value of the asset at the date of the balance sheet. An asset can thus appreciate substantially in value and yet " depreciation " still be charged annually. The addition of the phrase " diminution in value " in paragraphs 5 and 27 of the Schedule has thus robbed the definition of a reserve in paragraph 27 of some of the precision it would otherwise have had.[17] When reading a balance sheet we know that an amount in excess of what the directors think is " reasonable necessary " is a reserve. But necessary for what ? Depreciation as commonly understood ? Or diminution in value ? Presumably either interpretation will do. However, this point is perhaps less important than it would seem, for, as we shall see, the reference in paragraph 27 to provision for " renewals " is alone sufficient substantially to reduce the effectiveness of that paragraph.

15. Thus, if we turn to paragraph 5 (2) (b) of the Schedu which recognises replacement provision accounting as alternative to depreciation accounting, and read this conjunction with paragraph 27 (2), we are led to the co clusion that whether an allocation for " depreciation " wholly a provision or is in part a reserve may depend on t form of book-keeping adopted by the directors. Let assume that the conventional provision for depreciation an asset, if based on the original cost, would be A, but based on the estimated replacement value would be B. the directors adopt the usual book-keeping method, a show the depreciation in the balance sheet as a deducti from the fixed assets, any excess of B over A which they aside will be (it seems) a reserve and must be shown as su in the balance sheet. If, on the other hand, they choose show the whole allocation on the left-hand side of t balance sheet and call it a renewals or replacement pr vision, then the whole amount of B will be a provision the eyes of the law. It must be noted, however, that if wh they *do* replace the asset they choose to capitalise the outl on the new asset and write off the old asset against t replacement provision, any balance left on the provisi account turns into a reserve and must be shown as suc although had they left the old asset balance in being a debited the replacement cost to the replacement provisi there would have been no reserve (except to the extent, any, that replacement provision was over-estimated).

16. This anomaly in the Schedule seems, incidentally, make redundant some of the recent discussion regardi the precise treatment of allocations for additional repla ment costs, since it appears that, provided the right wo are chosen and the right book-keeping entries made, t full amount of a replacement value provision can regarded legally as a charge against profits and as provision and not a reserve. It should be noted that t particular anomaly would not have arisen had the Coh Committee recommendations been adopted as th originally stood, for the Committee had proposed that t replacement method of accounting should be available on to public utilities.[18]

17. It is not possible to consider here the fundament problems of depreciation policies raised by the foregoi discussion. It seems that the ambiguity in the Act has aris because we have not yet faced squarely up to the implic tions of different policies. Indeed, this is just one part the general lack of coherence in the body of accounti thought which has become apparent in recent years a arises largely from fundamental contradictions in o concepts of the purpose and basis of the balance she The question in particular of calculating a depreciati rate for a particular asset is fraught with difficulti Whether or not it will be possible in the next few years bring greater consistency to the assumptions which under our accounting conventions, we must recognise, I think, th personal judgment and opinion enter so much into preparation of final accounts that the conventions and ba adopted in any particular accounts should be clearly a

---

15 The two requirements cannot be separated, for the " cost " of goods sold can only be defined in terms of some arbitrary and stated standard.

16 *The Companies Act, 1947*, Institute of Chartered Accountants, paragraph 85.

17 The Cohen Committee used " depreciation " in the recommendation which led to paragraph 5 (1) (b) and " diminution in value " in the precursor of paragraph 27 (2) ; (Cmd. 6659, pp. 59-60).

18 Wrongly, I consider. My point is not that directors should not free to choose their own depreciation policy, but that the Act at pres does not call for a clear enough explanation of the basis and effec different policies, each of which may alter the significance of " reserve " balances. Sub-paragraph (4) (a) of paragraph 5 of 8th Schedule goes part of the way, but not far enough.

equivocally stated. Thus in relation to asset valuation information might include :

a) A statement of the cost of the assets shown under each heading, as at present. This statement could be given with advantage · even where there had been a subsequent valuation. In the latter case the 8th Schedule allows the valuation to replace the statement of cost. This seems such an obvious loophole (although admittedly it does not yet seem to have been taken advantage of much) that if a note of original cost is not always to be shown (and I suggest this is desirable in order to preserve the continuity of the balance sheet record) the provisions of paragraph 5 (1) might well be strengthened by requiring—as the Institute of Chartered Accountants has already recommended—the date and source of any valuation to be stated, but with this addition, that unless the valuation represented a bona fide market valuation by independent valuers the original cost should also be stated.

b) A statement, forming part of the general statement of conventions and accounting bases adopted by the company (see paragraph 4 above), of the method of dealing with depreciation. The annual rate (if any) used in each case, the method of application (for example, straight-line), the extent to which obsolescence had been taken into account in assessing the rate (for obsolescence is probably in many cases more important than wear and tear) should all be given. This, it is true, might require the separation in the balance sheet of groups of assets whose basis of valuation happened to be different, and one can conceive cases where this would be a complicated and difficult business. We are here up against one of the basic difficulties referred to earlier of how much information is " practicable." The importance of this information for the rational assessment by shareholders of the worth of their shares is undoubted.

It is, perhaps, relevant at this stage to turn to paragraph 11 (7) of the Schedule, which requires the directors to state in the balance sheet if, in their opinion, any of the current assets have not a realisable value in the ordinary course of business at least equal to their stated book values. One may ask why this requirement should be limited to current assets. If it has become clear to a board of directors that the value to the company in the long run (that is, in the ordinary course of business) of any fixed asset or group of fixed assets is below the stated balance sheet value—and it is admitted that there will be many borderline cases where it would not be expected that the directors should give such an opinion—then it cannot be said that the accounts show a true and fair view unless this fact is made clear to the shareholders. Where the company has a white elephant in the balance sheet and the directors have no doubt that it *is* a white elephant, it is surely their duty to say so and make no attempt to estimate the present value to the company. Certainly in many cases conscientious boards would do this now, but one wonders whether enough consideration is given to this question.

Goodwill, etc.

In paragraph 5 (2) of the Schedule there is an exemption from the normal basis of balance sheet presentation of fixed assets in respect of goodwill, patents and trade marks. This dispensation for some reason does not extend to such items as development expenditure which are by their nature very similar if not indistinguishable from these. On the other hand one may ask why it is necessary to exempt goodwill, patents and trade marks from the general provision requiring a statement of assets at cost with a deduction for amounts subsequently written off. It is true that in the case of items of this kind original cost is even poorer evidence in assessing the present value of the asset than in the case of many other assets, but it is still difficult to see why a record of the original amount expended on goodwill, etc., should not be shown as much as for other assets. Reserves must be shown separately in the balance sheet. If, instead of being transferred to reserve account, profits have been used to write off goodwill, why then should they disappear from the balance sheet ? Again it is hard to understand why a mere difference in book-keeping technique should alter the record presented to the shareholders. The same argument applies to so-called fictitious assets, such as preliminary expenses.

Investments

20. Under paragraph 5 (2) (c) if " the market value (or, in the case of investments not having a market value, their value as estimated by the directors) " is stated, it is not necessary to show cost and subsequent depreciation of investments which are fixed assets. Now, by value one usually understands market value. Presumably the intention here, however, is to emphasise the difference between current values, which may fluctuate, and the directors' estimate of the *present value to the company* of the investments, taking a relatively long view, that is, the basis of valuation commonly believed proper for any fixed asset, the " value to the company as a going concern " basis of the textbooks. Thus we arrive at the odd conclusion that if, for example, trade investments which happen not to be quoted are considered by the directors to be standing at a reasonable amount in the balance sheet, details of cost and subsequent depreciation need not be shown, although the basis of the directors' valuation is perhaps no different from that in respect of other fixed assets whose cost and subsequent depreciation *must* be shown. Is there in fact any reason why the cost and subsequent depreciation basis should be departed from because assets happen to take the form of investments in other companies ? It may be that the intention of paragraph 5 (2) (c) is that the directors should estimate current *market* value in cases where there are no *quotations* or *dealings*. The paragraph does not, however, say so. We may also note that the Act does not define trade investments. Here again it can no doubt be said that most accountants know when an investment is a trade investment and when it is not. Nevertheless, there must be borderline cases. Here it seems that our criterion should be whether the investment is intended to be held permanently (subject to its continued income-earning capacity), for if so it is surely *ex hypothesi* a trade investment.

21. While discussing trade investments one can note a more serious defect in the Act : namely, that 49 per cent. of the equity of a company may be held, perhaps as the sole asset of the owning company, but no disclosure is required of the underlying assets and liabilities represented by the investment or of the proportion of the undistributed income attributable to the owning company's interest. It is thus possible to avoid the elaborate provisions of the Act in relation to group accounts by reducing holdings in other companies to just under 50 per cent. of the equity. Although this percentage does not give formal control, in most cases it will give *de facto* control. It would seem desirable that the

provisions of the Act should be extended to require the inclusion in annual accounts of a statement giving minimum information in relation to such holdings. This might take the form of a statement, suitably amended, like that required by paragraph 15 (4) of the Schedule in relation to the profits of non-consolidated subsidiaries. A difficulty might arise in attempting to define at what point an investment became sufficiently important for this information to be given. This could perhaps be dealt with in terms of a given proportion of the gross revenue or net worth of the investment-owning company represented respectively by the profit arising from or the cost of the investment in question. Alternatively, and this represents surely a minimum requirement, the investment-owning company should be required to give sufficient details of its holdings and of the income derived therefrom to enable both to be reconciled without difficulty with the separately published accounts of the companies held. This would at least put the shareholders in the position of being able to obtain for themselves the same information as that suggested above, except, of course, where the subsidiaries happened, as they well might, to be overseas companies.

Taxation

22. Another paragraph which, although it has proved valuable in practice, still seems to be insufficiently precise is 11 (10) of the Schedule. This paragraph requires the basis of computation of the United Kingdom income tax allocations to be shown in the balance sheet and can be linked with paragraph 14 (3), requiring similar information in relation to the profit and loss account. This is usually interpreted as requiring a statement of the fiscal period in respect of which the tax provision or reserve is made. This information is not, however, usually sufficient for an adequate interpretation of the accounts. In particular it is often difficult to relate the tax charge to stated profits for particular periods. The introduction of high initial allowances has increased this difficulty, making the charge for income tax (and profits tax too) bear in many cases even less relation than before to the profits shown in the accounts. As far as the writer can see the only satisfactory way round this obstacle is to require a reconciliation of taxable profits with accounting profits and for the former to be related to the provisions and reserves appearing in the accounts. This may seem a radical suggestion, but if one is to get a clear trend of the profits available for distribution it is hard to see how it can be avoided. The reconciliation would not need, of course, to be in great detail.

Arrangement of Act

23. The somewhat haphazard way in which the various accounting provisions have been arranged in the main Act and in the 8th Schedule deserves a brief note, for we can hope that matters will one day be improved. No doubt this arrangement is due in part to historical accident. For example, the provisions of the Act regarding the keeping of books of account are contained in three widely separated Sections, numbers 147, 331 and 436, the requirements of two of which, numbers 147 and 331, overlap. The segregation of most of the detailed accounting provisions in the 8th Schedule has been valuable, and it is a pity that it was not possible, perhaps owing to drafting difficulties, to include therein all the accounting provisions, including some of the less general parts of Sections 147 to 163. The Schedule, too,

could have been arranged more logically. The provisi relating to the balance-sheet statement of investments, instance, are contained in no fewer than five differ paragraphs : 5, 8, 11, 15 and 28.

Documents Annexed

24. Section 149 (7) (a) refers to information which allowed to be given in documents annexed to the bala sheet or profit and loss account. This raises the gene question : " Where does the balance sheet end ? " F sumably the answer is when the two sides are totalled ; this is correct, the implication is that any information specifically allowed to be given in statements or docume annexed must appear on the face of the balance sheet abe the totals. This would appear to make technically ille the presentation of, for instance, the details regarding fix assets and depreciation (required by paragraph 5 (3) of 8th Schedule) in separate schedules not shown on the fa of the balance sheet, since it is not stated that this inform tion can be given in documents annexed. It would ha been more satisfactory if the references to documents a statements annexed had been eliminated and a gene provision inserted providing that so long as a true and f view was given any information required by the Act co be contained in supporting schedules to the balance sh or profit and loss account. It would also make for tidir and the avoidance of error if the present provision allow material information to be given in the directors' rep (Section 163) were abrogated. It is surely undesirable that the auditors should sometimes have to report on a p of a document not normally subject to their report and that the balance sheet should sometimes be incomple unless read in connection not with the directors' report a whole (which would perhaps be unexceptionable) with a part of the directors' report, perhaps only a senten to be sought out from surrounding irrelevancies.

Board of Trade Powers

25. I will end by referring briefly to the various powers the Board of Trade (under a number of Sections of the and paragraphs of the Schedule) to vary the accountin provisions in relation to particular companies. T flexibility gained by the insertion of these powers in the is no doubt an advantage. Nor are there signs wanting t the Board of Trade is ready to grant indulgences. The however, are powers which should not lightly be exerci and the hope may be expressed that in such cases the Boar advisers consider with great care any adverse effect on interpretation of the accounts which may result. There danger here for auditors, for it would surely be no defen in answer to a charge that accounts reported on as true a fair were not so, to reply that such and such a requirem had been waived by the Board of Trade ; the provisions sub-Section 1 of Section 149 of the Act cannot be set asi

Conclusion

26. I am only too conscious that these remarks, which necessarily condensed, raise many problems which ther not space here to discuss. Nor are most of the ideas I ha made use of new in themselves : I can only hope that th discussion in the context of the accounting provisions of Act may make some small contribution to the developm of these.

Printed by T. Whittingham & Co., Ltd., Pixmore Avenue, Letchworth, Herts.

Reprinted from ACCOUNTING RESEARCH, Volume Two, Number Two, April, 1951.

A NOTE ON RESERVES, PROVISIONS AND PROFITS

By H. C. EDEY

I—INTRODUCTION

It is the object of this note to consider briefly whether those parts of the Companies Act, 1948, which relate to reserves and provisions have contributed significantly, in the words of the Cohen Committee when recommending their inclusion in the new Act, to the "adequate disclosure and publication of the results of companies."[1]

The gist of the relevant paragraphs of the Eighth Schedule to the Act can be summarised thus:[2]

(a) Depreciation or replacement provisions in respect of fixed assets must be disclosed in the profit and loss account in aggregate and under asset headings in the balance sheet. (But so far as the balance sheet is concerned there are saving clauses in relation to depreciation of goodwill, patents and trade-marks, investments and "difficult cases" where the figures are hard to obtain.)

(b) The aggregate amount of provisions for liabilities (as defined below) must be shown in the profit and loss account and balance sheet.

(c) The aggregate amount of reserves (see also below) must be disclosed in the balance sheet, distinguishing between capital and revenue reserves.

(d) The changes in reserves from year to year, and the applications of provisions not used for their original purpose, must be explained, and it must be shown how these affect the profit and loss account.

Reserves and provisions are defined (the former negatively) in paragraph 27 of the Eighth Schedule, which reads:

27.—(1) For the purposes of this Schedule, unless the context otherwise requires,—

(a) the expression "provision" shall, subject to sub-paragraph (2) of this paragraph, mean any amount written off or retained by way of providing for depreciation, renewals or diminution in value of assets or retained by way of providing for any known liability of which the amount cannot be determined with substantial accuracy;

(b) the expression "reserve" shall not, subject as aforesaid, include any amount written off or retained by way of providing for depreciation, renewals or diminution in value of assets or retained by way of providing for any known liability;

---

[1] Cmd. 6659, para. 101.

[2] The requirements are modified for banking, discount, assurance and most shipping companies. Individual exemptions may also be granted.

(c) the expression "capital reserve" shall not include any amount regarded as free for distribution through the profit and loss account and the expression "revenue reserve" shall mean any reserve other than a capital reserve;

and in this paragraph the expression "liability" shall include all liabilities in respect of expenditure contracted for and all disputed or contingent liabilities.

(2) Where—

(a) any amount written off or retained by way of providing for depreciation, renewals or diminution in value of assets, not being an amount written off in relation to fixed assets before the commencement of this Act; or

(b) any amount retained by way of providing for any known liability;

is in excess of that which in the opinion of the directors is reasonably necessary for the purpose, the excess shall be treated for the purposes of this Schedule as a reserve and not as a provision.

These provisions of the Eighth Schedule must be read in conjunction with the overriding requirement of Section 149 of the main Act that the annual balance sheets and profit and loss accounts shall give a "true and fair view" of the company's state of affairs and profit or loss.

II—THE BALANCE SHEET

The term true and fair cannot be interpreted in an absolute sense. Thus, for example, a "true and fair" balance sheet may, it seems, contain an item "Goodwill £45,000," without implying that goodwill is really worth that sum: in fact it may be worth either nothing or much more than £45,000. Wynn-Parry J. has said "The legend in the balance sheet does no more than accurately represent the state of the freehold property account in the books of the company."[3] Compare this view (which related to a pre-1948 balance sheet) with that of the Cohen Committee: "A balance sheet . . . does not as a general rule purport to show the net worth of an undertaking . . . or the present realisable value of such items as goodwill, land, buildings, plant and machinery. . . ."[4] Buckley quotes this paragraph and says of the "true and fair view" clauses of the Act: ". . . *semble* this is not inconsistent with the nature and functions of a balance sheet as described [in paragraph 98 of the Cohen Report]."[5]

On the other hand, if we turn to paragraph 101 of the Cohen Report we find it stated, under the heading *Undisclosed Reserves:* "The objections urged against undisclosed reserves can be summarised as follows. As the assets are *undervalued* . . . the balance sheet does not present a true picture of the state of the company's affairs."[6] The apparent contradiction by the Committee of

---

[3] *In re Press Caps Ltd.* (1949), 1 Ch. 434 CA.

[4] Cmd. 6659, para. 98. The Committee does not, however, appear to have been entirely clear on this matter, for it implies in the same paragraph that the balance sheet does purport to show the "going concern" value of the assets ("net worth" presumably being identified with market values). But going concern value, if it means anything, is the whole value of the business to its owners, including the value of goodwill, and can only be assessed by capitalising the profit expectations of the owners (or their representatives).

[5] Buckley on the Companies Acts, 12th Ed., page 966.

[6] My italics.

its remarks three paragraphs earlier must presumably be explained by limiting the meaning of "undervaluation" in paragraph 101 to the result of under-stating the profit of a given period and thus reducing the book value of assets, or increasing the book amount of liabilities, below or above what they would otherwise have been: "An undisclosed reserve is commonly created by using profits to write down more than is necessary . . . assets . . . ; by creating exces-sive provisions for bad debts or other contingencies; by charging capital expenditure to revenue; or by under-valuing stock in trade."[7] It seems that the Committee was here concerned, not with the balance sheet as such (which, so far as fixed assets are concerned, it evidently regarded, like Wynn-Parry J., as little more than a receptacle for ledger balances) but with the *desideratum* that the profit and loss accounts should disclose as accurate a picture as possible of the current profits of the company from its normal trading activities and in particular that it should no longer be possible for ". . . undisclosed reserves accumulated in past periods . . . [to] . . . be used to swell the profits in years when the company is faring badly. . . ."[8] The account should give ". . . a fair indication of the earnings of the period. . . . The [profit and loss] account should be drawn up in accordance with accepted accountancy prin-ciples consistently maintained."[9] All this is in accordance with the trend of accounting thought in recent years.[10]

We can conclude that, so far as the balance sheet is concerned, the Cohen Committee did not intend, and the Act does not (it seems) require, an inter-pretation that would exclude all hidden reserves. Assets may be undervalued, for example because prices in general, or of particular assets, have risen; valuable goodwill may not appear in the balance sheet because it has been built up since the company was formed, or because it has been written off.[11] The main effects on the balance sheet of the parts of the Act relating to reserves and provisions can then be summed up as the limited, though useful, ones of:

(a) disclosing the amount of those liabilities which are only capable of rough estimate,

(b) preventing the inflation of liabilities by the inclusion in their total of distributable profits, and

(c) analysing in more detail the derivation of the balances on some asset

---

[7] Cmd. 6659, para. 101.

[8] *Ibid.*

[9] Cmd. 6659, para. 103.

[10] "The accounting profession is in more or less general agreement on the significance of the income account and is of the opinion that if the income accounts are correct each year, the balance sheet will take care of itself": J. W. Smart, C.P.A., in *Public Account-ing Practice in the United States*—address at the Chartered Accountants' Summer Course, July, 1948.

[11] It seems doubtful whether the debit to profit and loss account from year to year of expenditure on advertising, research and similar outlays which may be creating a valu-able goodwill was intended by the Cohen Committee to be included in that "charging capital expenditure to revenue" which they condemn in paragraph 101 of Cmd. 6659.

accounts by showing the relation between original expenditure on the assets (or later valuations) and amortisation or replacement provisions so far made, thus providing shareholders with a rather better basis for guesses of present values and of the adequacy of depreciation provisions.

In view of this limited achievement it is perhaps unfortunate that the Act requires auditors to report of balance sheets that they give a true and fair view of the state of the company's affairs. Many laymen would, if they knew the facts, probably consider that balance sheets do nothing of the kind. The Cohen Committee may have been justified in rejecting the idea that the balance sheet can show "net worth" for this figure is, after all, anybody's guess.[12] It is surely time, however, for balance sheet headings to indicate clearly and unequivocally those items which are nothing more than a record of past outlay minus certain arbitrary deductions.

III—THE INVESTOR'S REQUIREMENTS

It seems then that it is in the profit and loss account that we should expect to find the main contribution of the reserves and provisions clauses of the Act. Do these bring this account closer to providing "shareholders and investors and their advisers" with "the information to enable them to estimate the real value of the shares"?[13] Our first step is to decide what this information is.

Over the long period (that is, a period sufficiently long to establish a trend and eliminate the result of speculative operations) the market value of a share depends, *ceteris paribus,* on the assessment, by buyers and sellers, of:

(a) The merits of alternative uses for their funds (for example, the current yield on Government securities of varying maturity dates).

(b) The dividends likely to be paid on the share in question.

Here we are concerned with (b). Many investors will no doubt rely on the opinions of others for the assessment of the value of their shares. Others may neglect their holdings altogether. For our purpose it will be reasonable to consider the attitude of the professional investor. We can, I think, assume the latter will attempt to assess the probable level of dividends on his shares in the indefinite future, though his estimate will no doubt take the form of a fairly close assessment of the probable dividends for the next year or two plus a more or less vague idea of the trend thereafter. (But however short the period for which an accurate forecast is attempted some kind of implicit assumption must be made of the value of the shares at the end of the period, which in turn implies an assumption of the probable level of dividends thereafter.[14]) If the company is one which will probably be liquidated within a foreseeable time, say 20 or 30 years, as may be the case for example if its object is the exploitation of a gold mine, the investor may even make some

---

[12] But it would undoubtedly be of value to shareholders to have in the margins of the balance sheet estimates of (a) present replacement values and (b) scrap values of the various assets, since these would give some rough idea of the limits within which "net worth" lay though, of course, it would be necessary to make allowance for goodwill.

[13] Cmd. 6659, para. 101.

[14] These forecasts may of course take the form of guessing other people's estimates.

attempt to estimate *all* the future dividends (or at least some kind of "average" level of dividend), including the final dividend in liquidation.

For the assessment of future dividends reports of past profits and dividends are part of the evidence, but nothing more. The social, political and economic conditions of the world in general, and of the company's own region and trade in particular, are as important. The proportion of reported profits likely to be paid out as dividends requires an assessment of probable directorial policy (and, in the United Kingdom today, of Government policy). For the moment, however, we are considering only the first of these things.

The shareholder (or his adviser) may then be assumed to start, for want of a better basis, with last year's reported profit (or perhaps with the figures for several years) and, applying his knowledge of outside conditions, and such extra information as the directors may give him, to guess which components of the profit balance are likely to change and by how much. He will thus arrive at some estimate, necessarily very rough, of the order of magnitude of next year's reported profit, and so on for the following years, the aura of uncertainty around his guess rapidly increasing as the period lengthens. For this kind of guess (which is only different in degree from the kind of estimate the Board will have to make when budgeting for the future) the most suitable presentation of the profit and loss account would take the form of an analysis of revenue and expenditure in substantial detail and as far as possible into homogeneous groups in the sense that the components of each group were likely to vary in the same way in response to changes in other figures or in outside conditions.[15]

IV—THE CAPITAL AND REVENUE PROBLEM

That it is in this direction we must look for improvement in the technique of presenting information to shareholders is emphasised when we examine the attempt of the 1948 Act to achieve the same thing. The legal provisions we are considering attempt to meet this problem by defining certain types of bookkeeping entry and requiring their disclosure in the interests of allocating the "correct" revenues and outlays to each year of account and of disclosing those items in the calculation of which there is a substantial degree of estimate. There is here an implicit assumption that so far as other items of outlay and revenue are concerned the distinction between "capital" and "revenue" expenditure can be accurately made and that in particular the balance of profit and loss account before deduction or addition of such items, the so-called "trading profit," is a meaningful figure.

In some sense future earning power—and presumably we must base our capital-revenue allocations on estimated changes in this earning power—is

---

[15] It is presumably with the object of facilitating such studies that we segregate "exceptional" items in the profit and loss account. This segregation, however, is only the first step in a development of profit and loss presentation which we may hope will be carried much further. And cf. "General rules for initial recording of cost data" in Chapter 6 of *Management Planning and Control,* B. E. Goetz (McGraw-Hill Book Company, 1949).

dependent upon *all* past expenditure and revenue, since all the decisions of which these are the reflection can be assumed to have some effect on the future of the company.[16] The justification for devoting particular attention to so-called depreciation and replacement provisions is no doubt the practical one that these are often likely to be the more important determinants of future revenues and outlays. This may not always be the case. Consider, for example, the acceptance of a large contract on relatively poor terms because it is expected to establish a connection which will bring more business later. The difference between the net revenue on this contract and the net revenue that could have been earned now had it not been undertaken represents the creation of an asset which will not, however, be entered in the books. Nor will there be any single item of expenditure which can be pointed to as "asset creating." There seems no complete solution to this difficulty within the framework of the conventional form of annual account. Even if full details of the contract were disclosed and the reasons for accepting it explained, a later change in managerial policy or expectations could change the situation completely. The answer seems to lie rather in the linking of analysis of the past with the presentation of budgets, as will be noted later.

In this connection we may recall our footnote 11 (page 135) on the significance of expenditure on development and of cognate outlays (such as expenditure on research and advertising)—expenditure which is incurred with the object of either *maintaining* revenue-earning power at something like the present level or *increasing* it in the future. It is doubtful whether a consistent directorial policy of charging to revenue items of this kind, which are intended to *increase* profit, would be challenged by the auditors on the grounds that thereby a hidden reserve ("goodwill") was being created. Nor do I think I am wrong in saying (though I stand to be corrected) that such items expended to "renew" goodwill are not likely to be regarded as "renewals" for the purpose of separate disclosure in the profit and loss account in accordance with the Eighth Schedule. It might be said that this latter point is only part of the more general question "At what point does maintenance become renewal?" And indeed, why should the complete replacement of an asset require to be included in the separately disclosed depreciation provision while piecemeal replacement does not? The answer to this is probably that the latter is likely to be relatively insignificant in relation to total reported profit. This argument, however, cannot be applied to our case of development expenditure and we must conclude that where such expenditure is likely to *add* substantially to earning power (goodwill) then its non-disclosure in the profit and loss account is equivalent to feeding hidden reserves to the credit of that account and will

---

[16] Unless we are prepared to use market values of assets as a criterion, we must necessarily invoke estimates of future earnings when deciding whether capital is being "maintained." Precisely what meaning shall be given to the term "maintenance of capital" (and, therefore, "net profit") must be decided before meaningful allocations can be made between "capital" and "revenue." (See, for example, "The Nature and Measurement of Income," R. S. Edwards, *The Accountant*, 1938, and *The Valuation of Property*, J. C. Bonbright, McGraw-Hill, 1937. The former has been reprinted in *Studies in Accounting*, ed. W. T. Baxter, Sweet and Maxwell, 1950.)

mislead the shareholder. The Eighth Schedule, as it now stands, *could* be interpreted as requiring such debits to be treated as reserve appropriations, on the grounds that they represent outlays more than are, in the opinion of the directors, "reasonably necessary" for the "renewal" of goodwill. Accounting thought, however, is so used to regarding goodwill, development expenditure, and the like as in some way "spurious" that the renewal of goodwill is not likely to be an acceptable concept and such an interpretation is probably not in accordance with "accepted accounting principles." As, in any case, the separation of the "improvement" element of expenditure from the "maintenance" element is a matter whose assessment is highly subjective, and assessments are likely to vary more widely in this case than in others, we must conclude that the case for the detailed analysis of profit and loss items, plus managerial explanations of the object of the expenditures, is further strengthened. Where it is not a question of charging actual expenditure, but of reserving or providing for future expenditure of the same nature, the question "reserve or provision" poses itself more directly. It may even be that in such cases the position is reversed and the tendency is rather to regard the whole allocation as a reserve although in fact it may include a substantial element of goodwill "renewal" provision.[17]

V—THE DEPRECIATION PROBLEM

Let us turn now to the question of depreciation and replacement provisions proper. The Act has paid particular attention to these, and, whatever other problems of interpretation there may be, it is interesting to consider the probable effectiveness of its requirements. From the point of view of the shareholder attempting to estimate future dividends, the interpretation of depreciation and replacement provisions, as indeed of all other items in the account, can be conceived as the answering of two questions: (a) what effect is the current depreciation policy likely to have on future revenues and outlays (that is, future "profits" before depreciation) and (b) can the current depreciation or replacement provision be regarded as a good measure of similar provisions in the near future?

The point of the first question can be illustrated by the example of a gold mining company, where the knowledge that zero depreciation is provided will obviously be an essential factor in guessing at the surplus available for dividend in ultimate liquidation, while on the other hand the amount allotted annually for finance of further development will be an important factor (when coupled with the information provided in the report) in estimating future annual dividends.[18] Where, as is usual, the venture is a continuing one, there being no intention of liquidating within the forseeable future, the depreciation

---

[17] Whether or not goodwill, development expenditure, advertising outlay and so on appear in the balance sheet is not relevant for we have already seen that the determination of profit is regarded in accounting opinion generally as a matter separate from balance sheet presentation.

[18] It is perhaps to the accounts of mining companies that we should look for a model. These customarily contain a detailed analysis of current revenue and expenditure, and give average realised prices of products. Average operating costs per unit of output or

provisions represent amounts that will be re-invested by the directors, and as these in total are higher or lower so, other things being equal (a big assumption, it is true), will future dividends also be higher or lower. It is in this context that the *basis* of the provision, whether it is on original cost, at replacement level, and so on, is relevant.

So far as (b) above is concerned, unless we know the *period* (or rate) and *pattern* (over time) of allocations, then *in the absence of managerial explanation* last year's "net profit" will, even if the basis of depreciation is given, be a correspondingly poorer guide to future accounting net profits and therefore to future dividends or to the assessment of future "cover" for dividends (the latter is likely to alter the stock market capitalisation rate for calculation of share values). This is saying in another way that the shareholder should know how the directors propose to allocate expected profits to accounting periods through the arrangement of their depreciation policy. (It is true, of course, that the directors' ploughing-back policy is equally important. This indeed raises the question whether gross rather than net revenue is not the more significant figure (cf. our mining company), and whether the division of the difference between profit before depreciation and dividends (that is, gross saving by the company) into (a) depreciation and (b) net profit ploughed back, has much meaning. This depends a good deal upon the directorial attitude to profit determination and may perhaps be a worthwhile subject for investigation later on when the 1948 Act has been in force sufficiently long. This, however, is a digression.)

How far are the provisions of the Eighth Schedule effective in helping the shareholder to answer the questions posed above in relation to depreciation and replacement policy?

So far as the general basis of depreciation is concerned, the Schedule evidently envisages that alternative policies can be followed, for in different places it speaks (a) of amounts provided "for depreciation or diminution of value" (Eighth Schedule, para. 5 [1] [b]), (b) of provision for "renewals" (*ibid.,* para. 5 [2] [b]),[19] and (c) of "some method other than a depreciation

---

per ton of ore crushed, as appropriate, are often stated, but in any case can usually be calculated from the figures given. Depreciation is usually not provided (except, perhaps, on the less important assets), but annual appropriations from operating profit are made for the finance of further development. The purpose for which the finance is needed is commonly explained in considerable detail and the accounts are accompanied by many statistics of production, payability of ore, ore reserves, etc., and by a detailed engineering report. The shareholder is thus given every opportunity to form his own opinion on the probable future earnings of his company and of the depreciation quota he should deduct from his dividends in order to meet his personal criterion of capital maintenance. Moreover, quarterly operating reports in less detail are usually provided.

[19] It is interesting to note that the words used in para. 5 (4) (a) (which requires that the means by which the *replacement* of fixed assets is provided for shall be stated in cases where the "depreciation or diminution in value" basis is not adopted) suggest that the object of *all* provisions of this nature is *replacement* and not *amortisation*. In a continuing business this may well be a more rational approach, but the Act itself seems to waver between the two conceptions. The Cohen Report on the other hand came down definitely in favour of the "depreciation or diminution in value" concept and

charge or provision for renewals" (*ibid.,* para. 14 [2]). However, paragraph (12) (1) (a) of the Schedule (which requires the statement in the profit and loss account of "the amount charged to revenue by way of provision for depreciation, renewals or diminution in value of fixed assets") does not distinguish between the alternative methods of depreciation (or amortisation) and renewals (or replacement) provision nor does it mention "other methods," and the accounts therefore may leave the shareholder in ignorance of the basis in use. It is true that the shareholder may be able to deduce this information from the balance sheet, since "replacement" or "renewal" provisions will presumably appear among the credit balances (although it is seldom possible to reconcile the profit and loss charge at all exactly with the figures in the balance sheet). Also, if the recommendation of the Institute of Chartered Accountants[20] has been followed, allocations "to finance replacements at enhanced costs" will appear, not as provisions, but separately as reserves. In any case (a) it appears that all companies do not follow the Institute's recommendation and (b) there are varying interpretations of "enhanced replacement costs," while the interpretation adopted is often not made explicit in the published accounts concerned.

It seems then the Act does not ensure that the actual basis of depreciation shall be disclosed to the shareholder. Yet it is this basis which is relevant as one of the important determinants of future revenue and outlay. So far indeed as provisions in relation to current assets are concerned no information at all may be available, as such provisions need not be disclosed either in profit and loss account or balance sheet, and it may be noted that the Act, therefore, apparently does not require disclosure of charges made for "renewals" of stock or work in progress at replacement price level.

Let us turn from the question of basis to that of period and pattern. If the current revenue and outlay from year to year remain fairly constant the use of straight line depreciation evidently tends to allocate accounting profit evenly over the years and the reported profit of year 1 will provide a reasonably good yardstick for estimates of years 2, 3 and 4 and so on. If, however (on the same assumption as to revenue and outlay), the depreciation charge is so calculated as to fall more heavily in the earlier years of heavy capital expenditure the reported net profit of year 1 will not give a good idea of the likely net profit in later years, and shareholders basing their expectations on the former may be misled even if they guess correctly the trend of gross revenue. It is true that where the directors base a high depreciation charge, in the earlier years, on the greater certainty of the level of net revenue in those years it could fairly be said that net profit may in fact measure accurately the profit *as the directors conceive it.* But on the other hand there may be a tendency to write off heavy expenditure, particularly on "development," quickly on grounds of "prudence" which may amount to an understatement of even what the *directors* call profit. It seems doubtful whether even in the latter case

---

would have excluded the replacement concept except (on administrative grounds) in the case of public utilities (Cmd. 6659, p. 59).

[20] Recommendation No. XII on Accounting Principles.

the auditors would be prepared to oppose the rapid writing off of (for example) large development expenditure on the grounds that it was more than "reasonably necessary." Nor in fact would they, it seems, be entitled to do so unless they considered, not only that the charge was more than "reasonably necessary" but that it was in excess of what the *directors themselves* considered to be reasonably necessary.[21] Then again, it may be that current revenue and outlay in year 1 is not likely to be a good measure of these items in years 2, 3, 4, etc. In this case a straight line depreciation rate might result in a reported profit that fell steadily. In short, if in the next n years the directors expect a total gross revenue[22] from a particular project of p and estimate total depreciation in relation to that project (on a given basis) at d, then "fair" reporting of annual "profit" requires a statement of how much of d will be allocated to each year of the n years. The larger d is in relation to p and the larger p is in relation to the total gross revenue of the company, the more important is disclosure of this kind likely to be. The provisions of the Eighth Schedule do not ensure that this information is given.

Whatever policy the directors may adopt, it seems that the annual depreciation or replacement allocations can legally be classified as provisions, and not as reserves, provided only that they do not exceed what, in the opinion of the directors, is "reasonably necessary." Provided the policy is consistently followed, it seems that the auditor in such cases cannot interfere. Yet depreciation provisions which A might consider "necessary" (say on grounds of "prudence"), might be considered by B to involve a substantial secret reserve. Where the activities of the company were few, and the asset accounts correspondingly simple and few, the balance sheet might provide the shareholder with much of the relevant information. For example, he could see that, in relation to last year, expenditure on, say, jigs and dies, etc., had risen by x, depreciation thereon by y, and hence deduce an approximate depreciation rate. If the directors had explained the purpose of outlay x and defined the basis of y (for example, as recovery of original cost) the shareholder would at least have a good start in the very chancy game of estimating the worth of his shares. But if the company's business was large and complex, then in the absence of a detailed analysis of the depreciation provision and the relevant balance sheet asset item (in addition to the other information) the shareholder would be left in the dark on what might well be a new and important project. It is not, of course, suggested that the "correct" depreciation provision should be that which spreads the accounting profit uniformly over time. It is useless to discuss the "correctness" of the various depreciation concepts without first deciding on a definition of profit, and it may well be that the quest for such a "correct" depreciation concept is a search for a chimera which it would be better to abandon.

---

[21] It is interesting to note that the decision as to "necessity" is (by para. 27 of the Eighth Schedule) to be made by the directors, the people whose propensity to create secret reserves it is the presumed intention of these provisions of the Act to check.

[22] i.e. profit before depreciation.

VI—CONCLUSION

The 1948 Act has attempted, by defining provisions, which are charges against profits, and distinguishing them from reserves, which are not, to arrive at a "truer" net profit. This attempt is, it seems, of limited value and is in a sense dangerous, for it carries the underlying suggestion that by careful definition, a "true" concept of profit can be derived, and that accurate measurement of this will be possible. It would indeed be possible to define "profit" rigidly,[23] and this might not be wholly disadvantageous. But it would be an unfortunate development if such a step were not accompanied by requirements for a much more detailed analysis of accounts and especially for their accompaniment by fuller explanations and statements of assumptions. The well-prepared accounts of the future will be, no doubt, those from which it will be possible to extract alternative profit figures according to different criteria, but which themselves may contain no single item labelled "net profit."[24]

We have already noted that in kind the information needed by shareholders in the assessment of the value of their investment does not differ from that likely to be used by the management as a guide to their conduct of the business. This suggests that the distinction commonly made between accounting for management and accounting for publication, between "management" and "financial" accounting, is perhaps a bad one. There is little doubt that one of the most valuable aids to the shareholder or investor in his attempt to assess the value of his shares would be a detailed and reasoned statement by the directors of their estimates of future profits and dividends.[25] The most useful form this could take would be that of a summarised cash budget covering a number of years and showing expected sources of new finance and expected dividend payments. The annual accounts could form the basis (perhaps through the link of a source and disposition of funds statement) for a comparison of last year's budget with actual achievements, and so on. It can perhaps be hoped that enlightened boards may move towards supplying such budgets. We cannot, however, expect rapid progress. And indeed there are considerable difficulties. Boards may hesitate to commit themselves when a subsequent unfavourable turn of events could bring down wrath upon their heads. Meanwhile, given the existing framework of accounting conventions and legal requirements, the compulsion of acting within the bounds of the possible, our aim must be the more pedestrian one of piecemeal improvement.

London

---

[23] For example, in terms of the profits tax computation.
[24] See Edwards, *op. cit.*
[25] Following a line of thought opened up by R. S. Edwards and others in recent years.

Printed by Jordan & Sons, Limited, Chancery Lane, London, W.C.2

INCOME AND CAPITAL IN INCOME TAXATION— DISTRIBUTIONS BY COMPANIES

By HAROLD EDEY

Introduction

This article is part of a study of the measurement of business income under the United Kingdom tax laws. It seemed desirable, for the reasons given below, to discuss certain aspects of the way in which stockholders[1] are taxed when they receive distributions from their companies,[2] before examining the measurement of the business profits from which some of these distributions are made. Any discussion of the concept of taxable income must deal with the various meanings of "income" and "capital." But it is not possible to sort out the various shades of meaning which "income" and "capital" have acquired in income tax law without referring to the company distribution cases; and until these meanings have been sorted out one cannot appreciate fully the implications of the words in profit measurement cases.

It has not always been clearly recognised by the Courts (or, if recognised, has not been acted upon) how many distinct meanings (some very subtly shaded from others) these words have, both in law and in accounting practice.[3] In tax law the two words have gradually acquired the general meaning (in addition to all the other meanings) of "taxable" ("income") and "non-taxable" ("capital"). It has therefore become easy to fall into the logical fallacy of drawing from the "capital"

---

[1] By "stockholders" I mean all holders of company securities, whether shares or debentures; and by "securities" all titles of this *genre,* whether or not they carry a legal charge.

[2] The discussion is restricted to companies legally "resident" in this country. "Residence" implies, broadly, that the "central direction and control" of the company is in the United Kingdom. On this see any standard textbook on income tax.

[3] There is no general definition of "income" in the Income Tax Acts and it has long been judicially recognised that many amounts which would in ordinary language not be called "income" are, nevertheless, taxable. Yet: "Income tax . . . is a tax upon income" (*London County Council v. Attorney General* (1899/1900) 4 T.C. 265 (H.L.) per Lord Macnaghten at p. 293) and "The real question, for the purpose of deciding whether the Income Tax Acts apply, is whether the . . . sum is capital or income" (*Westminster Bank Ltd. v. Riches* (1945/1947) 28 T.C. 159 (H.L.) per Lord Simon at p. 187). The idea expressed in these propositions appears repeatedly in income tax litigation; it seems, however, to have served little purpose (beyond fogging the issue), for the Revenue Judges have in practice not relied on any single clearly-stated definition of these concepts. On the contrary, they have (as the section of the law discussed in this article shows) been most catholic in their choice of logical foundations for so-called capital-income decisions. A consistency in the use of the words is certainly not one of the features of the case law.

nature of a sum of money, when "capital" is used in *any* of its senses, the conclusion that it must therefore be necessarily non-taxable; and likewise with "income." The Courts have recognised this danger explicitly; and they have tended to be chary of any one test of taxability. Nevertheless, this fallacy has not always been avoided, and at times the "capital" or "income" nature of an item in some irrelevant context has been at least one of the points given weight in the judgment. In such a case, even if the incorrect use of the word does not affect the decision, the error is recorded and, at best, will increase the labours of readers; while at worst it will lead later to inconsistent judgments and to uncertainty in the law.[4]

A knowledge of the mechanism of taxation of corporate distributions is thus relevant to problems of accounting measurement of income. But it is also necessary for a complete understanding of the relationships between shareholders and the companies of which they are the nominal owners; the same is true of any examination of the part played by the corporate form of enterprise in the promotion of national saving. A study of this section of income tax law reveals, indeed, some curious anomalies, and raises doubts about the extent to which Parliament has, when it re-enacts each year the income tax legislation, a full appreciation of the nature of the present arrangements.

The topic of this paper is, then, terminological and other aspects of the rules of income taxation when the effective control of valuable resources passes from company directors into the hands of individuals who are able to choose whether they shall allot those resources to personal consumption or to investment elsewhere—that is to say, when there is a change of *effective* ownership, in favour of natural persons, of corporate property. The paper is also, however, necessarily concerned with certain rearrangements in the ownership of company securities which are sometimes called "distributions," even though at the time of the "distributions" the company parts with none of its assets: so-called "bonus issues" and "rights issues." On the other hand, because the corporate entity is then disregarded, the special case in which income of a company under the control of

---

[4] Some of the relevant rules of law have been discussed recently by Miss O. M. Stone in "What is Income?" (*The Modern Law Review*, April, 1952), of which I have made considerable use. On this topic see also A. Farnsworth, *Income Tax Case Law* (Stevens and Sons Ltd., 1947), Chapters 7 and 9, and the same author's (with J. P. Hannan) *The Principles of Income Taxation* (Stevens and Sons Ltd., 1952), especially Chapter 6.

I think Miss Stone, in her article, implies that it is possible to achieve a useful definition of "income" and "capital" which would enable the terms to be used consistently in all branches of the law. I am doubtful about this. What is to be taxable or non-taxable should depend on the conscious intention of the legislature and not on rules of nomenclature found convenient in other contexts. An example of confusion the use of such words as "capital" can cause has been seen recently in the public discussion on the taxation of authors' copyright royalties and of proceeds of sale of copyrights. It has been said that it is wrong to tax the latter because they are "capital"—the magic word which transmutes taxable sums into non-taxable ones. But authors' copyrights are the fruits of their labour like any other earnings. If they choose to sell them outright rather than collect royalties there is no reason (given the present tax system) why they should not be assessed to income and sur-tax on them. It may, of course, be unjust to assess the results of several years' work in one year when the tax rate is as steeply progressive as ours; this, however, is quite a different question.

a few shareholders is treated not as corporate but shareholders' income, even though the income may not have been distributed,[5] is not here discussed; nor are inter-company distributions.

Only non-corporate shareholders whose total statutory income exceeds £2,000, and who are therefore within the sur-tax range, feel the direct impact of taxation on distributions of companies resident in the United Kingdom (though, of course, all shareholders are indirectly affected by taxes assessed on the *company*). The liability of shareholders to standard rate tax (that is, income tax other than sur-tax) is exhausted by the direct assessment of the company to income tax on its statutory profits, distributed or not.[6, 7] The question has, however, a rather wider interest than this might suggest. If, for example, the assessment of standard rate tax on companies were discontinued in favour of a direct dividend tax on distributions, the problem of deciding *which* distributions were taxable as "dividends" would become even more important than at present, for it would affect the liability of all taxpayers, whether or not within the sur-tax range.

The Tests for Taxability

The rules which determine the taxability, in the hands of the recipients, of distributions by U.K.-resident companies may be summarised as follows:

(a) Any "dividend" that does not result in the release of assets by the company is not taxable "income."[8] "Capitalisations" of profits (in the technical sense in which the word is used in company law), and in particular so-called bonus issues (or scrip issues) of shares or debentures of the company, are not considered by the tax law to give rise to "income" unless (probably) the issue takes the form of debentures (*quaere* Preference shares) repayable within a short period of time.[9] So-called "rights issues with bonus elements" to existing stockholders similarly attract no tax liability.[10] All these transactions have in common the absence of

---

[5] Under the Income Tax Act, 1952, s. 245.

[6] As a corollary, the rules that relate to sur-tax assessment determine whether a taxpayer liable marginally at *less* than standard rate can reclaim standard rate tax "deemed" to have been paid on his behalf by the distributing company.

[7] It is a well-known feature of United Kingdom income tax law that stockholders do not become liable to tax on profits (or entitled to relief for losses) made from *dealing* in securities unless the dealing can be said to amount to the legal carrying on of a business, in technical phraseology "trading" (which is a question not of law but of fact). This rule is of very long standing. Such profits are an example of one type of "capital profit." I do not propose to examine here the history of the exemption of this type of profit from taxation. For completeness it should also be mentioned that there is an exception to the general rule in that profits from "bond washing"—the systematic sale of certain classes of securities cum dividend in order to avoid receipt of cash dividends—are assessable to sur-tax (Income Tax Act, 1952, Section 237). See also below (page 325) in connection with interest on bills and promissory notes.

[8] *I.R.C. v. Blott* (1919/21) 8 T.C. 101 (H.L.).

[9] *Aykroyd v. I.R.C.* (1942) 24 T.C. 515, discussed below.

[10] These are merely issues of new securities to existing stockholders at a given price; their issue involves no formal "capitalisation" of profits or release of resources by the company; and so far as the new shares are of a class already in issue and the issue price is below the present market value of the existing shares (as it usually is, and is almost invariably intended to be), rights issues resemble so-called "splits," that is, increases in the total number of

any release to stockholders of the company's resources.

(b) Dividends of any kind deemed to have been paid out of funds not taxable in the *company's* hands, including so-called "capital profits," are not taxable income in the hands of shareholders.[11, 12]

(c) Distributions to stockholders in the liquidation of the company;[13] or by way of reduction of "capital";[14] or by way of repayment of redeemable securities (even if they are redeemed above issue price), are not taxable income in the stockholders' hands.[15, 16]

(d) Any other distribution by a company to its stockholders, whether in cash or in specie, is treated as taxable income in the hands of the recipient stockholder.

Were the law self-consistent it would be possible to derive from these rules one or more general principles for the taxation of company distributions. This cannot be done. All these rules are indeed consistent in the sense that whatever tax may be laid upon the *company*, shareholders do not incur liability in respect of its profits until it has placed resources in their hands.[17] This seems not un-reasonable if one thinks of a shareholder's interest as a kind of quasi-loan to

---

shares of a given class without any change in the quantum of rights attaching to the class as a whole (except, perhaps, voting rights), rather than true bonus issues.

[11] *Vide Neumann v. I.R.C.* (1932/34), 18 T.C. 332 (H.L.).

[12] But for the purpose of profits tax (assessed on the *company*) a company cannot avoid the higher rate on distributed profits by claiming that it is only distributing "capital profits." Any distribution to shareholders except a return of "capital" (and even this is subject to Section 31 of the Finance Act, 1951—see below) is regarded as a "gross relevant distribution." The effect of this is that until the company has paid the full rates (i.e., those applicable to *distributed* profits) on all taxable profits since 1947 (that is, while the company has a balance of "non-distribution relief" in hand) any distribution to shareholders will be regarded as being made partly or wholly out of those taxable profits. (Finance Act, 1947, Section 35, and *Lamson Paragon Supply Co. Ltd. v. I.R.C.* (1951) 32 T.C. 302.) A payment of share premiums on redemption is a reduction of "capital," however, for this purpose, and is not caught by Section 35 (*I.R.C. v. Universal Grinding Wheel Co. Ltd.* [1953] 3 W.L.R. 29).

[13] *I.R.C. v. Burrell* (1923/24) 9 T.C. 27 (C.A.).

[14] This is apparently covered by *Burrell's Case.*

[15] *Lomax v. Peter Dixon and Son* (1943) 25 T.C. 353 (C.A.).

[16] But, again, distributions in liquidation of sums in excess of paid-up share capital plus share premiums paid in cash are regarded as "gross relevant distributions" for *profits* tax purposes. Moreover, a combination of capitalisation of profits (whether of "capital profits" or not) and reduction of capital (in whatever time order these may occur) will now, under the Finance Act, 1951, Section 31, be regarded as amounting to a "gross relevant distribution."

[17] Even this consistency ceases, however, at the frontier of the company. If company *A* holds, *inter alia*, all the voting shares of company *B*, the assets of *B* are as much under the control of the directors of *A* as *A*'s own assets. But should *A* distribute, to its own shareholders, some of the shares it holds in *B*, while yet retaining its control in *B* (e.g., by distributing non-voting preference shares in *B*), then, though the practical effect is similar to that of issuing bonus preference shares in *A*, no real resources being unlocked, yet sur-tax will be payable (under rule (d) above), on the value of the shares received by the shareholders of *A*, as on a cash dividend. Inconsistencies of this kind are inevitable when the rights of shareholders may, without infringement of the law, vary so widely from company to company, so that, because it is hard to cover all contingencies, legislation affecting these rights must sometimes appear inconsequential.

the "directors-in-office" of the company in exchange for a promise of "interest" (dividends) contingent upon the earning of profits and upon the willingness of the directors to pay it. This view is probably a fairly close approximation to the facts of the case in relation to most public companies in these days and has considerable significance for a policy of Governmental encouragement of corporate saving. The inconsistency arises because the principle does not hold in reverse. It is only applied in favour of the taxpayer, not of the Revenue. Sums in excess of their original investment may, in certain cases, be placed in the hands of stockholders without liability to tax arising. We shall now discuss these rules in detail.

Bonus Issues

When bonus issues are made the process is, for company law purposes, described as "capitalisation" of profits; the new titles issued to shareholders have also been treated as "capital" for the purpose of deciding relative rights of life tenants and remaindermen in trust cases. Perusal of the tax judgments suggests strongly that this use of the terms "capitalisation" and "capital" influenced some of the judges in their decisions on the *taxability* of the transactions. Nevertheless close study suggests that the basic test applied has not been (or at any rate, has not remained) merely one of verbal analogy, but has become one of substance. It is true that the leading authority, *Blott's Case*, was founded on a trust case[18] in which the decision that a bonus dividend was capital as between life tenant and remainderman was based on the intention of the company to "capitalise" the profit. Some of the judgments in *Blott's Case* and later tax cases suggest pretty strongly that they were swayed by the mere use of the word "capitalisation." Lord Cave's judgments in *Blott's Case* and in the later case *I.R.C. v. Fisher's Executors*[19] suggest, however, that the *ratio decidendi* for holding bonus shares non-taxable was the absence of any release of assets by the company. There is no "magic" of capitalisation here: merely a straightforward extension of the principle that while cash dividends, because they put funds into the hands of the shareholders, may be taxable, undistributed profits are not.[20] On the other hand, consistency demands that when, eventually, resources *are* released by money payments to stockholders in respect of any bonus issues made to them at an earlier date, that is, by repayment of debentures,

---

[18] *Bouch v. Sproule* (1887), 12 A.C. 385.

[19] (1924/26), 10 T.C. 302 (H.L.).

[20] An interesting example of the irrelevant introduction by the Court of the idea of "capitalisation" is to be found in *Parker v. Chapman* ((1927/28) 13 T.C. 677 (C.A.)) Here a shareholder allowed the company to apply commission due to him *in another capacity* in payment for new shares. He was held to be taxable on the commission. The Court of Appeal reasoned that it was the *creditor*—in this case also a shareholder—who "capitalised" the amount, and not the *company*. In fact it is hard to see how the issue of shares was in any way relevant. The shareholder had received commission: this was taxable just like a salary or any similar payment. But he had not received the payment *qua* shareholder, and if he chose to invest the money in the company this was his own concern. The Court was, of course, right. The money had been invested and in this sense "capitalised"; but the point is that this had really nothing to do with the case and illustrates the tendency of the Courts to be drawn off by the capital-income red herring.

or of share capital (in a formal "reduction of capital"), or in liquidation, liability to tax should arise just as it would in respect of any cash dividend. Except (probably) for the case of short-term debentures (and here any liability to tax will, it seems, arise on *issue;* not on later *redemption*)[21] this is not at present the law. There is little doubt that this is at least in part due to a spurious association of "capital" in a company law sense (which may have been built up out of earlier profits) with "capital" sums which are so called merely because they are not taxable. (See the section below on distributions of "capital" funds.)

Contrariwise, the distribution of a dividend in the form of shares of *another* company, like a money dividend, is treated for tax purposes as "income," for here there *is* a release of assets.[22] In *Pool's* case Sankey, J., found it necessary to add to the release-of-assets test the qualification that, to be taxable, assets released must be derived from taxable profits, or as he put it, must not be "capital." This proviso was not, of course, necessary to the decisions on bonus shares where, since no distribution of the assets had taken place, the question whether assets distributed were "capital" or "income" did not arise. "Capital" in the sense in which Sankey, J., used the word had no reference to any question of "capitalisation of profits"—as in the bonus share cases—but referred to the taxability while in the *company's* hands of the fund from which the dividend was distributed,[23] and would have been equally relevant in the case of a distribution of *money,* as we shall see.

Thus, in the "bonus share" cases, taken by themselves, a consistent principle can be found which, whatever the judges may have *said,* does not depend on mere verbal juggling with the words "capital" and "capitalisation."[24] In these cases the terms have become mere verbal appendages, contributing nothing to the argument. It is not so with the other rules relating to the taxation of company distributions.

Distribution of "Capital" Profits

Dividends in cash or in kind are normally, for sur-tax purposes, "income" in the shareholders' hands. If, however, they are "deemed" to be paid out of "capital profits" of the company, they are not taxable. This rule has received judicial approval and has not been challenged in the Courts by the Revenue authorities. Yet it can only be rationalised by regarding it as a relic of an earlier

---

[21] In *Whitmore v. I.R.C.* (1925) 10 T.C. 645, bonus debentures were held non-taxable though repaid within two months of issue, but this is probably no longer good law. The decisions in *Aykroyd v. I.R.C.* (1942) 24 T.C. 515, and in *Associated Insulation Products v. Golder* (1944) 26 T.C. 231 (C.A.) (in which the Court of Appeal, by implication, approved *Aykroyd's Case*) suggest this.

[22] *Pool v. Guardian Investment Trust Co. Ltd.* (1921), 8 T.C. 167.

[23] This is discussed below.

[24] In the equivalent American cases liability of the recipients of stock dividends (bonus shares) to Federal income tax appears to depend upon whether the issue changes the recipients' proportionate rights in the company. (See *Koshland v. Helvering* (1936) 298 U.S. 441 and Lasser K. (ed.) *Handbook of Tax Accounting Methods,* D. Van Nostrand Co. Inc. 1951, p. 46.)

rule now judicially discountenanced : namely, that the company earns its profits and pays its tax as agent of the shareholders,[25] and that consequently if the law leaves a profit untaxed in the hands of the company that profit should not, when distributed, be taxable in the shareholders' hands.[26] This view is inconsistent with the established principles of the bonus share cases and generally with the idea of non-taxability of *undistributed* profits. If what a company earns but does not distribute is, for that very reason, not taxable income of the shareholders, why should not what it *distributes* (other than original paid-in funds) be taxable, however it may have been earned? Asymmetries of this kind may sometimes be justified on practical grounds. It is particularly interesting, however, that in this connection there is a *formal* inconsistency in the law. An appeal to *company* law would show that dividends paid out of so-called "capital profits" *cannot* really be "capital," for it is illegal for a company to distribute "capital" except in the formal legal processes of reduction or liquidation. Hence what is here "not-capital" in the company law[27] is "capital" in the income tax law.[28] Now, there is, as I see it, no particular reason why revenue law *should* follow company law. The inconsistency arises because the Courts *have,* as we shall see, sometimes relied on the description of a transaction in other branches of the law in order to establish its taxability or non-taxability, without defining such terms as "capital" in relation to each context in which they have been used.[29]

Distribution of "Capital" Funds

When we turn to the taxation of distributions to shareholders made in liquidation or in the process of a legal reduction of capital we find that the tax rules *are*

---

[25] *Vide* Stone, *op. cit.,* and Farnsworth, *Income Tax Case Law,* Chapter 7. The old idea still persists in the rules whereby the company is assessed to standard rate income tax on the whole of its "taxable income," the recipient of dividends incurring no further liability for standard rate tax. However, whatever the origin of this practice, it can be regarded today as a method of "double taxation relief," compensating the shareholder for the fact that the very high rate of tax levied on the company (which includes profits tax and perhaps Excess Profits Levy as well as standard rate income tax) has substantially reduced the fund out of which dividends can be paid and has therefore probably reduced the level of dividend the directors are prepared to distribute.

[26] In certain cases profits, apparently untaxed in the hands of the company, will in fact be "deemed" taxed, and when distributed will be "income" of the shareholders (see *Neumann v. I.R.C.*).

[27] And see Stone, *op. cit.,* on trust law, which here follows company and not tax law.

[28] But if the dividend is paid by an *overseas* company the *company law* rule is allowed to determine the taxability of the sum received in the United Kingdom (*I.R.C. v. Reids Trustees* (1947/49), 30 T.C. 431 (H.L.)).

[29] The non-taxability of "capital profits" when distributed to shareholders raises the further question of how meaningful it is to impute a particular cash distribution to a given source of funds. There are, of course, artificial rules for tracing the progress of sums of money passing through accounts, e.g. the Rule in *Clayton's Case*; but such ideas become very unreal when applied to a miscellaneous collection of constantly-changing assets like a business. The profits tax rules (see footnotes 12 and 16) have recognised this. (See also the recent case of *Hatton v. I.R.C.* [1953] 1 W.L.R. 729, in which Upjohn, J., held that a dividend could not have been paid out of interest on tax reserve certificates (which, in itself, is not taxable) because (it seems) the interest could only be earned by applying it in payment of tax liabilities; and if it was so applied it was no longer free for distribution.)

based on the terms used in company law. In *Burrell's Case*, the leading case on the non-taxability of distributions in liquidation, the *ratio decidendi* was based on the fact that the assets which represented the undistributed profit at the time of liquidation were part and parcel of the joint stock or common fund which represented the *capital* of the company (*vide* Pollock, M. R., at page 40).[30] "Capital" here described the funds which would pass through the liquidator's hands and would, after payment of the company's debts, be divided among the shareholders in accordance with their contractual rights. But "capital" for Revenue law purposes could only be sensibly construed to mean "non-taxable." Why should the first description of a given amount imply the second? It is queer that company law nomenclature should be ignored in considering the taxability of dividends paid out of profits *before* liquidation begins but should be applied in connection with distributions *in* liquidation.

Premiums on Redemption

If debentures and Preference shares are repayable at a figure above the price of original issue (whether because they are repayable at a premium or were issued at a discount, or both) the excess (which I shall call here a premium) is not taxable in the hands of the recipient stockholder unless the latter is "trading" in securities, that is, is a stockjobber or a bank or something like that. This appears to be a very old rule in income tax law[31] and probably has the same origin as the rule whereby the profits of dealing in securities are only taxable in similar circumstances. Yet the similarity between these two types of transaction is less than it might appear. Premiums on redemption are (unlike profits on *dealing* in securities) another case of a release of assets by a company, just like a cash dividend or a dividend in specie. They are in fact the actuarial equivalents of periodic dividends and interest. It is true that the premiums happen to be called "capital" payments; but this is merely a way of describing the method of payment. Indeed, some discounts and premiums *are* taxable, namely when the period of credit is relatively short and there are no accompanying periodic payments, that is, in the case of discount on bills or interest on promissory notes.[32] It is not easy to find a logical distinction between such payments and discounts and premiums on the longer-dated obligations called debentures. In order to make the distinction it is, for example, necessary to show that the difference between the issue price and the redemption price of a security, whether called discount (when the issue price is below the quite arbitrary "par" or "nominal" value) or premium (when the redemption price

---

[30] It is of interest to accountants that the decision in the well-known *Spanish Prospecting Co. Case* [1911] 1 Ch. 317, was distinguished in *Burrell's Case* on not very clear grounds. It was necessary to the Court's decision to do this because the *Spanish Case* showed that even if a company was in liquidation it was possible to separate "profit" from "capital" funds and the Court in *Burrell's Case* decided that this separation could not be made for the purpose of assessment to sur-tax of a shareholder receiving the dividend.

[31] *Vide* Lord Greene, M.R. in *Lomax v. Peter Dixon and Son* (1943) 25 T.C. 353 (C.A.) at page 365.

[32] *Vide National Provident Institution v. Brown* (1919/21) 8 T.C. 57 (H.L.) and *Bennett v. Ogston* (1930) 15 T.C. 374.

is above "par"), is neither "discount" nor "interest" in the sense in which the word is used in the Rules of Case III of Schedule D,[33] which expressly charges "All discounts" and "interest of money." To find that such sums (that is, discounts and premiums) are not "discount" or "interest" in this sense seems to have been equated by the Courts with finding that they are not "income" but "capital" and therefore excluded from taxable gains on "general principles." In *Lomax v. Peter Dixon and Sons* the question at issue was whether discount and premiums on interest-bearing notes securing a loan to an overseas company were taxable as "income arising from possessions out of the United Kingdom."[34] In the High Court, Macnaghton, J., had held that the amounts in question were "income," but in so holding he had felt it necessary to distinguish the notes in question from ordinary "debentures," a distinction rejected in the Court of Appeal, which reversed his decision. Lord Greene, M. R., delivered the judgment of the Court of Appeal. His judgment is of interest because it is an example of what, with great respect, one can only call a rationalisation of a proposition for which there is no clear legal authority, but which the judge is convinced is right.

If the relevant transactions in this case could not be distinguished from those in the *National Provident Case*, that is, from transactions in short-dated bills, they would be taxable; even if they could be so distinguished there seems to have been no authority other than long usage for their exemption, but the Revenue were prepared to concede this point on the grounds that discounts and premiums on *debentures* were not taxable—an unusual case of the Revenue conceding a point which, in view of the *National Provident Case*, was, as we shall see, quite strongly in their favour. Lord Greene held that the notes were indistinguishable from debentures. Despite the Revenue's concession of the point, however, he went to some length to rationalise the exemption of debenture discounts and premiums from taxation. Indeed it is difficult to separate in his judgment the questions: (a) were the notes "debentures" and (b) are premiums and discounts on debentures "capital"? On the latter question the Solicitor General, in conceding the non-taxability of debenture discounts and premiums, had explained that such amounts were regarded as capital sums borne by the company *because of the risk attached to lending.*[35] Lord Greene laid considerable emphasis on this point in his judgment. His view, like the Revenue's, appeared to be that the part of the lender's return which can be ascribed to the *risk* of lending, as distinct from "pure" interest, is non-taxable or "capital" *provided* that the contract is drawn so as to make this part of the return a discount or premium and not periodical interest. This distinction between the rewards of "waiting" and of "risk-bearing" has no logical justification in this context. It seems that here, too, both judge and Revenue were following a false verbal analogy: the Revenue explanation of their forbearance

---

[33] Income Tax Act, 1952, Section 123.

[34] Income Tax Act, 1952, Section 123.

[35] It is of considerable interest that the reason given by the Revenue for exempting such amounts differed from that proffered by them in *Wilson v. Mannooch* (1937) 21 T.C. 178 (per Lawrence J. at page 184) where they relied merely on the fact that such amounts were not "annual" profits.

suggests that it was felt a reward for risking *capital* must itself be *capital*. This argument can obviously be extended immediately to the reward for *lending* capital, and would exempt all interest. Moreover, if this is the reason for exempting premiums and discount why should it not apply equally to *periodical* payments? This had never been suggested. Lord Greene himself was careful to point out that even discounts and premiums might *not* be "capital" if the periodical payments did not represent a reasonable commercial rate of interest (by which he presumably meant the return exclusive of "risk premium"). He had to make this distinction because of the House of Lords decision, in the *National Provident* case, that discounts on short bills (where the "periodical" rate is zero) *are* taxable. Yet in that very decision distinctions between reward for risk and pure interest and between "income" and "capital" were said to be irrelevant (see Lord Sumner at pp. 96-97).

In another case, *Bennett v. Ogston*,[36] to which Lord Greene referred, Rowlatt, J., had held that interest on a moneylender's loans embodied in the "capital value" of promissory notes was assessable as income after his death.[37] Here the interest clearly must have included an allowance for risk. This case Lord Greene distinguished on the verbal grounds that as the whole of any discount on the face value of notes would be "interest" under the Moneylenders Act it must be "interest" and therefore "income" for tax purposes, an interesting contrast to his statement that "all discounts" in the Income Tax Act did *not* include "discounts" on debentures.[38]

To summarise: the *National Provident* decision had suggested that "discounts" on the issue of loans, whatever their nature, were "profits" and might be assessable. Although the case was not decided on these grounds this is consistent with the "release of assets" principle. Lord Greene was unable to accept that this ruling could extend to discounts on "debentures," but gave no authority for this beyond saying that the Revenue had never sought to tax these sums, and pointing out that the opposite decision must, since it would put debentures on the same footing as bills, render taxable not only discounts and premiums but also any profits of dealing, by whomsoever made.[39] This he reasoned could not be good income tax law: the best evidence of this was the storm in the City such a decision would raise! He did not, however, define a "debenture" unless a definition is implied in his remarks about the relation of discounts or premiums to a "reasonable" commercial rate of interest. None of the arguments seem very convincing.

The above discussion has been concerned with debentures, but there is no doubt that the same general principles apply in the case of the redemption of fixed-dividend *shares* at a price above original issue price. The Revenue has not sought to make these taxable (except in the hands of persons "trading" in securities).

[36] (1930) 15 T.C. 374.
[37] Under Case III.
[38] Lord Greene could not distinguish this case on the grounds that the moneylender was *trading* in money (which would make *all* premiums and discounts assessable) for he was dead and the trade had ceased.
[39] This followed from the *National Provident* decision.

Conclusion

It is a good deal easier to point out logical inconsistencies in the income tax legislation than to suggest satisfactory changes. The existence of *prima facie* anomalies in the law is alone not a sufficient reason for making alterations; anomalies can become irrelevant when broader considerations are brought into the argument. The form which the legislation should take can only be usefully considered in relation to the final aim or aims of the taxing system; this is a social and political matter.

Some of the anomalies that have been described may represent, from some points of view, fortunate gaps in the sweeping tax net of this country, to be justified, perhaps, because they may increase the incentive to undertake business risks. It seems desirable on principle, however, that "gaps," however useful, should be overt rather than covert; freely created by the legislature rather than the result of the luck of litigation and embodied in a mass of indigestible and often mutually contradictory precedents relating to an antiquated Statute. Our present system taxes people heavily, but allows some of those who are knowledgeable, and are prepared to devote sufficient "non-productive" energy and trouble to the task, to avoid some of the burden. *Lacunae* in the tax legislation the benefits of which can only be enjoyed by relatively complicated legal processes—for example, of capital reduction or liquidation—and which may set a premium on going out of business, are unsatisfactory, even if they are thought to bring net advantages with the law as it now is. It would be better to close the gaps and use the consequent gain in revenue to reduce taxes on business.[40]

The aim of this paper has been not to suggest substantive changes in taxation, but to indicate the misleading nature of some of the terminology of Revenue law. It is not certain how far the misuse of such ill-defined terms as "income" and "capital" have contributed to the creation of the particular anomalies discussed here. One cannot say that a judge would have reached a different conclusion in any given case had these words not been introduced. Nevertheless, even when they have not been necessary for the decision, once words with so many possible meanings have been embodied in a precedent they are likely in future to play some part in obscuring the original intention of Parliament. It is desirable that draftsmen of the taxing statutes and, I submit with respect, judges, should as far as possible avoid expressions of this kind, and should aim instead at describing Parliament's intentions in terms of the *procedure* by which the taxable *quantum* is to be ascertained. This might have the incidental advantage of bringing to Parliament a clearer appreciation of what it is doing when it enacts Income Tax Bills and the like.

London.

---

[40] For example, if all company distributions to stockholders in excess of the original paid-in money (or money's worth)—possibly adjusted for purchasing power changes—were made taxable as dividends it would be possible to lower the rate of tax on non-distributed profits of companies without risking additional dissaving made possible by the use of technical methods of avoidance based on the oddities of the law discussed above. This might be a way of encouraging business saving provided it was accompanied by a relaxation of the rigour of the rules subjecting undistributed profits of "controlled" companies to sur-tax and, eventually, to estate duty. A general tidying-up of the rules seems desirable first, however, so that the results of given actions can be estimated more accurately.

ACCURACY AND INACCURACY

IN

PROFIT CALCULATION

I

THE Revenue case, *Patrick* v. *Broadstone Mills, Ltd.*,[1] should be
of interest to practising lawyers, to jurists and to economists, for, in
the writer's opinion, and with respect, the Court of Appeal, by affirm-
ing Vaisey J.'s decision (which reversed the decision of the Special
Commissioners of Income Tax) (a) failed to follow a long-standing
precedent of the House of Lords; (b) provided an interesting case
of judicial legislation in economic matters; (c) introduced a new
uncertainty into Revenue law, and, therefore, into the pursuit of
business, and (d) thereby raised important questions of principle
with respect to the drafting, and subsequent judicial interpretation,
of statutes relating to economic matters where measurement is
involved.

The facts are complex, and merit a fairly lengthy exposition in
order that the essential nature of the issue at stake may be laid bare.

II

The business of the company was cotton spinning. In order to
carry on the business it held stocks of raw cotton. At any given
time some of this cotton clothed the spinning machines and some
waited by the machines, ready for use. A certain minimum
physical quantity of both of these categories of stock was held in
order to ensure continuity of production. This minimum quantity
was called the Base Stock. Additional stocks were sometimes held,
but were not relevant in this case. The question at issue was how
the Base Stock should be valued for profit calculation purposes
under the Income Tax Acts.

In order to calculate annual profit for income tax purposes it
was, of course, necessary to deduct from the company's sales
revenue, *inter alia*, a figure in respect of the cost of the cotton
used in order to produce the yarn that was sold. The problem
the court had to decide was, in essence, how this deduction was
to be calculated. The company, in effect, calculated its gross profit
in any year by deducting from its sales revenue the money outlay
occasioned by the need to replace the raw cotton embodied in the

[1] [1954] 1 W.L.R. 158.

yarn sold.[2] In any given year it did not consider it had made a profit until it had recovered sufficient money to maintain the level of the Base Stock.

As a matter of arithmetic, effect could be given to the above view of profit either by leaving the Base Stock out of the profit calculation altogether (*i.e.*, by omitting it from the trading account) or by bringing it into the profit calculation, but at a constant valuation (which normally would represent the cost of the Base Stock when first set up, perhaps many years ago), so that the same amount was first added and then deducted in the account.[3] In either case the effect would be to calculate the profit by deducting from the sales revenue the outlay for the period in question in replacing the cotton sold.[2]

On the other hand, the more usual methods of accounting for stock measure the cost of goods sold in a given year by some kind of approximation to the outlay originally incurred on the physical stock embodied in the goods sold. In a relatively small number of cases the goods sold are actually identified with particular lots of raw material and their cost fixed accordingly. More commonly, the cost will be determined by averaging in some arbitrary way the price of goods in stock at the beginning of the period and of goods bought during the period; or it may, for example, be assumed that the first lot of materials coming into stock will be the first to go out into production (" first in, first out "), and be priced accordingly; and there are other methods. The arithmetic involves the apportionment of part of the outlay on purchase of materials during the accounting year to the closing stock, an appropriate credit being made in the trading account; while the value of the opening stock, derived from purchases in the previous year, is added to the expenses in the trading account. To the cost calculated in one of these ways will be added the amount, if any, by which, on a bona fide estimate, the corresponding valuation of the closing stock exceeds its " market value " (the interpretation of which also varies). These methods are described collectively as the " cost or lower market value " basis of stock valuation.

It is thus apparent that " cost or lower market value " is, strictly speaking, not a method of valuation, but a rather ill-defined set of methods. The interpretation put upon " cost " and

---

[2] It can be assumed, for the purpose of the discussion, that the quantity of raw cotton bought always equalled the quantity embodied in yarn sales, or, in other words, that the company did not hold any other stocks than the Base Stock. The company did, in fact, hold additional stocks, but there was no dispute about their valuation or about the "cost" of yarn sold so far as its production absorbed stock held in excess of the Base Stock.

[3] In fact, the Base Stock on the machines was omitted entirely from the trading account and the Base Stock awaiting use alongside the machines was brought into the trading account at a fixed price. In both cases the arithmetical result in any given year was, of course, the same.

" market value " varies, and the choice of interpretation is arbitrary. The recommendation on the valuation of stock in trade issued by the Council of the Institute of Chartered Accountants lists no less than five ways of calculating " cost " and two ways of calculating " market value " for the purpose of a " cost or lower market " valuation.[4] Even if the many possible sub-classifications are ignored, this gives ten possible combinations. This is of some relevance in view of the emphasis laid by the court, as will be seen, on the concept of " accuracy " in profit calculation, with the consequent implication that there must be a " best " method of stock valuation.[5] The court did not select for approval any particular definition of cost or lower market value.

When a " cost or lower market " valuation is used, the amount deducted from sales revenue will, in a period in which prices are rising, usually be less than the amount needed to replace the stock embodied in the goods sold; for the amount so deducted will reflect costs of purchases at a rather earlier date, when prices were lower. When prices are rising the more usual form of profit calculation will thus produce higher " profits " than the Base Stock method, and, within limits, contrariwise when prices are falling.

A further implication of the Base Stock method, noted by a Revenue witness, is the fact that where this method is used the balance sheet fails to reveal a " hidden reserve." In this, however, the Base Stock method differs from others only in degree; it is common knowledge that, except when prices have fallen, most balance sheets fail to record part of the market value of the assets, including stock, that they list, since these are usually not included at a figure in excess of cost.

It may be noted that whatever method may be followed, the " hidden " value must eventually be brought into account for tax purposes when the business use of the stock comes finally to an end.[6]

III

The Revenue's case rested, essentially, on the contention that, in consequence of the company's method of stock valuation, the accounts failed to show the " full amount of the profits "[7] of the relevant accounting year.

No particular significance appears to attach to the word " full "

---

[4] Recommendation X of Recommendations on Accounting Principles of the Institute of Chartered Accountants in England and Wales.

[5] Indeed, one of the *curiosa* of this case is that it is possible to argue that the Base Stock method *is* a variant of the cost or lower market method of valuation, since the Base Stock is in fact normally valued at the cost, in the market, of raw material acquired at some date in the past, and is retained at that value subsequently, provided it does not exceed the current market valuation (on some interpretation of " market value ").

[6] Under Income Tax Act, 1952, s. 143.

[7] See Income Tax Act, s. 127.

and it was not used by Singleton L.J.[8] in the passages which appear to contain the kernel of the court's judgment.[9]

Singleton L.J.'s reasoning can, if it has been correctly understood, be summarised thus:

(1) The correct method of calculating profit is that which gives the most accurate result.

(2) It is not possible to calculate profit accurately without taking into account the value of stock at the beginning and at the end of the relevant accounting period.

(3) The most accurate method of valuing stock for this purpose is to take it at cost or lower market value.

It followed that, as the company had used the Base Stock method of valuation, it could not succeed, and the Special Commissioners, in deciding otherwise, had misdirected themselves in law.

In essence, therefore, Singleton L.J. held that the company's case failed because it depended upon a method of profit calculation less accurate than that proposed by the Revenue.

In the following passages it is hoped to show that, with respect, this reasoning is neither in accord with precedent nor a satisfactory interpretation of the statute law.

Accuracy is a word to which no significance can be attached until it has been decided what it is that is being measured. It is not, for example, helpful to say, *before it has been agreed how long a mile is*, that such and such a measure is more accurate than another for the purpose of determining a mile.[10] To define " profit " by saying it is that which is obtained by using the most accurate measure is to commit an error of logic. Accuracy would, no doubt, have had a meaning if the court had been applying the rules of some standard method of profit computation founded on the relevant statute. It is well known, however, that the Income Tax Acts are silent on what constitutes profit, and the courts have, hitherto, tended to avoid the suggestion that the statute is satisfied by a standard set of accounting procedures and by no other.

Were the question " What is profit? " to be decided *ab initio* it may be that the courts would feel that, in order to ascertain the intention of Parliament, as expressed in the words of the statute, they should have recourse to those most concerned with investigating economic phenomena in a dispassionate way. It was long ago decided, however, in the House of Lords, that the views of political economists as to what constitutes " profit," however

---

[8] The discussion here is confined to the first judgment, delivered by Singleton L.J. Of the concurring judgments, that of Birkett L.J. did not break additional ground and that of Hodson L.J. was limited to the expression of concurrence.

[9] At pp. 173–4.

[10] This implies being able to describe a given *operation* or *procedure*, such as laying down a particular, legally approved or otherwise generally accepted, yardstick one thousand seven hundred and sixty times.

worthy of attention in other respects, are not relevant in determining how income tax assessments are calculated.[11] This is perhaps
as well, for the courts might find it difficult to decide which set
of opinions among those held by economists were those that
Parliament had in mind.

The question is, in any case, not open. " Profits," said Lord
Halsbury L.C. in 1892, " must be ascertained on ordinary principles
of commercial trading." [12] This dictum has met with repeated
approval in the House of Lords and elsewhere.[13]

This leaves the question whether, as a matter of fact, " ordinary
principles of commercial trading " were applied in this case.
Evidence was given by an eminent professional accountant that,
although accounting views varied as to which was the " best "
method, the Base Stock method of valuation adopted by the
company was " a recognised commercial accountancy basis " and
" a good method of accounting." He also testified that " an
accountant would give an unqualified certificate to accounts as
giving a true and fair view of the profits of a company whether it
employed the one method or the other so long as the company had
adhered to one method consistently." [14] It was found as a fact by
the Special Commissioners that the company's method of stock
valuation was in accordance with sound commercial practice and
this was not disputed by the Revenue or by the court. There
was no suggestion of inaccuracy in the *application* of the method
of valuation used. Singleton L.J.'s judgment implies clearly
that it was the *method* and not the actual calculation that was
" inaccurate."

The facts in the *Broadstone Mills* case seem, therefore, to place
that case within the area covered by Lord Halsbury's dictum, and
it must be concluded, with respect, that it was wrongly decided.[15]

---

11 *Coltness Iron Co.* v. *Black* (1881) 6 App.Cas. 315; 1 T.C. 287.
12 *Gresham Life Assurance Society* v. *Styles* [1892] A.C. 309, 316; 3 T.C.
185, 189.
13 See, for example, *Lowry* v. *Consolidated African Selection Trust, Ltd.* [1940]
A.C. 648; 23 T.C. 259, where the company was held to be debarred from
treating as a deduction in the calculation of profit the difference between the
market value of its own shares which it had issued to employees and the
(lower) price of issue. Lord Maugham, in delivering judgment, said: " It is
well settled that profits and gains must be ascertained on ordinary commercial
principles, and this fact must not be .forgotten " (p. 661) and again " in its
essence I think it is only necessary in this case to ascertain the profits and
gains on ordinary commercial principles " (p. 662). It is significant that Lord
Romer in his dissenting judgment argued that on commercial principles the
deduction claimed by the company should be allowed (pp. 691–695).
   For a recent case on the valuation of stock in trade in which this principle
was applied see *I. R. C.* v. *Cock Russell and Co., Ltd.* [1949] 2 All E.R.
889; 29 T.C. 387.
14 *Per* Singleton L.J. at p. 165.
15 Singleton L.J., in discussing the question of " accuracy " attached some
importance to the judgment of Lord Loreburn L.C. in *Sun Insurance Office*
v. *Clark* [1912] A.C. 443; 6 T.C. 59, which seemed to imply that there is
some absolute standard of profit calculation and that the test of " correctness "
in profit calculation for tax purposes is the degree of accuracy achieved in

This seems to dispose of the matter. The case raises some interesting points of principle, however.

IV

The difficulty of the argument from " accuracy " is that until a standard of profit has been laid down, " accuracy " can have no significance. The court in this case had, no doubt, some kind of standard in mind. In view of Singleton L.J.'s references to the importance of valuing stocks at the beginning and end of the year, " profit " was presumably correlated with changes in the value of some of the company's property. But, on this basis, the type of valuation approved by the court would often fail to pass the court's own test. Nearly all forms of the cost or lower market method fail to take into account unrealised appreciation in stocks held at the end of the accounting period, and are hence " inaccurate." Nor is it an answer to this criticism that " commercial principles " do not recognise the inclusion of unrealised appreciation in the profit calculation, for it is of the essence of the judgment in this case that these principles may be ruled out if they lack " accuracy."

It is true that it has long been the more usual practice of accountants when computing business profit to make some kind of adjustment for changing stock values of the type evidently envisaged by the Revenue and the court in their use of the term " cost or lower market value." The adjustment is, indeed, analogous with the similar adjustment that is made for changes in the amount of outstanding trade debtors, it being customary to assume that revenue includes amounts receivable as well as amounts received, and that, therefore, where there is, for example, an increase in the amount of book debts, it is necessary to add this increase to the cash receipts in order to arrive at the " correct " revenue figure. As in the case of stock, to the extent that this is not done the balance-sheet fails to take account of a " hidden reserve," in this case of debts not included. It has not, however, up to now, been thought that adjustments in this respect are in every case an essential element in computing taxable profit. They are certainly usual, but this is not because the income tax legislation requires such treatment, but because it is the common commercial practice. It has long been the custom in some professional practices to ignore, not only changes in stock and professional " work in progress," if any, but also changes in book debts, it being assumed that cash fees received are an adequate measure in any given year of the gross revenue of that year,

approaching this standard. It may be doubted, however, whether in view of the earlier *Gresham Life Assurance* case this was an essential element of the judgment. To the extent that it was, the reasoning, though not the judgment, in the *Sun Insurance* case is open to the same criticism as that in the *Broadstone Mills* case.

provided always that the same basis is followed from year to year. It cannot be argued that, in this respect, professional practices are on a different basis from trading businesses. In both cases the Act requires tax to be charged on the " full amount " of the profits. (I.T.A. 1952, s. 127.) It is of interest to note that the *Broadstone Mills* decision would, if upheld, seem to provide good authority for charging to tax, on the grounds of " accuracy," the outstanding uncollected fees of any of Her Majesty's counsel at the time of their elevation to the bench or retirement.

Nor is this all. The distinction between the Base Stock method of valuation and the more usual type of calculation can be expressed broadly as the distinction between (a) a concept of profit based on surplus remaining after providing for the maintenance of business at the same *level of activity* or on *the same scale* (here represented by the fixed minimum physical level of stock), which an economist would describe in terms of the preservation of the value of the stock in *real* terms; and (b) a concept of profit based on the surplus remaining after preservation of the *value of the business* (or, in this case, the *stock*) *in terms of money*. If accuracy is to be the test, some accountants would be prepared to give evidence that the Base Stock method is *more accurate* than any cost or lower market value basis, since, as indicated above, its use produces a figure of profit approximating more closely to a profit calculated in terms of purchasing power, as distinct from money.

This suggests that there is something fundamentally unsound in the implicit assumption of the court that there exists a " standard " or " true " profit in the sense of some unique figure which can be found in any given case, and to which a more or less accurate approximation can be made. Even had there been no precedent requiring the application of commercial principles to profit calculation, the decision in the *Broadstone Mills* case would have been unsatisfactory.

The ideas conjured up in the mind by such words as " profit " and " income " do not relate to " things " of the " real world " of the kind which we assume exist because our senses tell us of them. They refer to the result of a class of operations or procedures carried out by men for particular purposes. The precise details of the operation in any given case are governed by the aims of the people concerned. In the case of business accounts the aim is to arrive at an agreed or approved assessment of changes in certain types of interests in property during a given period. This is necessary in order to determine such questions as the amounts that are to be withdrawn by partners from a business at the end of a given period, or the relevant rights of different classes of shareholders; and to satisfy such rules of law related to interests in property as the law relating to the divisible profits of companies, which, in theory at least, protects the property rights of creditors as against those of shareholders. The rules of calculation are necessarily in some degree arbitrary because, although behind the relevant contracts or rules of law lies the general idea of profit as an increase in the value of property, the value of a given property right is a thing on which two persons will seldom agree unless it is calculated on some predetermined arbitrary principle. It would, no doubt, be possible to compute profit annually on the basis of a careful valuation of the property concerned, such as is made when a business is sold or for estate duty purposes. This, however, would be impossibly costly and impracticable. Hence, for commercial purposes, rule-of-thumb practices are accepted for year-to-year calculations.[16]

Similarly, in the law of trusts, certain rules regulate, as a matter of convenience, the allocation of given property rights between life tenants and remaindermen. The application of the rules is susceptible of amendment by the settlor to suit his own views of how his property should be administered. The settlor decides what is " income " whether his decision is implied by his acceptance of the established rules of law or is explicit in the trust instrument.

In income tax law, the question " What is profit ? " must be assumed to have been decided by the legislature. It might reasonably be expected that the decision would be based on a consideration of the economic effects expected to result. This assumption is of considerable importance in relation to the judicial interpretation of revenue law. If Parliament fail, as they have done in this context, to describe the procedure by which taxable profit is to be calculated, is it to be surmised that they have left it to the courts to decide what is the " correct " or most " accurate " method of calculation required to achieve their presumed economic aim ? This surmise would be tantamount to a supposition that Parliament intended to delegate legislation on certain economic matters to the courts. Or is it rather to be assumed that Parliament, having laid down no procedure of calculation, intended that the word " profit " in the context we are discussing should mean the kind of figure that reasonable business men and accountants would accept; aware no doubt that a certain lack of uniformity would result, but satisfied that, taking one year with another and one business with another, both justice and the economic aims of the legislation would be satisfied ? This, it must be presumed, was believed by the House of Lords in 1892.[17]

In the *Broadstone Mills* case it was a criticism of Vaisey J. in the High Court that the method of calculation adopted by the company involved the bringing into account of a " mere arbitrary " figure; a similar comment was made by Singleton L.J. in the Court of Appeal. Yet the arbitrariness so introduced (and no commercial

---

[16] On this see the very clear discussion by Fletcher Moulton L.J. in *Re Spanish Prospecting Co., Ltd.* [1911] 1 Ch. 92, at p. 98 *et seq.*

[17] A third possible view, that an economist's definition is implied, has already been mentioned.

profit calculation is without its arbitrary elements) is small compared with the arbitrariness which will be introduced into the revenue law if, as has happened in this case, the court is to appropriate to itself the right of prescribing accounting rules.   Thereby a large additional uncertainty will be added to the problems of business men, for who will be able to tell whether an accounting rule of profit calculation accepted for fifty years will not be challenged in the courts, when, owing to the particular conjucture of prices and other circumstances, it happens to suit the Revenue to do so?

H. C. Edey.*

---

* Lecturer in Accounting and Business Finance at the London School of Economics and Political Science.

Reprinted from *The Accountants Journal*, April and May 1956

COMPANY ACCOUNTING IN THE NINETEENTH AND TWENTIETH CENTURIES[1]

By H. C. EDEY, B.Com., A.C.A.
Reader in Accounting in the University of London

In 1855, one hundred years ago, it first became possible in this country to form limited liability companies by the now familiar process of registration. Business corporations enjoying limited liability had, indeed, been known for a much longer period, but owed their existence to Royal Charters or to special Acts of Parliament. This procedure has always remained available but it was, and is, an expensive and protracted affair.

The history of company accounting as we know it really began, however, eleven years before 1855, when the first 'Companies Act' – the Joint Stock Companies Act of 1844 – was passed. Although the principle of general limited liability was not to be conceded until 1855, the important features of corporate entity and transferable shares were thenceforth obtainable by the simple process of registration.

Several noteworthy features characterized the legal requirements relating to company accounting during the period from 1844 to 1855. In the first place, the spirit of the legislation was in some respects remarkably close to that of today. The Act of 1844 required companies to keep books of account; to present a 'full and fair' balance sheet at each ordinary meeting of shareholders; to appoint auditors whose duty it would be to report on the balance sheet, whose report would be read at the meeting, and who were entitled to examine the books and question officers of the company. The balance sheet was to be filed with the Registrar of Companies. On the other hand, a profit and loss account was not required. (This omission must not, however, be taken to imply that revenue accounts were at that time considered of no value: the legislation of 1844 relating to banking companies – which were excluded from the provisions of the general Joint Stock Companies Act – required an annual profit and loss account as well as a balance sheet.)

So far as these requirements went the date might well have been 1948 and not 1844. There were, however, apart from the absence of the profit and loss account from the list of required documents, certain fundamental differences. In the first place, no attempt was made to specify the contents of the balance sheet. This omission might perhaps be of less importance today when a substantial body of generally accepted accounting doctrine exists; but in 1844 there was no such collection of precepts to give unequivocal meaning to the phrase 'full and fair'.

Secondly, the Registrar of Companies was given no

[1] Most of the factual information in this article has been drawn from public Acts of Parliament. I should like to acknowledge the assistance I have obtained from *The Development of the Law of Company Accounts in England between 1844 and 1944*, a London University thesis by P. PANITPAKDI, which has in particular saved me much time both in planning the article and in searching for references.

power to enforce compliance with the requirement of balance sheet registration and had no control over the contents of balance sheets filed.

Finally, no provision was made for *professional* audit; indeed, although the public accountant was already on the scene, it seems that in those days the auditor would normally have been a layman acting on behalf of the shareholders. In the Companies Clauses Act of 1845 (which related to parliamentary companies) we find, for example, permissive power granted to the auditors to employ accountants at the expense of the company. A similar provision was later to be included in Table B of the 1856 Companies Act (Table B was the equivalent of what is now Table A of the 1948 Act).

It is perhaps not surprising that by the early 1850s it had become clear that there was evasion of the law, including the special manufacture of balance sheets for registration purposes. In such circumstances today legislation would no doubt follow, aimed at closing the gaps which had become apparent. The time we are considering, however, was one in which great weight was laid on freedom of private enterprise from control. There were many who thought that the disclosure of company accounting information was a matter to be left to be decided between shareholders and directors. As for creditors, they were, after all, free to choose whether or not they entered into contractual relations with a company.

No change was in fact made in the accounting and auditing regulations when, in 1855, amid a good deal of controversy, the principle of limited liability for registered companies (other than banks and insurance companies) was introduced, even though some voices were heard to say that the legal right so granted should be paid for by the provision of accounting publicity. The principle of freedom from regulation was to be taken further, however, for the following year, when earlier legislation was amended and consolidated in the Companies Act of 1856, Parliament struck out of the company law the whole of the compulsory accounting and auditing legislation of the 1844 Act.

The first century of general limited liability thus began with companies completely unfettered in accounting matters. The difference between this situation and the scene as we see it today is a significant commentary on the change in political and social outlook that has taken place. Nevertheless, we must preserve our sense of balance. It would not be true to say that responsible men of affairs of a hundred years ago rejected all State control in such matters. Compulsory accounting and auditing requirements were never abandoned in the legislation intended to be applied to parliamentary companies. (Among those would be railway companies:

railway stocks at that time represented an important part of the securities market). Moreover, when soon afterwards limited liability was introduced for banks and insurance companies (the failure of any one of which was likely to cause particularly severe loss to the community) one of the conditions imposed was the half-yearly publication of a statement of assets and liabilities and of called-up and paid-up capital. It must be remembered, too, that in the 1850s probably few people evisaged how great a part the limited company form was soon to play in the economic life of the country. At that time it was probably expected by most people that it would be the exception rather than the rule.

The hundred years from 1855 can, from our point of view, be divided into two periods. The first, covering the forty-five years to 1900, was marked by a complete absence of statutory regulation in matters relating to accounting and audit for companies incorporated under the general company law, the only exceptions being those carrying on a few special classes of business. The second period, from 1900 to the present day, saw a gradual return to the kind of regulation that Parliament had approved in 1844, with this difference, however, that it was worked out, as Act followed Act, with increasingly greater precision and attention to loopholes.

The Companies Act of 1856, and the consolidating Act of 1862 which replaced it, contained model sets of articles of association – the forerunners of Table A of the Companies Act, 1948 – in which were exemplary clauses on accounts and audit. There was also a remarkably up-to-date standard form of balance sheet, though not of profit and loss account. Such an account was, however, required – the words used were a 'Statement of income and expenditure'. It was to be so drawn up as to reveal 'a just balance of profit and loss'.[1] These provisions are very interesting for they anticipated in many respects the legislation which was to follow much later. Nevertheless, although they may well have had considerable influence on accounting thought, they were no more than permissive. Any company which chose to adopt its own articles could ignore the model set and any company which adopted the latter and proceeded to ignore it had thereby committed no breach of the general law – though auditors who failed to observe the duties imposed by such articles ran the risk of successful legal action against them should their neglect injure the company. (It must be remembered that legal actions against auditors before 1900 so far as they did not arise out of the general law of contract rested in most cases only on company articles and not, as they would now, on the auditing provisions of the Companies Act as well.)

The important exceptions to this absence of regulation before 1900 were insurance and banking companies. We have already seen that some minimum accounting disclosure was imposed upon them by the

[1] For a more detailed discussion of the changes in accounting and auditing law during the period 1844 to 1900 including the provisions of these model articles readers are referred to a joint essay by EDEY and PANITPAKDI in *Studies in the History of Accounting* (Ed. Yamey and Littleton), to be published by Messrs Sweet & Maxwell.

early legislation. They were later, however, subjected to more stringent regulation. The Life Assurance Companies Act, 1870, imposed upon companies carrying on life business the obligation of preparing, registering and providing, on request, to shareholders and policy-holders, annual revenue accounts and balance sheets in prescribed forms. Quinquennial actuarial valuations were also introduced. Special legislation for this class of company has continued to the present day. The Companies Act, 1879, reintroduced a compulsory annual audit for all banking companies registered thereafter as limited companies.

The immediate cause of the latter Act was the failure in 1878, in conditions of fraud, of the City of Glasgow Bank. Under the 1879 Act the auditor was required to state whether, in his opinion, the balance sheet was a 'full and fair' balance sheet properly drawn up so as to exhibit a true and correct view of the state of the company's affairs as shown by the books of the company. These requirements did not differ greatly from those of the 1856 model set of articles, and no doubt served as the basis of the equivalent section of the 1900 Act which made an annual audit compulsory for all registered companies. The well-known *London and General Bank* case (in which the auditors were held to have been guilty of misfeasance) related to an audit under the Companies Act, 1879. This case made clear that the phrase in the Act 'as shown by the books of the company' did not (as had been suggested) restrict the auditors' duty to a mere arithmetical check of balance sheet against books.

During the latter part of the nineteenth century there was a good deal of active public support for company law reform in accounting as well as other matters. This movement undoubtedly drew a good deal of its inspiration from the fact that fraud and sharp practice were a less unusual feature of company finance than is the case today. It was not until 1900, however, that the annual audit became an established part of the law.

In the inquiries that preceded the Companies Act, 1900, proposals had been made for the introduction of annual registration of accounts and of compulsory circulation of accounts to shareholders as well, but these did not find their way into the Act. The latter did not even include an express direction that annual accounts were to be prepared, but this was implied by the auditing requirements. The absence since 1856 of a compulsory audit had not, of course, meant that it was unusual for the accounts of well-known companies whose shares were publicly held to be audited. The professional auditor was by now an accepted part of the scene. There was indeed some support at the time for making an audit by *professional* accountants obligatory, but this measure was not destined to reach the Statute Book for another forty-seven years.

Only seven years were to elapse before the next major development. The Companies Act, 1907, took the decisive step of requiring the annual filing of an audited statement in the form of a balance sheet containing a summary of the company's capital, its liabilities, and its assets, giving such particulars as would disclose the general nature of such liabilities and assets and how the values of the fixed assets had been arrived at. The document filed did not, however, have to include a statement of profit and loss. Private companies were now defined for the first time (in much the same terms as at present) and were exempted from the requirement to file a balance sheet. It was also provided that any shareholder should be entitled to receive, on payment, a copy of every audited balance sheet laid before the company in general meeting; debenture-holders were given the same rights, except in the case of private companies or companies registered before the Act.

An alteration was now made in the form of the auditors' report. Under the 1900 Act the auditors had been required (a) to sign a certificate at the foot of the balance sheet stating whether or not all their requirements as auditors had been complied with, and (b) to make a report to the shareholders on the accounts examined by them and on every balance sheet laid before the company in general meeting during their tenure of office. The report was to state whether in their opinion the balance sheet – the words 'full and fair' of the 1879 Act had disappeared – was properly drawn up so as to exhibit a 'true and correct' view of the state of the company's affairs as shown by the books of the company. It was to be read before the company in general meeting. This distinction between the auditors' certificate and report was now abolished. Henceforth a single statement – the report – would be made. This would either be attached to the balance sheet or there would be inserted at the foot of the balance sheet a reference to it.

The 1907 Act also made some changes in the wording of what was now to be the auditors' report. Instead of the reference to the auditors' 'requirements', the report was to say whether or not the auditors had obtained all the information and explanations they had required. After the words 'true and correct view of the state of the company's affairs', the wording now became: 'according to the best of their information and the explanations given to them, and as shown by the books of the company'. It was thus made explicit that more than a mere checking of balance sheet against books was required by the law.

Another new clause provided that no new auditor might be appointed unless due notice of intention to nominate him had been given to the company by a shareholder and the company had given due notice thereof to the retiring auditor and to the shareholders. This would prevent the removal of an auditor without the general body of the shareholders becoming aware that this had been done.

Two other well-known accounting requirements passed into law in the 1907 Act. The balance sheet had in future to show, to the extent that they had not been written off, the amounts of commission paid in respect of shares or debentures and of discount allowed in respect of debentures. Secondly, the accounts of the company – the balance sheet was not specifically mentioned – were to show the capital on which, and the rate at which, interest had been paid out of capital during the period to which the accounts related; this followed the granting of power to pay such interest under prescribed conditions.

The 1907 Act was followed by a consolidating statute, the Companies (Consolidation) Act, 1908. This Act was provided with a new Table A in which the model balance sheet which had appeared in Table A of the 1862 Act no longer found a place.

In some degree history repeated itself after 1907, for the Companies Act of that year left much latitude to those who wished the balance sheets of their companies to give little information away. Quite apart from the absence of a profit and loss account, there were the generally accepted practices which allowed the deliberate creation of secret reserves and which permitted the grouping in the balance sheet in one aggregate figure of diverse types of asset. Furthermore, the balance sheet filed with the Registrar might, it seems, bear no recent relationship to the date of filing and, indeed, the same balance sheet might be filed year after year. Nevertheless, a decisive step towards the principle of accounting disclosure had been taken, and although over twenty years were to elapse before there was to be any significant further development, the eventual lines of that development were already implicit in the law.

The next major statutory change in the company law was made by the Companies Act, 1928, the provisions of which came into force under the new consolidating Act of 1929. The new Act followed a period in which there had been much discussion on the presentation of company accounting information and during which two company law amendment committees had sat. The new accounting and audit provisions, with which many readers will be familiar, contained three significant innovations. One of these related to the disclosure of information in prospectuses of new issues. The contents of prospectuses had long been regulated, but this was the first time that the law had required reports (by the auditors) on the past profits and dividends of the company whose securities were to be issued or offered for sale, and (by accountants named in the prospectus) on the past profits of any business that was to be acquired from the proceeds of issue. (The period to be covered by the reports was to be three years as compared with the five years required under the 1948 Act and the ten years now required by the London Stock Exchange.) No statement of assets and liabilities was, however, yet required.

The second major innovation was the formal recognition of the growing importance of holding companies. The Act, despite a good deal of support for making compulsory the device of the consolidated balance sheet – there was weighty opposition as well – did not require the preparation of any form of group accounts. It did, however, define a holding company and require disclosure in general terms of the manner in which profits and losses of subsidiaries had been accounted for. Though in itself of relatively little value, since no indication of the size of profits had to be disclosed, this paved the way, and by its very inadequacy drew attention to the need, for the elaborate provisions of the 1947 legislation. The Act also provided for the first time for the separate statement in a holding company's balance sheet of investments in, and loans to and from, subsidiaries.

The third departure from earlier practice which is of particular interest was the requirement that in addition to the balance sheet an annual profit and loss account should be laid before the company in general meeting. For very many years there had been much opposition to enforcing disclosure of profit and loss information, usually on the grounds that this was private and that disclosure would injure the competitive position of companies. Even now public companies were not compelled to file a copy of the profit and loss account with the Registrar, though a full balance sheet had to be filed and it ceased to be possible, as earlier, to file out-of-date balance sheets. Nor was the auditors' report explicitly extended, as it was to be in 1947, to the profit and loss account, though it could not be ignored that the profit and loss account balance formed part of the balance sheet, and, as the *Royal Mail* case was to show, auditors could ignore its contents only at their peril. Moreover, the Act did not, despite an attempt in Parliament to introduce such a clause, regulate the contents of the profit and loss account – and in this it is clear that it had the support of a good deal of current business and accounting opinion – and this to some degree vitiated the new provision. Nevertheless, the requirement that the profit and loss account must be submitted to shareholders was a real advance and this, combined with the effect of the *Royal Mail* case (mentioned below), led to the provision of a good deal of information valuable to the investor – information, it may be noted, of a kind that had been available to the shareholders of railway companies and other public utilities for many years.

The question of secret reserves had attracted a good deal of notice in the years leading up to the new Act, but this topic received no attention in the Act. It might well have been otherwise had the legislation followed instead of preceding the *Royal Mail* case. The definition of, and distinctions between, reserves and provisions, and the requirements for their disclosure, which are such a significant part of the 1948 Act, found no place. The Act did, however, go very much further than before in prescribing the form and contents of the balance sheet – so much so that anyone acquainted with the Companies Act, 1948, can feel he is on familiar ground when he reads the Act of 1929.

Space does not permit the listing of the detailed provisions with respect to the balance sheet. Among those that now appeared for the first time were requirements for the disclosure of loans made to directors and officers, of loans made by the company for the purchase of its own shares for the benefit of employees, of discount (so far as it was not written off) on any shares issued under the new power given by the Act to make such issues under prescribed conditions, and of particulars relating to redeemable preference shares (also now legalized for the first time). Henceforth, also, a distinction between fixed and floating (later to be called 'current') assets was to be observed in the balance sheet. Preliminary expenses not yet written off were to be separately stated, as were goodwill, patents and trade-marks so far as their value could be ascertained.

The disclosure in the accounts of directors' remuneration paid by the company or any of its subsidiaries now became for the first time obligatory, though the value of the provision was reduced by the express exclusion of remuneration of the managing director

and of remuneration paid to any other director in respect of any salaried post held by him.

A number of changes were made in the provisions affecting auditors, of which perhaps the most significant were (*a*) a provision that rendered void indemnity clauses in a company's articles of the type which had played a part in the *City Equitable* case in 1925, and (*b*) a provision that allowed the auditors to attend general meetings before which accounts examined by them were to be laid, and to make at these meetings any statement they desired with respect to the accounts.

Another interesting feature was the reintroduction into the company law, after more than seventy years, of explicit provisions imposing the duty of keeping proper books of account.

Two years later came the *Royal Mail* case, in which the auditor of the Royal Mail Steam Packet Co was brought to trial on the charge of aiding and abetting in the publication of false annual reports with intent to deceive. The essence of the case, as most readers will know, was the crediting to profit and loss account of profits relating to earlier periods, hitherto undisclosed, in such a way as to suggest that current profits were much greater than was in fact the case. (The accounts in question had been prepared under the pre-1929 law.)

The auditor was acquitted of intent to deceive, but the case had a great impact on accounting thought. In particular it became evident that good accounting practice could not remain indifferent to the form and contents of the profit and loss account despite the absence of express provisions relating thereto in the Companies Act, 1929. This case, and the growing pressure for the provision in company accounts of information adequate to allow the investment merits of company shares and debentures to be reasonably estimated, were no doubt among the factors which led the Cohen Committee on Company Law Amendment to say in their 1945 report:

> 'We consider that the profit and loss account is as important as, if not more important than, the balance sheet, since the trend of profits is the best indication of the prosperity of the company and the value of the assets depends largely on the maintenance of the business as a going concern.'

This statement perhaps better than any other made in the Cohen Report summarizes the spirit of the innovations introduced into company accounting law by the Companies Act, 1947, which was based largely upon the extensive recommendations of the report. The contents of the Act, embodied in the present consolidating Act of 1948, are well known to all accountants and demand no discussion here. It is an interesting thought that, unfamiliar as many of the technical expressions to be found in this Act would have been to the members of the 1841–1844 Select Committee on Joint Stock Companies (of which Gladstone was latterly chairman and the recommendations of which led to the 1844 Act), those same members would probably have found little to surprise them in the general import of the present-day accounting and auditing provisions of the company law. The major differences are of technique rather than of aim; the history of the growth in technique is largely the history of the growth of the accounting profession.

H. C. Edey

VALUATION OF STOCK IN TRADE
FOR INCOME TAX PURPOSES

THIS article discusses the present state of income tax law as it affects the valuation of the stock in trade of businesses at the beginning and end of their accounting periods. Occasion will also be taken to discuss the valuation of stock in trade withdrawn from a business for the private use of the business proprietor or added to the business from the private resources of the proprietor. Other questions affecting stock in trade, including such matters as what is to be included under that head, the imputation of value when stock is acquired or sold *en bloc* with other assets for a single sum, its valuation on the commencement or discontinuation of the business, etc., will not be discussed here. The article is prompted by two recent Revenue decisions each of which carries the weight of high judicial authority, namely the decision of the Judicial Committee of the Privy Council in the case *Minister of National Revenue* v. *Anaconda American Brass, Ltd.*[1]; and the decision of the House of Lords in *Sharkey* v. *Wernher.*[2]

These decisions are of particular interest because in each case the judgment invalidated a long-standing accounting practice. The *Anaconda* decision, being a Privy Council judgment, is not formally binding on the United Kingdom courts; in practice, however, it would almost certainly be followed. This is the more true as the principle on which the case was decided seems to be the same as that recently approved by the Court of Appeal in *Patrick* v. *Broadstone Mills, Ltd.*,[3] which itself was mentioned with approval by the Privy Council in the *Anaconda* case. The latter arose on a point of Canadian income tax law, but there is no reason to suppose it is not fully applicable to our own tax law.

METHODS OF VALUATION

I shall assume it is generally accepted that in the computation of the profits of businesses whose activities include the purchase and sale of goods, whether for income tax assessment or otherwise, the annual business expenses should include the opening stock valuation and should be reduced by the closing stock valuation. It is easy to see that failure to make these adjustments would often produce absurd

---

* The writer is Reader in Accounting, The London School of Economics and Political Science, University of London.
1 [1956] 2 W.L.R. 31 ; [1956] 1 All E.R. 20.
2 [1955] 3 W.L.R. 671 ; [1955] 3 All E.R. 493.
3 [1954] 1 W.L.R. 158 ; [1954] 1 All E.R. 163 ; 35 T.C. 44.

results. The profit of a business that began the year with large stocks which it then sold without replacement would evidently be over-stated if the stocks used up were not counted as part of the expenditure just as much as if they were money. Similarly, the profit of a business that was consistently increasing its stocks would evidently be under-stated if the cost of acquiring the additional stocks was charged as a business expense without making allowance for the value of those in hand at the end of the period. It is true that it would be possible to *define* profit in such a way that opening and closing stock values were ignored, but such a definition would not be accepted by business men or accountants for most practical purposes.

The necessity for taking account of stock may be agreed. This still leaves open, however, the question of the method of valuation, and it is to this that we must now direct our attention. We may divide the methods used in business practice into three groups, of which the first is by far the most widely used in this country. These groups may be called—

(a) The *cost or lower market value* method;

(b) The *net selling value* and the *long-term contract* methods;

(c) The *base stock* and *last-in, first-out* (LIFO) methods.

The cost or lower market value method will be discussed in greater detail below when it will be pointed out that the name covers a number of different practices. For the moment it is sufficient to say that it implies a valuation of stock on the basis of either cost or market value, whichever is the lower, where both cost and market value, however calculated, are closely related to price levels ruling at the time of valuation or at the time of the most recent purchases of stock.

The net selling value basis of valuation is an unusual one, the use of which is believed to be largely confined to certain tropical agricultural producers—notably tea and rubber companies—and some mining companies. The stock of saleable product is valued at the price at which it is realised after the end of the accounting period, net of any expenses attributable to the realisation. The long-term contract basis of stock valuation is restricted to the kind of business suggested by its name. When this method is used, partly completed work under contracts is valued on the same general principles as when the cost or lower market value basis is used, but with this difference, that to the cost figure is added a conservatively estimated proportion of the profit margin expected to be ultimately realised on the contract. Both the net selling value and the long-term contract types of valuation may, though not necessarily, result in valuations higher than would be given with the cost or lower market value method. This will be the case if known or expected net realisation value is higher

24

than cost. If, however, the contrary is true, the valuation will be the same as with one or other of the variants of the cost or lower market value method.

ANACONDA: THE LIFO METHOD

The base stock and LIFO methods of valuation are essentially the same and the two terms are sometimes used interchangeably. As any differences between the two methods are matters of detail rather than of principle the discussion will be confined to the method at dispute in the *Anaconda* case, that is, the so-called LIFO method. The principle lying behind this method is not difficult to understand, but is apt to be obscured by the rather complicated accounting technique. Let us start by setting out the description of this method of stock valuation given by Viscount Simonds in the *Anaconda* case.[4]

"It must in the first place be explained that Lifo does not mean that the metal last to be received into stock is in fact the first to be processed and sold. On the contrary, the actual physical flow of the raw material is regarded as irrelevant: that which was purchased in previous years and was in stock at the opening of the relevant financial year or that which was purchased during that year may have been processed and the products sold during that year: this of no account. It is to cost that Lifo looks, and in the simplest terms it means that the cost per pound of the metal most recently purchased and added to stock is the cost per pound of metal content to be charged against the next sale of processed metal products. It is the necessary corollary of this that to the stock which is in fact in hand at the end of the year there must be attributed the cost of metal which has not yet been exhausted by the cost attributed to metal consumed; this has been called the unabsorbed residue of cost."

An alternative way of looking at this procedure is to regard the initial purchase of stock in much the same light as a purchase of a fixed asset, the assumption being that where it is necessary to carry a certain quantity of stock the original outlay on this minimum quantity is the figure at which the latter should be carried in the books. Replacements for stock that would otherwise be run down by sales are, therefore, regarded in much the same light as renewals of fixed assets, and their cost is debited accordingly to profit and loss account as an expense. Thus sales are *deemed* to be made from the most recent purchases and the original purchases, valued at their original prices, are *deemed* to remain in the business. This does not necessarily correspond with physical reality, but the fact that the actual

4 [1956] 2 W.L.R. at pp. 35, 36.

goods in stock may not be physically the same as the original purchase is not regarded as relevant since it is the *economic* and not the *physical* aspect with which we are concerned. Stocks will thus be valued on the basis of cost at the date of purchase of the oldest goods deemed to be in stock. If the physical quantity in stock is always the same, opening stock will be valued at the same figure as closing stock, both will cancel out, and the cost of the annual purchases will be charged as a business expense.

So long as current market prices and also those at which the latest purchases have been made exceed the original cost price adopted in the LIFO stock valuation, the LIFO method will produce a lower valuation for stock than would the normal cost or lower market value basis. This will reduce taxable profits in every year in which prices continue to rise, since the undervaluation of closing stock in relation to the price level at the end of the accounting period will tend to be greater than the undervaluation of opening stock in relation to the price level at the beginning of the period.

The economic justification of the LIFO method rests on the fact that if stock is sold when the outlay on replacing it is £100, the sacrifice to the business—in other words its expenditure—is also £100 and not the original cost of the stock, let us say £90. The latter figure *is no longer economically relevant*.[5] Hence, runs the argument, if the selling price was, say, £120, the economic profit is only £20. This is the figure that the LIFO method of accounting will produce. In accounting terms we say when using the LIFO method:

	£	£
Sale		120
Cost of stock sold:		
Opening stock valuation, representing original cost price of the stock	90	
Stock bought to replace stock sold	100	
	190	
Less: stock still in hand valued at same price as original purchase	90	100
		20

The argument so far seems perfectly valid. The sacrifice from using stock must indeed be measured at the time of use by reference to current price levels. Yet the stock was acquired at a lower price level. By valuing its stock on the basis of an old price level the business has not taken credit in its accounts for the rise in money replacement

---

5 *Cf.* Lord Radcliffe's views in *Sharkey* v. *Wernher*, see *post*, p. 35.

value of the original stock which has taken place while it has been held. In terms of money values, the business is better off by £10. On the other hand, this £10 is not what economists call " real profit " for it does not (provided it is due to a *general* rise in price levels) represent any increase in general purchasing power over physical goods.[6]

I think it may be helpful to pose the question in another way. The result achieved by the LIFO system is not dependent upon valuing the closing stock on the basis of the original cost of goods bought in an earlier accounting period—in some ways a confusing and unsatisfactory procedure. Instead the business might say " The cost of the most recent purchases of goods of the amount and type we now have in stock was £100: this is, therefore, applying the cost or lower market value basis, the valuation to be used in the accounts for the closing stock. On our original purchase of the stock we sold we only spent £90 (say in the previous year) and it was brought into opening stock this year at that figure. As, however, its replacement cost was £100 we will *revalue it before sale* on that basis, *i.e.*, at £100, when including it in the account, so that the latter may include, as an expense, the true current economic cost of the sale. The difference of £10 between the old and the new book values is a special capital profit to be shown as such in the balance sheet." The account would now say:

	£	£
Sale		120
Cost of stock sold:		
Opening stock valuation at original cost price of the stock	90	
Add: increase in money value during the year, to be treated as capital profit	10	
Current replacement cost of opening stock	100	
Cost of replacing stock sold	100	
	200	
Less: closing stock in hand valued at cost or lower market value	100	100
Profit		20

In other words the results of the LIFO method of undervaluing closing stock in relation to current costs may equally well, and perhaps more clearly, be achieved by raising the value of opening stock to reflect current replacement costs. The question then to be asked is: is that rise to be taxable?

[6] If there has been no *general* rise in prices but the business's own stock has risen in value, the profit is real, for the business now has more purchasing power than before in relation to other commodities.

27

PRESENT LAW SUMMARISED

The recent decisions mean that except in the most unlikely event of a new House of Lords decision which did not follow the *Anaconda* decision of the Privy Council, stock in trade may not (in the absence of new legislation permitting the practice) be valued for tax purposes on the LIFO or any similar basis which departs radically from the more usual cost or lower market value procedure.[7] In other words these cases have decided that closing stock must not be valued at a figure substantially below that which would be produced by the cost or lower market value basis. The legal principle of the *Anaconda* judgment—its *ratio decidendi*—discussed below, leaves in my view no room for doubt that no other form of accounting adjustment (such as an upward revision in opening stock figures) that would achieve in a different way the same result as the use of the LIFO method is now available to the taxpayer.

This leaves the questions first, of whether the *Anaconda* decision invalidates the net selling value and long-term contract methods of stock valuation, and secondly and more important, of how far variations in practice may occur in the application of the cost or lower market value basis without becoming inconsistent with the new judicial precedent.

The Revenue authorities are, of course, in any case unlikely to attack the net selling value and similar methods, since when prices are rising they must tend as compared with other methods to raise assessable profits without corresponding depression when the reverse is true. Moreover, the analysis given below suggests that the court would accept this method and it will not be discussed further.

Case law, old and new, provides little guidance on the second question, that is, on the precise interpretation of the now judicially approved cost or lower market valuation basis. Before we give attention to the possible range of variation in the latter's application it will be convenient to examine the principles of law to be drawn from the *Anaconda* decision. It is not easy in a few words to do justice to Viscount Simonds's judgment, but in essentials it seems to amount to the following propositions.

(a) That the true income is to be ascertained as nearly as it can be done.[8]

(b) That the true income is that calculated by ordinary principles of commercial accounting so far as these are not modified by express provisions in the taxing Acts.[9]

---

[7] There is no question of the propriety in appropriate circumstances of LIFO and similar methods of valuation for the purposes of company accounts—this was made clear by the court both in the *Anaconda* case and in *Patrick v. Broadstone Mills, Ltd.*   [8] *Anaconda Case* [1956] 2 W.L.R. at p. 38.

[9] *Ibid.*, at p. 38. I shall call this the " ordinary commercial principles " rule.

(c) That ordinary principles of commercial accounting require that stock should be valued at the beginning and end of the accounting period at cost or market price, whichever is the lower.[10]

(d) That therefore the LIFO method does not produce the true income and is consequently inadmissible.

The decision in *Patrick* v. *Broadstone Mills, Ltd.* must, I think, be assumed to be based essentially on the same reasoning.[11]

When this argument is examined closely, however, it seems to provide no general guide to the way in which cost or lower market value is to be interpreted in practice. The principle given under (a) above—that " true income " is to be sought—does not help, for the term is without precise meaning until " income " has been defined. The principle given under (b) above, that true income is that calculated under ordinary commercial principles, brings us back to the original problem: which, if any, of the different applications of the cost or lower market rule is to be preferred?

It is not clear how much weight the court placed on the fact that a LIFO stock valuation tends to understate the increase in the money replacement value of a business's stock—that is to say, how far the court has refused as a matter of principle to identify " true income " in the income tax sense with the economist's conception of " real income." It may perhaps be safe to assume, as I have implied above, that the court did not rely on this distinction, but based its decision on the departure of the LIFO method from the methods of stock valuation long established as most usual for business purposes. Indeed, it was surely only by adopting as the essential test of validity the consistence of the method of stock valuation adopted by the tax-payer with the long established " ordinary commercial principles " that the court could avoid rejecting one of the oldest established and best known principles of the income tax law.

It may be added that if the court's decision were indeed based, not on ordinary commercial practice but on the proposition that LIFO gives a poorer approximation than other methods to " true income " in the economic sense, it would be in conflict with a good deal of economic opinion.[12]

---

[10] *Ibid.*, at pp. 38, 39.

[11] See H. C. Edey, " Accuracy and Inaccuracy in Profit Calculation," (1954) 17 M.L.R. 229, where I have attempted to show that the alternative, a *ratio decidendi* based on an attempt to ascertain " true income " without reference to any standard of income, leads to a logical contradiction. But on this see the discussion below.

[12] But some economists would argue that there is no such thing as " true income," income being a category the nature of which depends upon the purpose for which it is used. From this point of view income in Income Tax law should depend upon the definition adopted by Parliament and this in turn should depend

It must be admitted on the other hand, however, that the court went to considerable pains to demonstrate that in their view the LIFO method of stock valuation was unsatisfactory on general accounting grounds—namely, that the accretion in stock value failed to reach the profit and loss account [13]—which was hardly necessary if the practice was to be rejected because it was not an "ordinary commercial principle." This is rather an important point, for if it is now established that it is for the court to say what is "true income"—and this without taking evidence on the nature of income—a new and serious uncertainty faces taxpayers for the principle would surely not be restricted to stock valuation.

Moreover, even if we can assume that the court has preserved the form of the "ordinary commercial principle" rule, it is difficult to avoid the conclusion that the range of variation in accounting practice acceptable is now smaller than some people at least have thought it to be in the past. There is no doubt whatever that the LIFO method used by the Anaconda company (and the Base Stock method used by Broadstone Mills, Ltd.) were "accepted commercial practices" in the ordinary sense of the words. It would not have been unreasonable to believe until a short while ago that even if these methods were on the whole unusual in business, yet in companies that adopted them consistently they were acceptable for tax purposes. Until recently this view had long been reflected in the practice of the Revenue authorities. It is also clear that for accounting debits or credits to be valid for tax purposes in one kind of business they do not always have to be valid for all kinds of businesses: to hold otherwise would lead to absurdities. It seems, however, that the ordinary commercial principles rule must now be applied in relation to the *most usual* commercial practice or group of practices. It is, perhaps, relevant (though no stress was laid on the point in the *Anaconda* case) that as originally formulated the principle was stated to be that of *ordinary* commercial principles.[14] The alternative formulation of "accepted" or "sound" [15] commercial practice is probably now to be avoided as misleading.

This indeed raises a further problem: suppose what have previously not been "ordinary commercial practices" of accounting then become so? If, for example, the majority of British businesses

upon the economic effects that are desired by Parliament, that is, on economic policy considerations. This view leaves the argument in the text unaffected, since if "true income" does not exist the court cannot ascertain it.

13 *Anaconda Case* [1956] 2 W.L.R. at p. 39.

14 See *Gresham Life Assurance Society* v. *Styles* [1892] A.C. 309, *per* Lord Halsbury L.C. at p. 316, and *Anaconda Case* [1956] 2 W.L.R. at p. 38.

15 *Cf. I. R. C.* v. *Cock, Russell & Co., Ltd.* [1949] 2 All E.R. 889, *per* Croom-Johnson J. at p. 892.

adopted the LIFO method of accounting for stock, would the application of the *Anaconda* decision lead to the conclusion that the method was thenceforth acceptable for tax purposes? The question may not be pressing but it seems to be one that requires answering.

COST OR LOWER MARKET METHOD

It is common knowledge in accounting circles that " cost or lower market " covers a number of practices, in each of which either " cost " or " market " means something different.[16] Let us first consider " cost."

Meaning of cost

Cost may mean unit cost—the actual outlay attached to the particular physical assets in stock. (It is only practicable to determine cost in this way when the stock consists of a relatively small quantity of distinguishable goods, such as motor-cars.) Or cost may be derived by use of the first-in, first-out (FIFO) method in which the goods sold are deemed to be those that were first acquired or made during a given period. Or cost may be the average cost of stock owned or acquired during the accounting period. Or cost may be the standard cost for a given period, probably the last accounting period; this implies a predetermined or budgeted, that is, *expected*, cost for the period, which can normally be assumed to approximate fairly closely to cost as it would be calculated by one of the other methods just mentioned. Refinements and variants of these methods may be found in practice.

Cost calculations may, more particularly in manufacturing businesses, vary in another way. The cost of goods in stock may be interpreted as a due proportion only of the direct production or prime costs—the cost of material and labour physically identifiable with the units produced—or of prime costs plus a proportion of other works expenses—or of the latter plus a proportion of general administrative expenses. This leaves scope for variety of practice in the expenses grouped under each head and in the way—which cannot but be arbitrary—in which total annual expenses are allocated to the product including that part of the latter which consists of stocks of work in progress and finished goods.

It is doubtful whether the *Anaconda* case provides very much in the way of guidance in deciding to what extent each of these practices is acceptable for tax purposes. It can be said that the FIFO method

---

[16] See The Institute of Chartered Accountants in England and Wales, *Recommendations on Accounting Principles*, Recommendation X.

is definitely acceptable and the Average Cost method probably so.[17] It is also unlikely that the court would have rejected the Unit Cost method as, like FIFO, it has an appearance of arithmetical accuracy which fits in well with the general flavour of the *Anaconda* judgment. In any case, however, these three methods have the blessing of long usage to commend them, and it is hard to believe that they do not all fall within the range of ordinary commercial usage approved by the court. This is the more true as it is by no means established that the FIFO method commended by the court has ever been the most common method used in practice: it is at least as likely that some form of average cost calculation has always been as, or more, usual.

As for Standard Cost, this is more doubtful, for it certainly cannot claim to have been very common in the past nor to be the most usual method now. Nor has it the same attractive arithmetical accuracy, for its adoption is bound to result in the stock valuation prices being in some cases different from any " actual " past price. Fortunately— for the method has great conveniences—there are grounds for thinking the *Anaconda* decision does not exclude it. It may not be unreasonable to construe " ordinary commercial practice " in relation to stock valuation not as covering any single method or set of methods, but rather as referring to any practice which will give results substantially the same as one or other of the methods discussed in the previous paragraph, the exact method of calculation being a matter of reasonable convenience.[18] A Standard Cost basis of valuation can indeed, provided the standards are reasonably chosen, be regarded as a special kind of average cost calculation. Provided the results of using Standard Cost for valuation purposes in a particular instance could be shown not to differ significantly from those that would have been obtained from one or other of the FIFO, or the Average Cost, or the Unit Cost methods, it hardly seems likely that the court would reject it.

There is still the question of the definition of cost: to what extent does the law require that the stock valuation should, in the case of manufacturing businesses, include a proportion of the annual overhead expense? One may guess with respect to business practice— which may be relevant in applying the ordinary commercial principles rule—that the most common rule is to add to prime cost a proportion of works overhead expenses, but not of general administrative

---

[17] The latter is suggested by some words of Viscount Simonds [1956] 2 W.L.R. at p. 39.

[18] " Reasonable convenience " may perhaps be regarded as an acceptable paraphrase of " as nearly as it can be done," the words used by Lord Loreham L.C. in *Sun Insurance Office* v. *Clark* [1912] A.C. 443, 454, which was cited by the Crown in the *Anaconda* case and seems to have been implicitly approved by the court in that case.

or other expenses; this is, however, no more than a guess. Apart from ordinary commercial practice, so far as the *Anaconda* decision points in any direction it seems to be in favour of the allocation of some overhead. To the extent that the decision must be assumed to have gone beyond the application of the ordinary commercial principles rule—and this interpretation raises logical difficulties as we have seen—it seems to be favourable to an income concept that takes into account the accruing money value of stock, so far as the latter can be attributed in some sense to past business outlays: this would support the inclusion of an overhead allocation in stock valuation.

Apart from what overheads are to be included in stock valuations there is also the question of how the allocation is to be calculated. It is not possible to say that there is any well-known rule about the principle on which the allocation of given overheads is to be made, and in view of the wide—and arbitrary—variations in practice it is difficult to see on what grounds the Revenue could resist any reasonable rule if consistently followed. The *Anaconda* case does not seem to help here.

Meaning of Market Value

This brings us to the interpretation of " market value " in the " cost or lower market value " formula. Here again there is variation in practice which falls under two main heads. Under the first of these market value is interpreted as the net realisation value on sale in the ordinary course of business. Under the second it means the current replacement value. Whether these two views differ so widely as to make one of them unacceptable is open to question, particularly as the adoption of the latter rather than the former will seldom do more than shift part of the tax liability into the following year of assessment. When market value is relevant, the use of the market replacement value basis will usually result in a lower closing stock valuation, and therefore a lower profit in the year when it is applied, but the opening stock of the following year will, of course, be valued on the same basis, and when the stock is sold the profit shown in the accounts will be correspondingly higher.

Possibly the net market realisation value is the more usual of the two methods, but there seems no other reason for favouring it and, since considerable inconvenience would otherwise result, it is to be hoped the court if occasion arose would decide that both methods are sufficiently well established to be acceptable. The " true income " criterion seems of little relevance here, for good arguments can be put up for either basis of valuation.

There remains the question whether the cost or lower market value

33

basis is to be applied to the stock taken as a whole or to each separate item. The latter is the more conservative practice and will, if it makes any difference, produce a lower valuation, and hence a lower taxable profit. The 1949 case *I. R. C.* v. *Cock, Russell & Co.* decided that the latter method was acceptable for tax purposes. The case was decided on the ordinary commercial practice principle, and although it was not taken beyond the High Court it is difficult to see how it could be reversed without either upsetting that principle or bringing evidence to show that this method of valuation did not fall within the category—a difficult task to achieve.

SHARKEY *v.* WERNHER

Although it is not directly relevant to stock valuations of the type just discussed, the recent decision of the House of Lords in *Sharkey* v. *Wernher* is of interest in this context because it too bears on the interpretation of the ordinary commercial principles rule.

It was common ground to both parties in the case that where there is a trade (in the Income Tax sense of a taxable business activity) and a transfer of stock is made from the business to the owner for the latter's private use, then in calculating the taxable profit some credit must be made in the business accounts for the value so withdrawn. The question at issue was how the stock withdrawn is to be valued for the purpose of the credit. The court decided (Lord Oaksey dissenting) that the correct basis of valuation in such a case is current realisable value, thereby approving an earlier decision, *Watson Bros.* v. *Hornby*,[19] in which stock had been transferred from the business whose profits were the subject of the assessment to another business carried on by the same taxpayer.[20] Despite *Watson Bros.* v. *Hornby* it had probably been considered by most accountants before *Sharkey* v. *Wernher* that the appropriate valuation basis in such cases was the cost of the stock.[1] This view seemed to be justified both on the grounds that this has long been ordinary accounting practice and also on the grounds that to credit any figure above cost would violate the Income Tax principle believed to have been established many

---

[19] [1942] 2 All E.R. 506 ; 24 T.C. 506.

[20] In this case the transfer was not to private use as in *Sharkey* v. *Wernher*, but to another business. The situation was, however, essentially the same as if the taxpayer had transferred stock from business A to himself as a private person and then retransferred them from himself in his private capacity to business B. (The latter was, at that time, assessed to tax (under Schedule B) in such a way that the value set on the transferred stocks could not affect its profits.) Realisable market value was substantially below cost and hence it was much in the interest of the taxpayer that the former should be the basis of valuation: this the court accepted.

[1] Exactly how cost should be calculated in any given instance, *e.g.*, how much should be allocated for overhead expense, has remained an open question which in view of the *Sharkey* v. *Wernher* decision is presumably no longer relevant.

years ago [2] that a person cannot trade with himself. It would be difficult to blame accountants for arriving at the same conclusion as the Court of Appeal itself did in *Sharkey* v. *Wernher*.

The principles on which the House of Lords reversed the Court of Appeal's decision seem to have been, first that the current realisable value is of all bases the least arbitrary: in Lord Radcliffe's words ". . . it gives a fairer measure of assessable trading profit as between one taxpayer and another, for it eliminates variations which are due to no other cause than any one taxpayer's decision as to what proportion of his total product he will supply to himself " [3]; and secondly that it is better economics to credit the business with the current realisable value—the current money's worth—than with some kind of cost figure which is a bygone and has no current economic relevance. [4]

Both these are appealing arguments; to what extent can they be reconciled with the views that have prevailed generally up to the date of this case and, if they cannot be so reconciled, to what extent do they introduce wholly new principles and how widespread are the effects of these likely to be?

A close examination of the judgments of Viscount Simonds and Lord Radcliffe suggests that in fact the application of the decision may be more limited in scope than might at first appear to be the case. In the first place, Lord Radcliffe said: ". . . we must not begin by assuming, without any evidence, that ' ordinary commercial accounting ' has any settled rule for such a case. . . ." [5] This implies that the court considered the ordinary commercial practice test to be relevant, though it must be admitted that it is not easy to reconcile the *Sharkey* v. *Wernher* decision with what has been undoubtedly a very widespread accounting practice of valuing stock withdrawals from the business on a cost basis.

This may be because more attention was devoted by the court to the second point, the question of whether a person can make a taxable profit by trading with himself. If this question could be answered negatively and the principle was applicable to the *Sharkey* case, the question of accounting practice could not arise, since the principle of ordinary commercial practice is not applicable to transactions which do not comprise a trade for Income Tax purposes. In such a case the valuation of the transferred stock could not exceed the expense debited in the accounts in respect of the stock—that is, could not be greater than the amount required to cancel out the costs incurred by

---

[2] See *New York Life Insurance Co.* v. *Styles* (1889) 14 App.Cas. 381 ; 2 T.C. 460, and *Re Glasgow Corporation Waterworks* (1875) 12 S.L.R. 466 ; 1 T.C. 28.
[3] [1955] 3 All E.R. at p. 505.
[4] See *per* Lord Radcliffe at pp. 504, 506.
[5] At p. 501.

the business in bringing the stock to the state in which it was transferred.

The essence of the court's decision on this point seems to have been that (a) the long-established rule regarding mutual trading is only relevant in deciding whether or not there is a taxable trade [6]; that (b) in this case there was unquestionably a trade [7]; that (c) there is ample precedent to show that where there is a trade the Income Tax code does on occasions require the assumption that a person can trade with themselves [8]; and that (d) it only remained to fix the most appropriate basis of valuation for the goods transferred by the taxpayer as trader to the taxpayer as a private person. For the reasons already given this basis was the current market realisable value.

It seems, therefore, that the scope of the decision is restricted to situations in which *there is already a trade*. It does not establish a principle that any transaction by a taxpayer to which a notional profit could be attached—for example, the painting by a taxpayer of his own house—gives rise to a taxable profit; first there must be a trade in the income tax sense and the case does not create taxable trades where none existed previously. On the other hand it does seem that where there is a taxable trade, then transactions of the taxpayer with himself may be treated on the basis that they are made on ordinary business terms. The principle is applicable " . . . to all those cases in which the Income Tax system requires that part of a taxpayer's activities should be isolated and treated as a self-contained trade." [9] The principle may, of course, benefit the taxpayer, as when he transfers private property *to* the business.

Effect of Recent Decisions

Neither the *Anaconda* case nor *Sharkey* v. *Wernher* have formally abrogated the ordinary commercial principles rule. Yet, on the other hand, and with all respect, in both cases the judgments give the impression that the court was, while paying lip service to this principle, seeking for some absolute concept of income by which it could judge the practice on which it was asked to pass. (This is equally noticeable in *Patrick* v. *Broadstone Mills, Ltd.*) It is difficult to see how these two views can be reconciled with one another unless " true income " means " income as determined by ordinary commercial practice "—and it is not certain that this is what the court intended. However this may be, the cases have established that the court will not hesitate to interpret ordinary commercial practice

[6] p. 502.
[7] pp. 500, 501.
[8] pp. 502, 503.
[9] *Per* Lord Radcliffe at p. 505.

narrowly—there is indeed some evidence that the court is prepared to go as far as to determine the point at issue by deciding what ordinary commercial principles *ought*, in its view, to be.

In conclusion it is perhaps not out of place to suggest that the time may have come for Parliament to lay down more precisely the rules by which taxable business profit is to be calculated. The principle for such an action must be to arrive at a definition of profit, both administratively acceptable and conducive to the fiscal aims of the Government. To leave the amount of the taxable quantum to the uncertainty of the judicial process is surely undesirable. To say this is not to criticise the court which at present is asked in effect to legislate in one of the most complex fields of economic policy. It is significant that the majority Report of the Royal Commission on the Taxation of Profits and Income made recommendations that, subject to certain conditions, would validate for tax purposes all of the main methods of stock valuation discussed above, namely, Unit Cost, FIFO, Average Cost, Standard Cost, Net Realisation Value or, in appropriate cases, a variant (defined in Appendix II of the Report) of the LIFO or Base Stock method, in each case subject to the application of lower market value where relevant to each item or group of items in stock and taking either of the two main interpretations of market value.

APPENDIX VIII

Memorandum by Harold C. Edey, Reader in Accounting, University of London

General

It is generally accepted that investors should be given every reasonable opportunity to select, for the investment of their money, the securities of those companies which are economically most efficient and which for that reason are, in a competitive economy, likely to be the most profitable. This is one of the major reasons for requiring companies to provide periodic accounting reports and financial statements in prospectuses. The 1948 Companies Act effected great improvements in the quantity and quality of financial information thus provided for shareholders. Certain deficiencies, however, remain and are the more apparent for the improvements of 1948. My submission is directed towards this aspect of company accounts. It will relate to annual accounting reports, but the comments will apply, *mutatis mutandis*, to prospectus statements.

It is sometimes said, when suggestions are made to increase the information available for shareholders, that particular measures of disclosure are undesirable because the information so disclosed is open to misinterpretation, and may therefore " mislead " the public. It is also sometimes said that provision of fuller information would make accounts too complicated for shareholders to understand. These arguments are, I believe, inappropriate in a free society. In my opinion the legislation should be based on the fundamental assumption that the public should receive as much information as is reasonably possible and should be allowed to make their own minds up on the basis of this information. Apart altogether from undesirable philosophical implications, such arguments also ignore the fact that expert advice can be sought from professional advisers or from the financial press, who are certainly unlikely to be misled if the accounts are sensibly prepared. Business is, after all, a complicated process. It is not always possible in financial reports to remove all the complications without seriously distorting the picture. Furthermore, directors can always supplement accounting information by more or less detailed explanatory notes if they think that the accounts are likely otherwise to mislead. It is also sometimes objected in relation to the disclosure of accounting information that competitors will be helped. Two points arise here. Firstly, competitors probably know much more about one another before accounts are published than this argument implies. Secondly, it is in any case in the public interest, making for smoother working of the pricing system, that competitors should become aware of exceptionally profitable opportunities in particular fields, and the like.

A Statement of Accounting Procedures

It is undoubtedly true that statutory accounting reports may be substantial documents. The addition of further requirements will certainly not reduce their size. I think that the Act might well include a requirement that each company, or at least each public company, should file annually with the Registrar a " Statement of Accounting Procedures " at the time of publication of its annual accounts. Such a statement could be designed to explain the bases and assumptions on which the less certain of the figures in the accounts had been calculated.

Explanations in such a statement could, because they were filed, be much more detailed than would be possible in the published accounts; and the Act's requirements could be correspondingly more comprehensive. Another advantage that could well accrue would be an increased flexibility in the use and development of accounting conventions. At present it is difficult for a company to depart from generally accepted accounting principles because, if it does, its auditors are likely, not unreasonably, to qualify their report. Yet there is room for improvement in some of these conventions. And in any case I take it as axiomatic that freedom to experiment is desirable. The procedures currently followed for financial accounts are not always convenient for internal management accounting purposes. But because it may be too expensive to duplicate internal accounting arrangements and prepare accounts on two different bases, companies may have to continue to prepare figures they do not really want because this happens to be in accordance with " normal procedures ".

For example, a manufacturing company might wish to change its internal accounting arrangements in order to value its raw material stocks at current market prices. This would be a departure from the more normal " cost or lower market value " rule: the auditors might feel they had to qualify their report if the company were to use this basis for its annual financial accounts. If my suggestion were adopted the company would state in its " Statement of Accounting Procedures " that this particular method of valuation had been followed, explaining the procedure used; and reference could be made to the " Statement of Accounting Procedures " in the auditors' report, thus drawing the attention of shareholders to the need to study this statement.

I shall give other examples later of the type of figure with respect to which I believe that a statement of this kind would be particularly valuable.

If this suggestion were adopted it could be implemented by requiring the Board of Trade to embody in a Statutory Instrument and appropriate form of words and instructions. A standing committee could be appointed to advise the Board; this could draw on the services of practising and industrial accountants, economists and financial journalists.

I think that the importance of not allowing rigid rules of financial accounting to strangle at birth improvements in management accounting practices cannot be over-emphasized. It is not easy to obtain evidence of the extent to which this has happened. My own view, however, is that financial accounting rules, together with income tax considerations, have had a considerable effect in limiting experiment.

Form of the Auditors' Report

This raises the question of the auditors' report.

I think it is unfortunate that the words " true and fair " are at present used in this report (and in the body of the Act). These words constitute, it is true, a term of art; but even so they are an unhappy choice. I believe that an appropriate form of words, incorporating a reference to the " Statement of Accounting Procedures " suggested above, would be:

" In our opinion the balance sheet and profit and loss account present a fair view of the company's affairs in the light of generally accepted accounting principles and the company's statement of accounting procedures filed under Section ... [and of the following modifications to generally accepted principles, explanations of which are contained in the said statement, namely ... [1]]."

The section in square brackets would be deleted where not appropriate.

It may be argued that to leave directors free to vary accounting methods would be to allow a latitude that could be abused. I do not think this is a convincing argument, firstly because even within the present body of accounting practice quite wide variations are possible in certain respects; and secondly because it would still remain in the hands of the auditors whether they should qualify the above form of words if it seemed to them that a departure from normal accounting principles did not arise from a *bona fide* motive, or if it seemed to them that the departure from the usual conventions was so radical as to make the accounts seriously misleading. (The effect of any change in the basis of accounting on the financial results of the year of the change must be disclosed under the existing legislation. This important provision would no doubt remain in force in any amended Act.)

Profit

It is unfortunately true that the concept of profit is not one that lends itself to a general definition that can be applied precisely in practice. Profit is customarily defined in accounting texts as " that which remains after provision has been made for maintaining capital intact ". But this definition does not convey a clear meaning until the word " capital " has been defined.

---

[1] Insert here a short description of the modifications (e.g., " the stock-in-trade has been valued on the basis of current market prices ").

The "maintenance of capital" could mean the maintenance of the saleable value of the company's undertaking as a whole; the maintenance of the current level of profit or of some other defined level of profit; the maintenance of the current level of dividends or some defined level of dividends; or the maintenance of the break-up value of the undertaking. It cannot be said that any one of these definitions would be freely accepted as the definition implied in practice. Yet it would be difficult to find any other general definition which would be accepted. /Probably the first of these definitions comes the nearest to what is generally considered to be the idea of maintaining capital intact. Quite apart from this, there is the question of whether the quantum that is to be maintained intact should be stated in terms of current money values or in terms of a constant level of prices, i.e. after adjustment for changing price levels.

The problem is solved in practice by applying a number of accounting precepts that have developed over a period of many years. These precepts are capable of fairly wide variation in application, however, and in a given company, in a particular year, the profit figure could vary quite widely depending upon the bases of calculation adopted and the assumptions made. This is one of the reasons why I think that these bases and assumptions should be stated, more precisely than has hitherto been the case, in a "Statement of Accounting Procedures" to be filed with the Registrar, as I have suggested above.

By reading such a statement in conjunction with the accounts the individual shareholder or his advisor would have a clearer picture of what was in the minds of the directors when profit was calculated, and would be able to make such adjustments to the figures as he thought appropriate if he did not wholly agree with the directors' approach. This is not a new departure in company accounting. The idea of showing depreciation separately in the profit and loss account, and in the balance sheet the original cost (or subsequent valuation) of a fixed asset before the deduction of depreciation, established by the 1948 Act, has the same kind of reasoning behind it. The shareholder can see how much depreciation has been provided in relation to original cost. He can make his own assessment of the situation and make such adjustments as he thinks appropriate. The suggestions made here merely take this approach a stage further with the object of making the information available more precise and therefore more useful.

I should like to draw a parallel here between the shareholder and the director. A director necessarily has access to a great deal of financial information. In particular he receives accounting reports drawn up in much greater detail than is usual for shareholders. He is thus able to supplement the relatively limited amount of information conveyed by the net profit figure—which he knows is dependent upon a number of calculations and assumptions in which the order of magnitude of possible differences of opinion is very high—by examining critically the component figures of the profit shown in the account given to him. Moreover, the director can supplement his information by asking searching questions with the reasonable certainty of getting satisfactory answers. But unless the accounts are presented to him in sufficient detail to show the component figures that, taken together, make up the profit, and unless the bases and assumptions on which these figures have been drafted are available, he will be handicapped in pursuing his enquiries. In the ultimate analysis the shareholder is interested in the same kind of financial information as the director, who is, after all, the shareholder's servant, and presumably has the same broad aims. In the limiting case of a controlling shareholder, indeed, it may become difficult to distinguish between the part played in control by the shareholder himself and that played by the board of directors. The aim of the company accountant, and the company law, should be, in my opinion, to place shareholders as closely as is reasonably possible to the position of directors, bearing in mind that they have less facility for intelligent questioning than the directors. It is, of course, out of the question to provide as much detailed information to the minority shareholder in a large company as is available for the directors. But I believe the accounts should deliberately go as far in this direction as is practicable. The attitude of mind of the financial accountant when preparing accounts for shareholders should be similar to that when he prepares accounts for directors and managers. In this sense, I believe that all accounts should be regarded as " management accounts ". The company law should, I think, be based on the same philosophy.

This question bears on such matters as a calculation of depreciation provisions in periods of changing price levels. There has been a good deal of controversy on the question of whether " profit " is to be correctly interpreted as a figure before, or after, adjustments for changing price levels have been made. Official pronouncements on the interpretation of the existing legislation have tended to suggest that the word " profit " should always mean a figure *before* a price level adjustment has been made. This has not been universally accepted by company accountants, but it has, I think, tended to make some accountants and directors refrain from introducing procedures which many people would have regarded as valuable. It is in my view undesirable that in such matters, company legislation should be capable of an interpretation likely to prevent accountants from presenting information which the weight of economic and financial opinion would regard as important to the investor.

I believe that the correct approach is to leave directors, advised by their accountants, to calculate the profit in accordance with the view that seems to be most appropriate and—most important—to make it clear to shareholders beyond a peradventure how they have made those calculations. I think that a general statement to this effect in the Act, or in the 8th Schedule, is desirable. This means that all calculations which lie within the area where opinion may differ, both with respect to the general method and the particular calculation or estimate, should be fully explained, e.g. in a " Statement of Accounting Procedures ".

In the following paragraphs I shall make some comments on particular items as ·they are affected by this general view.

Depreciation

My first comment relates to depreciation. In my view the provisions of the 8th Schedule of the Companies Act in effect already allow directors to show profit net of depreciation on the basis of current price levels, since they may make provision for *replacement*, even if they have not first revalued the assets. (There is no disagreement where assets have been revalued.) Nevertheless there seems to be uncertaintly on this point and I think the position should be made more explicit. I suggest that an amended 8th Schedule should be so drafted as to make it clear that there is no prohibition of the calculation of depreciation on the basis of current price levels if the directors think fit. Coupled with this I think that a fuller explanation of the method of depreciation should be supplied than has hitherto been the case, preferably in the " Statement of Accounting Procedures " suggested above. This explanation should cover (*a*) the question of the price level adjustment, i.e., whether such an adjustment has been made, and if so how it has been calculated; (*b*) the commercial life with the company that has been assumed for different classes of assets for the purpose of calculation of depreciation; and (*c*) the method of spreading depreciation over the commercial life of the asset, i.e., whether straight-line, reducing balance, etc. This explanation should relate to each class of fixed assets. Where more than one method is used in relation to a particular class of assets, the balance sheet value of the assets appertaining to each method of calculation should be stated.

It will be noticed that this suggestion refers not only to the problem of price level adjustment, but also calls for additional information than is now customarily provided with respect to depreciation calculated on the normal basis. One of the major difficulties of present practice with respect to fixed assets is that the shareholder is left very much in the dark about the approach the directors are taking in relation to the spreading of depreciation charges over time. This is particularly important, for example, where a heavy capital expenditure programme is undertaken and is then amortised over a short period: in the absence of explanation such a procedure may give for a time an unduly pessimistic view of the longer-term profitability of the company.

Expenditure on Research, Development, etc.

There are certain types of expenditure which are of particular significance for the longer-term prospects of the company. Expenditure on scientific research, on development, on advertising, fall into this category. Where such expenditure is charged to revenue the present legislation does not call for any accounting disclosure. Yet in some companies the failure to carry out heavy annual expenditure under one or other of these heads, or the failure to maintain a certain level of such expenditure, may be of great significance to the shareholder. I believe revenue expenditure under each of these heads should so far as possible be separately disclosed in companies' published profit and loss accounts. I am aware that this raises practical difficulties: it is not always easy to categorise expenditure of this type. It would, I think, therefore, be necessary to provide that this information should only be required to the extent that it was available in the company's books. This would not be a perfect solution but it would place more information of a particularly important type in the hands of many shareholders. It would be open to directors to add explanations if they thought the figures thus disclosed would be misleading in the absence of such explanations. It would also be interesting for shareholders to know whether their directors had in fact arranged for such expenditure to be separately analysed.

Stock Valuation

I think it unsatisfactory that the method of stock valuation, which may affect the profit figure a good deal, should not be stated in the annual accounts. I should like the suggested " Statement of Accounting Procedures " to show in some detail the method of stock valuation used, e.g., whether " cost and lower market value " has been used, and if so whether the formula has been applied overall or to individual stock items; and whether " lower market value " means estimated net selling price or estimated replacement value. An example of a situation where this information would be particularly important is that of a company carrying a large quantity of raw material at a time when prices had fallen heavily.

Profit on Hire-purchase Transactions

Companies carrying on hire-purchase or deferred payment business do not always disclose the precise way in which profit is allocated between accounting periods. The formula on which this allocation is made should, I believe, be included in the "Statement of Accounting Procedures ". Differences in formulae may make substantial differences in the figure of profit reported in particular years.

Sales Turnover

It is becoming increasingly accepted that the sales turnover figure is an element of the profit and loss calculation that is of particular significance when trends are under examination, and should be disclosed in the published information. This is now the accepted practice in America and is a growing practice in this country. I believe it should be required by the legislation.

A large company with many activities may make profits on some and losses on others. It is of significance to the shareholder to know when ground is being gained or lost on one particular activity. It is probably impracticable to call for separate profit and loss statements for different activities, but I see no reason why companies should not be asked to disclose the sales turnover figures for different major divisions of their business. This is not an easy matter to legislate on, since the definition of a separate activity is not easily arrived at. I suggest that for public companies whose shares are quoted a statement of the sales figures for distinct trading activities of the company should be required where these amounted to more than 20 per cent. of the total sales turnover. A " distinct trading activity " might perhaps be defined as one for which separate figures of sales are recorded by the directors for their own information. Here too there is no reason why the directors should not add explanations if they thought the figures would tend to mislead in the absence of such explanations.

Interest on Finance

The present legislation requires the disclosure of interest on debentures. But a substantial part of the finance of a company may consist of an overdraft or other non-permanent finance. It is of considerable investment interest to know the total burden on a company of its financing. I suggest that the profit and loss account should be required to disclose all interest paid, whether on debentures or on other loans and advances.

Reserves

The general balance sheet headings " revenue reserves " and " capital reserves " may each cover a long list of separate reserve balances. There is however a tendency in well-drafted balance sheets for this practice to be discontinued. Such balance sheets contain only a single item under the heading of " revenue reserves " and no more items under the heading of " capital reserves " than are necessary to comply with the existing legislation (which requires the share premium account and the capital redemption reserve fund, if any, to be stated separately).

Sub-divisions in the reserves have little economic or financial significance. I cannot see that any information is conveyed by such sub-divisions that could not be better conveyed by a short note, or a comment in the directors' report. I think that the proliferation of reserve balances is confusing to people who are not familiar with accounting figures. In my view there would be a considerable gain in clarity if all revenue reserves, including the profit and loss balance itself, were shown under a single head in the balance sheet with no sub-division.

I also think that the distinction between (a) items entering into the composition of profit and (b) appropriations to reserves tends to be fogged by the absence in the published accounts of a clear break between the profit and loss account proper and the appropriation account. This often applies even where the otherwise useful " narrative " form of account is used. I should like to see transfers shown in the annual profit and loss statement to (or from) revenue reserves, other than tax reserves, limited to a single net figure, representing the transfer of the balance of profit (or loss), after deduction of tax, to (or from) a separate account, to be called, say, the " Retained Profit Account ". The latter, following Canadian and American practice, would be presented as a distinct account, or in an entirely separate narrative statement. In this separate account or statement would be reconciled: (a) the opening balance of the retained profit from the previous year; (b) the profit for the year in question, net of all expenses and taxes; (c) the dividends paid or to be paid for the year in question; (d) any transfer to or from the capital reserve account or to nominal capital in respect of capitalised profit; and (e) the retained profit to be shown in the closing balance sheet. The latter figure would be the only revenue reserve balance in the balance sheet. The sharper distinction thus made between (a) the calculation and (b) the distribution of profit would I think make the profit and loss statement easier to understand, and the balance sheet would also be clearer.

Tax reserves are a rather special case. I suggest that the debit for tax on the profit of the current year should be shown in the profit and loss account " proper ". The fact that tax is from some points of view an " appropriation " of profit is not, I think, relevant in this context. From a shareholder's point of view his dividend must come out of what is left after payment of all tax.

The credit balance shown in the balance sheet for " future tax " should I think be treated as a separate item, *sui generis*. It would be appropriate I think to describe this balance as a deferred liability, but the exact name is not so important as making its significance clear. I shall refer in greater detail to the question of tax in a later section.

There is much to be said for getting rid altogether of the term " reserve " in connection with undistributed surplus. In certain contexts " reserve " means cash or investments, and many members of the public find it difficult to understand that " reserves " are not synonymous with " cash ". For this reason I have suggested the term " retained profit " for the revenue reserves. The term " capital surplus " is a possible substitute for capital reserves.

Capital Reserves

As regards the capital reserves, it would be simpler if the share premium account and capital redemption reserve fund could be amalgamated with the other capital reserves, but under the existing law relating to distribution of profits this would raise certain difficulties. Under the present legislation directors may transfer to capital reserve amounts which they " regard " as not free for distribution to the shareholders. If, however, they later stop regarding these amounts as not available for distribution they can, it seems, re-transfer them to revenue reserves.

One reason for transfers to capital reserve is presumably to sterilise certain so-called " capital profits ", which may be thought, having regard to judicial precedents, not to be available for dividend. A suggestion I shall make later with respect to the definition of divisible profits would, if adopted, make these precedents no longer relevant. If, however, the law remains as it appears to be now, it would seem more rational to regard the act of transfer of such items to capital reserve as *ipso facto* causing the amounts so transferred to become " capital " in the same sense as the share premium amount, that is, subject to reduction only by due legal process.

There is also a case for allowing, with the consent of shareholders in general meeting, a " voluntary " irrevocable capitalisation by simple transfer to capital reserve, of amounts that would otherwise have been free for distribution. The usefulness of formal capitalisation of distributable profits arises from the fact that it may improve the credit standing of the company: once profits have been formally capitalised, the amount by which the company's assets can be run down at any time by the declaration of a dividend is reduced *pro tanto*. This improves the security of creditors. At present the only method of irrevocable capitalisation available is the formal procedure of paying-up nominal capital which is then issued *pro rata* to existing ordinary shareholders, as bonus shares or otherwise. This involves expense and administrative trouble.

I can see no useful reasons for transfers to capital reserve account which can later be revoked by re-transfer to revenue reserve. I suggest therefore that directors should be allowed to transfer to capital reserve (or " surplus ") such amounts as they think fit, subject in the case of all amounts that would otherwise have been legally available for dividend to the approval of the shareholders in general meeting, the amounts thereby ceasing to be available for distribution and becoming subject to the requirements relating to reduction of capital. The share premium account and the capital redemption reserve fund, where they existed, would then not need to be kept separate, and any capital reserve in the balance sheet would consist of a single, undistributable total, available for no purpose except the payment-up of nominal capital. (I shall suggest below that the existing law with respect to the use of share premium and capital redemption reserve accounts be amended.)

No Par Value Shares

The case for no par value shares has been well put in recent years and I do not see any point in adding my own pleading to what is undoubtedly already in the possession of the Committee. It seems to me that the case in favour of this type of equity share is so overwhelming that there is nothing more to be said.

I should like, however, to make a brief comment on no par value shares. It has been suggested that no par value, while suitable for equity shares, is not a suitable device for preference shares. I do not agree. The idea of a par or nominal value seems to me unnecessary and indeed misleading, whether it be related to an equity share or preference share. It is quite possible for a preference share to be issued above par; to be quoted throughout its life at prices other than par; and to be repaid in liquidation or otherwise at a price other than par. It is unnecessary to have a par value in order to describe the dividend rate. It is just as easy to describe a preference share as a " 1s. per annum preference share " as to call it a " 5 per cent. preference share of £1 ". The concept of par or nominal value in relation to share capital seems to me wholly redundant.

Exactly the same principle applies to debentures, though here it is not so much a matter of legislation as of company practice. It is not the par value of a debenture which is relevant but the annual amount payable in interest per transferable unit, and the ultimate capital value repayable on redemption for the same unit.

Share Premiums

It seems now to be accepted that all amounts received on the issue of shares should be treated as not available for profit. Indeed it may be said that the acceptance of the non-distribution of the share premium was the final step in making the concept of nominal capital, as the minimum amount available for creditors when paid-up, finally obsolete. (A share premium account is, of course, only necessary when there is par value capital. If all capital is of no par value the total amount of the receipts from the issue of shares can be credited directly to the issued capital account.)

Once it is accepted that share premiums should not be distributed there seems to be no point in allowing the share premium account to be reduced for any purpose whatsoever except (*a*) the formal payment-up of shares, i.e. capitalisation by incorporation in the formal nominal capital: and (*b*) the formal process of reduction with the consent of the court. The present provisions whereby preliminary expenses, underwriting commission or discount on shares or debentures, or premiums on redemption of redeemable preference shares or debentures, can be debited to the share premium account seem to be an inconsistency. Preliminary expenses and underwriting commission represent either a valuable asset or a loss. If they are a valuable asset they should be left in the balance sheet. If they are a loss they should be debited to the profit and loss account, since otherwise capital is in effect reduced: i.e. debiting them to share premium account is no more and no less consistent than debiting them to share capital account. Debenture discount, and premiums on repayment of preference shares and debentures, represent a special way of paying interest. If, for example, a debenture is issued below its agreed repayment value, or a preference share is repaid above its issue price, the annual interest or dividend is correspondingly reduced. Annual interest and dividends are unequivocably a debit to profit, and cannot legally be debited to the share capital account or to the share premium account. There seems to be no justification for doing the same thing in an indirect way by paying annual dividends or interest and debiting the corresponding premium or discount to a share premium account. To do so is tantamount to distributing as profit part of the share premium account.

The same general argument applies to a capital redemption reserve fund set up on the repayment of redeemable preference shares other than out of the proceeds of a new issue of shares.

Pre-acquisition Profits of Subsidiary Companies

It is well known that when two companies merge, both of which have accumulated distributable profits, one or both of the companies, depending upon the manner of merger, may lose the right to distribute these profits. This is because when the shares of a company are bought the value of these is assumed to include the accrued profits of that company. If the acquiring company distributes these profits to its shareholders after the acquisition the actual value of the assets acquired is reduced *pro tanto*. Unless the balance sheet value of those assets is written down by a debit to the acquiring company's profit and loss account the balance sheet value would stand above the cost of the shares by the amount of the dividend. This violates a normal principle of accounting.

It would always be open to the acquiring company to obtain a formal reduction of capital, which would allow the distribution of this profit to take place. This does, however, involve the trouble and cost of a legal process. There does, therefore, seem to be a case for allowing profits which would have been distributable, had the merger not taken place, to remain distributable in the hands of the acquiring company, provided that the consideration for the shares acquired has been entirely in the form of share capital and there has been no cash payment or issue of fixed interest securities in consideration for the assets acquired.

Where the transactions are entirely in the form of an exchange of share capital between the acquiring company and the shareholders of the acquired company it is difficult to see that the interest of the creditors of the acquiring company can in any way be damaged by allowing a distribution of profits that would have been distributable in the absence of the merger. If, however, assets are parted with, or liabilities are incurred, by the acquiring company, it is open to argument that the subsequent distribution of pre-acquisition profits may in some sense represent a reduction in the assets available for creditors.

Perhaps an example will explain this more clearly. Let us suppose that Company " A " acquires all the issued share capital of Company " B " by paying the shareholders of Company " B " the amount which they think their shares are worth. It is a reasonable presumption that this cash payment is not less than the market value of " B ". " A " will therefore have parted with cash equal in amount to the value of the net assets, including goodwill, acquired. If now " B " pays a dividend to " A " out of pre-acquisition profits (i.e. in effect out of assets bought and paid for by " A ") and then " A " distributes this to its own shareholders, it can be said that " A " has parted with cash equivalent to the dividend twice, first to the original owners of " B " and secondly to its own shareholders. The value of " B " to " A " will have been reduced by the amount of the dividend and should, given the usual accounting conventions, be written down in its books. This writing down, equal in

199

amount to the dividend distributed by " A ", must be debited to the profit and loss account of " A ". This has the same effect as if the dividend had been distributed out of " A's " own existing profit fund and not out of the pre-acquisition profit of " B ", since an amount equal to the dividend will have been held back in " A's " books as the result of the writing down. If on the other hand " A " had merely issued its own shares in order to pay for the shares of " B " there would have been only one outgoing of cash, namely the payment of the dividend to the shareholders of " A ".

Dividend Law

The foregoing assumes that the convention whereby the value of a fixed asset is regarded, for dividend purposes, as no greater than its cost, is applied. If the cash price paid by an acquiring company is in fact a good bargain—the interest acquired is clearly worth more than the cash paid—there is evidently a case for allowing distribution of the difference. This raises the general question of how far recorded profits created by revaluing assets in an upward direction should be distributable, if at all.

My own view is that there is a case for allowing such profits to be distributed, provided the revaluation is *bona fide*, is carried out by a reputable person who is independent of the directors and shareholders, and the facts are clearly indicated in the annual accounts and in a statement accompanying the dividend. Indeed, such a procedure would, I believe, be within the law as it now stands.

The present dividend law is, and has been for a long time, inconsistent, in that in certain cases dividends may in principle be paid (however unlikely this may be in practice) even though the value (on any reasonable basis) of the net assets is clearly below the stated issued capital plus the share premium and capital redemption reserve accounts, if any. This is because the judicial cases relating to dividends established long ago that certain types of loss, for example the depreciation of wasting assets, and losses arising in earlier years, need not be taken into account in assessing the profit fund. This is not probably a very great problem under present day conditions, at any rate so far as public companies are concerned. How far it is relevant for private companies I have no way of knowing. I would suggest, however, that it would be more consistent if the law made it clear that it was illegal for directors to distribute dividends: (*a*) if thereby they endangered the solvency of the company in the short or longer run; and (*b*) if thereby they reduced the value of the net assets below an amount equal to the figure of issued capital plus the share premium and capital redemption reserve accounts, if any, or the share capital plus capital reserves if my suggestions above were adopted. The value of the net assets in this context would be defined as the value in the opinion of the directors of the assets of the company less the liabilities thereof, either on sale in the market or to the company in the ordinary course of business, whichever was the greater.

A saving proviso would no doubt be necessary in the case of mining and similar companies which had formally declared their intention not to provide for depreciation of their wasting assets.

One advantage of such a declaration of the law would be to make it plain that, subject to the above proviso, depreciation of fixed assets must be provided in the calculation of divisible profit, a point that is at present moot with respect to manufacturing companies.

Such a declaration would also remove the present anomalous distinction for dividend purposes between " capital profits "—which are in practice difficult to categorise—and other profits.

Balance Sheet Values

It has long been recognised that the market values of current assets, and the amounts of current liabilities, are of special significance. The size of the inward and outward cash flows in the near future—and therefore the company's liquidity—is determined in part by these. It has, however, been fairly widely assumed that the balance sheet values of the fixed assets are of substantially less importance.

The flow of take-over bids in recent years has provided ample demonstration, however, that the balance sheet values of fixed assets may be of great significance. Broadly speaking, conditions are favourable for a take-over bid when dividends distributed are relatively low in relation to the saleable value of a company's assets as a whole, net of liabilities, whether this be due to a deliberate policy of distributing only a small proportion of earned profits, or the inability or unwillingness of the directors to earn a competitive rate of profit on the assets under their control. The existence of either of these conditions may be hidden from the shareholders if the balance sheet substantially understates the current market values of the fixed assets. There is, of course, a range of uncertainty in any valuation; but the discrepancy between balance sheet and current market values may be sufficiently large to make this unimportant. In this kind of situation the shareholders may be unaware of a situation that may be known to a shrewd bidder.

It cannot be said that this state of affairs is satisfactory from a shareholder's point point of view. He may part with his shares on false assumptions about the company's position. Nor is it satisfactory from a national point of view that the earning of subnormal rates of profit on the current market value of assets should be hidden. The saleable value of assets reflects the price that other people are prepared to pay for those assets. In the ultimate analysis this price reflects the degree of usefulness that the community attaches to the assets, as reflected in the " voting power " of the money that people can spend. The competitive rate of return which can be obtained in the market on securities similarly reflects the usefulness attached by the community to capital resources. If directors fail to earn something approaching this market rate of return on figures approximating to the market value of the resources they control they are in effect reducing the level of the national income below what the market in general thinks it could be. Such a situation should be made apparent, so that share holders may exercise such rights as they possess in full knowledge of the situation.

It is true that the assessment of the market values of many assets raises difficult problems. As suggested above, however, the question is not that of making fine calculations. It is rather a matter of showing up situations where gross discrepancies exist. The problem varies in difficulty according to the type of asset. Where assets are fairly non-specific it is usually fairly easy to arrive at an approximate valuation, since in this case the market is likely to be relatively wide. Freehold properties in a large town are often good examples of such assets. Where the assets are very specific they may be of little value (except as scrap) to anyone other than a direct competitor of the company, and this makes the assessment of the highest market value obtainable more difficult. However, the fact that assessment is not easy should not prevent an attempt being made to give better information if, as I believe to be the case, this can be done without undue difficulty. Nearly all assets, other than freehold land, are insured. The basis of insurance is the replacement value. I suggest that companies should be required to state in their accounts, by way of note, the insured values of each class of fixed assets. It would be necessary no doubt in some cases for such figures to be accompanied by some explanatory notes in order to prevent them from being misleading to shareholders. This seems to me no great disadvantage. On the contrary, such an explanation is likely to provide useful information from an investment point of view.

It is worth noting in this connection that the current market values of some fixed assets at least may have significance for the liquidity position of the company: the assets may be available as security for loans, or for " sale and re-lease transactions ".

Over-Valuation of Fixed Assets

The foregoing relates mainly to the undervaluation of fixed assets. I think it can be argued from the existing legal precedents, and from the Act, that it is illegal to show in the balance sheet any fixed asset at a figure above the value which it is considered to be worth to the company. I am doubtful, however, whether in fact close attention is always given to this matter. In my view it should be made explicit that no asset may be carried in the balance sheet at a figure above the value at which (a) it is believed to be saleable in the market or (b) it is considered to be worth to the company in the ordinary course of business, whichever is the higher. (This already applies to current assets.) I agree that what an asset is worth in the ordinary course of business is not susceptible of precise measurement. Here too, however, we are not concerned with fine calculations, but with the avoidance of gross discrepancies. I think that the attention of directors and auditors should be expressly drawn to this point.

Revaluation of Fixed Assets

This raises the question of the revaluation of fixed assets. The present Act allows this to take place and it seems entirely desirable that this should be so. As valuations are always matters of opinion, however, I think it is desirable that when an asset is revalued the following additional information should be provided, either in the accounts of the year in question, or in the " Statement of Accounting Procedures " which I have suggested should be filed annually with the Registrar. The relevant information would be: (*a*) the manner and process of revaluation; (*b*) the name of the person who carried out the revaluation; and (*c*) the date or dates on which the revaluation was carried out.

It is I think generally accepted that unrealised appreciation of assets written into the books of a company may be used for the purpose of formal capitalisation, provided the valuation is *bona fide*. I think, however, that there is something to be said for making this clear by a declaratory provision in the amended Act.

Stock

I think the present information available with respect to the valuation of stocks of all kinds is insufficient to allow shareholders to make a full appreciation of their company's position. I think it desirable that stocks should be separately classified in the balance sheet under the heads of raw material and components, work-in-progress, finished goods, and other appropriate headings. Changes in the value of stocks held under each of these headings have their own particular significance. No doubt, however, it would be necessary to provide that such information would only be required if it were available in the company's books.

Balance Sheets: Miscellaneous

Under the present accounting requirements of the 8th Schedule it is not always possible to reconcile the opening and closing balances of any given class of fixed assets with (*a*) the amounts of any disposals; (*b*) the profit and loss debit for depreciation on that class of asset; (*c*) any profit or loss on disposal; and (*d*) the amount of any revaluation. It think it desirable that a reconciliation be provided for each class of fixed asset so that the logical continuity from one balance sheet to the next may be complete.

I think a similar reconciliation is desirable in respect of tax reserves and provisions (however named), deferred income (such as unearned interest on hire-purchase contracts) and long-term liabilities.

I think it is desirable that the balance sheet should give information about credit facilities, such as the right to overdraft facilities, which have been granted but have not yet been used. Such facilities form an important factor in assessing the liquidity position of a company. (It would no doubt be necessary to exclude from such a requirement trading credit likely to be available in the ordinary course of business; it would not be reasonable to require the assessment of this to be estimated.)

I think it is desirable that the statement relating to capital expenditure planned but not yet entered in the accounts should refer not only to contracts made, but to all capital expenditure which the board of directors has decided to incur, whether or not it has not been made the subject of a formal contract. This is important in relation to the company's liquidity position and its prospects generally.

The 1948 Act did not define current liabilities and current assets. I think this was probably a wise decision. It is difficult to find satisfactory definitions which are both useful and generally applicable. The present arrangements work quite well on the whole. However, there is, I think, one exception. A practice has developed of classifying investments separately from both fixed and current assets. I see no particular reason why this should be necessary. The Act allows trade investments to be valued on different bases from others and the directors have therefore to make up their minds which investments are trade investments and which are not. Once this decision has been made I see no reason why trade investments should not be included under fixed assets and other investments under current assets. This is, perhaps, not a very important point. If, however, a category of current assets is to be distinguished it seems reasonable to include in it such investments as are held as a temporary respository for liquidity. Investments in subsidiaries perhaps represent a special case.

There is something to be said for classifying the whole interest in a subsidiary under one head, even though this may include both permanent shareholdings and temporary advances.

Taxation

It is hardly necessary to point out that tax represents a very important outlay from the point of view of the shareholder, accounting at present for something of the order of 50 per cent. of net profit. For this reason alone it seems important that shareholders should be able to see as clearly as possible the impact of taxation upon their company, including the way in which it is distributed over different kinds of taxes, e.g., income tax, profits tax, and overseas tax.

There is another important point, however. The tax payable by a company provides perhaps a more objective check on the profit calculation than any other. A person who is reasonably expert in the field of income tax and profits tax can judge from the accounts of a company, provided the information relating to tax is sufficiently detailed and precise, how far the tax assessment is likely to have differed from the reported profit of the company. This provides additional information in the interpretation of the accounting results, e.g., with respect to the conservatism of the board of directors in their depreciation calculations, and so on. It is, of course, true that there are pitfalls in these comparisons, but it cannot, I think, be denied that the provision of precise figures relating to income tax and other taxes payable by the company will give the expert shareholder (or the shareholder provided with expert advice) information that is likely to improve his general understanding of the company's financial position. Indeed, it can be argued that companies should be required to disclose the quantum of the estimated income tax assessment on the profits of the year for which the accounts have been prepared, together with the agreed assessments relating to earlier years. I think that as a minimum the profit and loss account should show, under separate headings, all debits and credits in respect of United Kingdom income tax, United Kingdom profits tax, and overseas tax, if any, each classified by years of assessment. Where any items in the profit and loss account are recorded net of tax, or are not subject to tax, this should be stated. Where relief has been allowed from United Kingdom income tax in respect of overseas tax I think the accounts should show the net United Kingdom tax payable, if necessary with a note of the amount of the relief. Where initial allowances have been granted the accounts should indicate the net tax payable. No doubt the present practice of some companies of showing the United Kingdom tax that would have been payable if overseas tax relief had not been granted, or the United Kingdom tax that would have been payable had there been no initial allowances, is a useful addition to the information available to the shareholder. But I believe that the net tax payable under each head should also be disclosed. The amount of overseas relief granted, and the amount of relief from initial allowances, are both of interest to the shareholder and I see no reason why the information relating to these should be withheld.

In my view the practice of debiting in the profit and loss account tax that would have been payable had initial allowances not existed, and then showing this in the balance sheet under the heading of future tax reserves or some similar title, is unnecessarily complicated. I believe it is much simpler to charge each year the tax that is actually payable, or that will become payable in the following tax year as a result of the profit for the current year, and to leave the hypothetical question of the impact of current initial allowances on the tax in later years to an explanatory note.

I appreciate that the present approach of many accountants to this problem is to show a " normal " income tax or profits tax charge in relation to the profit of a particular year. But I think the effect of the methods described above is to make the accounts harder to unravel, even to accountants. Such information is better given, I believe, by way of note.

Similarly I think it is misleading to increase depreciation allowances (which in principle should be calculated independently of tax law) because certain initial or investment allowances have been obtained.

Investment allowances represent, in effect, reductions in tax. I think the net tax charge should be shown, the amount of relief from investment allowances being disclosed by way of note.

The foregoing relates to the profit and loss figures. I think the balance sheet should also, in the interests of clarity, show the amounts payable or estimated to be payable under each class of tax in respect of each year of assessment.

Subsidiary Companies: Names and Interests

It would, I think, be advantageous if holding companies were required to state, preferably in the " Statement of Accounting Procedures " or in conjunction with such a statement, the name of each of their subsidiary companies and the holdings in each of these by types of shares.

Modification of Accounting Requirements

At present it is open to the Board of Trade to modify, on the application of a company, under SS.149 (4) or 152 (3), the accounting requirements of the Act, to meet the circumstances of particular companies. I think it is desirable that the nature of all modifications of this type should be published annually in some detail, so that the question of whether all such modifications are in the interests of the investing public may be open to public discussion.

Special Exemptions to Banks and other Companies

In my view the present exemption which is granted to banks, insurance companies, and certain other companies, whereby they do not have to disclose accounting information required from other companies, is unjustified. It is argued that the special position of banks and insurance companies makes it particularly important that creditors should have faith in these institutions. For these reasons, it is argued, it is desirable to hide from shareholders and creditors information which, the law has decided, should be disclosed in general for other companies. This argument amounts to saying that one will have more faith in a company when one does not know what is happening to its profits and assets than when one knows that there will be full disclosure of any adverse event. Furthermore, the argument rests on the assumption that the public is essentially not to be trusted with information. I do not regard this as appropriate in a society such as ours.

Arrangement of the Accounting Provisions

I do not think the present arrangement of the accounting provisions in the Act and in the 8th Schedule can be regarded as the most convenient layout achievable. In this connection I should like to invite the attention of the Committee to the general approach to this problem in the (amended) Draft Report of the Commission of Enquiry into the Working and Administration of the present Company Law of Ghana. I had the privilege of being associated to some extent with Professor L. C. B. Gower when he was working on the report in question and it seemed to me that the presentation of the accounting provisions in the 3rd Schedule of that Report, though these are based, broadly speaking, on the 8th Schedule of the English Act, is nevertheless more systematic and is easier to follow.

The same report incorporates certain of the suggestions which I have made in this memorandum and should the Committee see merit in them they may feel that the Report would be useful from a drafting point of view.

14th May, 1960.

Thinking in Figures

by H. C. EDEY, B.Com, F.C.A.

Scientists have long been accustomed to describing their ideas by using numbers. This idea is familiar to men and women engaged in industry and trade, though the methods they have used have been of a simpler variety than those employed by many scientists. What was once called mercantile arithmetic – and for many people this included the elements of book-keeping – has for a long time been an everyday tool of their work.

But commercial mathematics are now leaving the elementary stage. Automatic computers have made possible calculations of a size and complexity never before possible. This has opened up the way for the application to business of analytical processes using mathematics as far beyond the old-fashioned mercantile arithmetic as the moon-rocket is beyond the bicycle.

In this Travers Lecture[1], Mr Edey examines some of the implications of this for business and management, and for business education.

SIX thousand years ago, in the valley of the rivers Tigris and Euphrates, in the southern part of the land we now call Iraq or Mesopotamia, temple priests, responsible for the revenues of the gods, wrote down on clay tablets their statements of receipts and disbursements. These ancient pictographic accounts – perhaps the oldest written records in the world – may well have been the source from which arose both writing and arithmetic. The whole of human literature and the whole vast edifice of modern mathematics perhaps originated in the needs of archaic mercantile arithmetic.

Ancient Accounting

Two thousand years later, in the same valley, in the city of Ur – the city from which Abraham began his wandering – and I quote from Sir Leonard Woolley:

'there were a host of secretaries and accountants responsible for the revenues and outgoings of the temple . . . countrymen would bring their cattle, sheep and goats, their sacks of barley and rounds of cheese, clay pots of clarified butter and bales of wool; all would be checked and weighed and scribes give for everything a receipt made out on a clay tablet and would file a duplicate in the temple records . . . animals had to be issued for the daily sacrifices, the priests and the temple servants required to be fed, wood or metal might be needed for repairs to the [temple] fabric, even oil for the oiling of the door hinges would be drawn from the stores and for everything issued the storekeeper made out an issue voucher giving the name of the applicant, the nature

and amount of goods required, their purpose and the authority on which the order was granted. Within the temple precincts there were regular factories where worked the women attached to the temple . . . the ledgers of the factory give a nominal roll of the women, the weight of wool issued to each at the beginning of the month, the lengths and weights of the specimens of cloth of various qualities which she produced at the month's end (a due allowance is made for unavoidable wastage in the process of manufacture), and then in parallel columns the amounts issued for her maintenance during the period, so much grain and cheese and cooking butter . . .[2].

These ancient accounts were not kept in money values, but in kind and, let me hasten to add, did not follow the rules of double entry, which did not yet exist; but we cannot doubt that the skills involved in keeping them – the inscribing of the cuneiform script in clay, the addition and subtraction of numbers – formed a worthy part of the curriculum of Sumerian education, and higher education at that, and ranked, we may surmise, level, as learned disciplines, with the astronomical studies to which we owe our 60 minute hour and our 360 degree circle – for unlike the

[1] John Ingram Travers, who was a partner in a firm of merchants in the City of London from which he retired in 1863, was active in promoting reform of the administration of the customs system. In recognition of his work in this direction the merchants and bankers of the City subscribed to a fund known as 'The Travers Bequest' to be used for providing lectures on commerce or commercial law.

[2] Woolley, *The Sumerians* (Oxford University Press): see also *Excavations at Ur*, by the same author (Benn).

Mr H. C. Edey, B.Com., F.C.A. the author of this Travers Lecture, is Reader in Accounting at the University of London and a Governor of the City of London College where he gave the lecture on April 4th.

electronic computer the Sumerians used a radix of sixty.

Three thousand years passed. During all this time I do not think that there was much change in the way that merchants or public officers of the civilized cities and states of Europe and the Near East handled their accounting records and mercantile calculations. There must have been indeed change in detail. Papyrus, or parchment, or waxed tablets might be substituted for clay. As time passed money values were more likely to be the units of account. But in the essential details of numbering, listing, adding and subtracting there was little change; and indeed the Greek and Roman number systems were inferior as tools of calculation to that of the Sumerians.

Rise of Double Entry

But around A.D. 1300 new ideas were arising in the Medieval city states of Italy. About that time a new accounting technique appeared that was to spread rapidly and become the standard of good accounting throughout Western Europe. We do not know just where double-entry book-keeping first arose or exactly how it came into being. It is, however, significant that not long before there had been a technical innovation of great importance – the introduction into Western Europe of a cheaper writing material, paper, and an innovation of equal importance in the tools of thought, for the Indian numbers brought to Europe by the Arabs were now coming increasingly into use; though, needless to say, the new-fangled numbers were deplored and successfully resisted for a long while by members of the Establishment of that time. But the simplicity of the new numbers made it possible for the writers of commercial arithmetics in Florence to develop improved rules for calculation[1], and may well have been decisive in suggesting the pattern of double entry[2]. It is characteristic of the period that the first known treatise on double-entry book-keeping – Pacioli's textbook of 1494 – should form part of a compendium on arithmetic, algebra and geometry, and their commercial applications.

The Italian merchant of that time was well trained in the arithmetic necessary for his business, including the use of compound interest and discount. He believed that accuracy and clarity were essential in business. As Sapori says, he was 'accurate in his computations and clear in his book-keeping'.[3] But he was also a man of culture. He took pains in recording matters of interest in the life around him whether relating to his business or personal affairs or otherwise. To quote Sapori again:

'The Italian merchant was orderly to the point of

meticulousness; he was a shrewd observer and a clear thinker. Being always willing to learn he reached a high level of strictly professional competence. But he also created, by harmoniously combining his various achievements in different spheres of knowledge, a genuine mercantile culture which was broad, solid, and magnificent.'[4]

Medieval Business Education

As for education, a merchant's son would receive his basic training in a public school where he would be taught reading and writing and the use of the abacus. He would then enter commerce to acquire the book-keeping skills, and the knowledge of merchandise and geography and other matters, that would fit him to become a successful merchant. The public school was a matter of concern to the authorities: it was there that a boy received his basic education that fitted him to take his part as a citizen and prepared him for success in a business career.

I do not think that the Florentine boy's education would have seemed to a Victorian merchant inappropriate for a good employee in his own accounting house – one who might expect to rise in the business and perhaps become a partner in due course. I doubt whether the nineteenth century commercial texts differ greatly, except in matters of language and detail, from what would have been appropriate in Renaissance Italy.

Nor, in essentials, has there been a great change since Victorian days. Perhaps of all professions today, that of the chartered accountant is the most obviously appropriate for someone who wishes to acquire a general skill in business. As you know it has not been unusual for a father who wishes his boy to take his place in a family firm to send him first to be articled to a chartered accountant so that he can become skilled in financial matters. I am not sure that in fundamentals the professional education of the present-day chartered accountant covers such a very different field, or is even so very different in kind, from that of the Italian merchant. Let us look at the curriculum.

The basis of the whole curriculum is a sound training in the principles of double-entry book-keeping. This is designed to make the accountant, like the Italian merchant, 'accurate in his computations and clear in his book-keeping'.

He must be trained in the techniques of auditing – in the checking and verification of accounts and accounting reports. Yet auditing, Sapori says, was a task that might well fall to the thirteenth century Italian merchant who would often be required, along with fellow merchants, to examine the accounts of outgoing public officials.

Needless to say the chartered accountant must – like his Italian merchant forerunner – acquire a general knowledge of commercial and financial affairs, and of the law as it affects commercial activities.

Of cost and management accounting the Italian

---

[1] Pledge, *Science Since 1500* (H.M.S.O.), page 48.

[2] Ste. Croix, 'Greek and Roman Accounting', in *Studies in the History of Accounting* (Ed. Littleton and Yamey), page 66.

[3] Sapori, 'Culture of Italian Merchants', in *Enterprise and Secular Change* (Ed. Lane and Riemersma), page 57.

[4] Ibid. page 65.

merchant was certainly concerned; though the nature of his business was such that detailed cost analysis beyond what was possible in his ordinary ledger – where, for example, he could separate the financial results of a given venture or activity from those of others, was hardly necessary. I do not think the training of the modern chartered accountant in cost accounting goes far beyond this. Mathematically speaking it requires no more than simple arithmetic.

Only perhaps when we turn to taxation do we find a really significant difference between the modern training of a chartered accountant and that of the Italian merchant. Yet even this is perhaps a question of degree rather than of kind. We may assume that the Italian was not unaware of the problems of tax.

The Italians went as far in their studies of compound interest and discount as is normal in business education today. I do not think it can be assumed that an English chartered accountant, a company secretary, or generally one who has studied business in commercial or technical college or elsewhere (I exclude such specialists as stockbrokers and actuaries) will necessarily have more than the slightest acquaintance with the standard compound interest and annuity formulae, or will be able to give a clear description of, for example, the significance of the gross redemption yields set against the Government securities that are listed daily on the back page of *The Financial Times*.

Generally, a Florentine merchant looking at the training of a modern professional accountant, a company secretary, or of others taking business courses today, would have little difficulty in understanding the nature of the course and the ideas governing its structure; and the techniques would be well within his range of knowledge.

Even the mathematical methods used by actuaries – the one class of people who have for many years consistently applied advanced mathematics to business problems – would not I suspect seem strange to our early Italians, once they understood the ideas lying behind the mathematics.

New Instruments and New Thought

I am not going to pretend that much of, shall we say, the average chartered accountant's work today is not far removed from the everyday detail of commercial life in Medieval and Renaissance Florence. The auditing or investigation of the financial statements of a complex group of companies requires a wide and specific knowledge of company law, revenue law, contract and agency law and their applications, of financial institutions and of their mode of operation, and of modern accounting methods. Nevertheless, in fundamentals, the change is not great. It is in detail rather than in kind.

There is an intimate connection between the growth in human knowledge and understanding and the development of instruments and tools. A new instrument is developed – the telescope, the X-ray tube, the electron microscope. At first it is crude and clumsy, but its potentialities are visible. Practical men – I am using the word not as an adjective of praise, but in the opposite sense to theoretical – develop the new instrument, improving as they go. New uses may be found for it, not at first suspected. The theoretical men are faced with a series of challenges. One is to fit the working of the new instrument into the general body of established theory – to explain why it functions as it does; sometimes this may not be necessary: the new invention may be a child of earlier theory, as the wireless was of Maxwell's theoretical work on electro-magnetic radiation. Another is to fit into the pattern of theory the new discoveries that the instrument makes possible. The theoretician himself may use the new instrument for testing the validity of old and new theories, as the big radio telescopes are now being used. Along with the new development in theory comes the need for new mathematical methods, or the application of methods already developed by the pure mathematicians, hitherto without an obvious use. Thus, new instruments produce new concepts and new concepts lead to new instruments, while both widen and deepen the fund of human knowledge and exend the tools of thought itself.

The Automatic Computer

The field of business is as open to this process as any other branch of human activity. We can see in the use of clay tablets in Sumer, and in the introduction of paper to Europe, examples of improvement in instruments – in the tools of intellectual activity and exploration. The men who first used pictographic inscriptions to express the ideas of numbers and things had made a step forward in the apparatus of thought so important that it is hard to find a suitable adjective to describe it. The introduction of arabic numbers was another such step. We may say that the rise of double-entry book-keeping was in a small way such a development, providing a systematic, logical, formulation for certain economic concepts. Seen in this light its growth in use, as the Italian cities moved towards the Renaissance, is part of the general pattern of growth in human knowledge and culture[1].

The time has come to speak of the electronic computer – or to use a better name, the automatic digital computer. I do not propose to say a great deal about the computer, deeply interesting though it is. Here I am concerned rather with the impact that I think this new instrument, along with modern mathematics, will have – and indeed is having – on business and on teaching for business. It would, in my view, be difficult to underestimate the importance of this new development. Life will never be the same again, any more than it could after the modern astronomical

---

[1] Cf. Yamey, Introduction to *Studies in the History of Accounting*, (op. cit.) pages 2–4.

telescope, by showing us the almost unimaginable vastness of the Universe, placed human life in a wholly new perspective.

Before I go on, however, I must distinguish between two, quite different, functions of the computer. The distinction is one well known to all who have to do with such matters.

On one hand, the computer provides us with a substitute for the clerical work of adding, subtracting, multiplying, dividing, writing down and transposing words and figures. It can indeed be regarded as a battery of very dull, but very accurate, obedient and fast clerks, each provided with an adding or multiplying machine, each able to read and write numbers, and to detect when one number is greater than or less than another, but little else. True, it is so much faster than any clerk or clerks that it can provide one with more accounting and statistical analyses, statements and summaries than could ever be obtained, or if obtainable, afforded, with older methods. (At this point I am irresistibly reminded of the story of the little girl who was asked to review a book on natural history. She wrote in her review 'This book tells me more about rabbits than I care to know'. If one is not careful a computer is liable to tell one more about one's business than one cares to know.)

Data Processing

This kind of activity is in itself of great importance. But it is not perhaps more than a development of the kind that started with the abacus itself, and had already gone far with the use of simpler mechanical and electrical computing machines. If it were possible, as I believe it soon will be, for a bank general manager to link all his branches by teleprinter to a central computer, so designed that the balance sheet for the whole bank is always on his desk before him, displayed, and continuously changing, on the screen of a cathode ray tube, this is really no more than one more step on a path long trodden, that leads back to Medieval Florence and the other Italian cities. Whether to use a computer for this kind of work is a matter of cost study. The decision is made, or should be made, just as one decides whether punched cards would be more profitable than hand-written ledgers (though it may be worth adding something on the credit side of the calculation for the benefits of research and experimentation). Double-entry principles are not rendered obsolete. They remain built into any accounting system that is put on to a computer. The auditor has to familiarize himself with the new routines. But no one, in these days, need even learn what binary arithmetic means. The modern computer may indeed do its work in binary, but it has been so built, or so taught – programmed is the appropriate word – that the figures and instructions fed into it can be in decimal notation; and what it has to report – its output – can be in the same form. All that one needs in order to use it is a dictionary, so that verbal instructions can be translated into appropriate numbers that the computer can read, and this the manufacturers will provide, under the name of a code manual.

New Mathematics of Business

But there is another side to the computer's work. It has made possible for the first time the solution, within reasonable time limits, of certain types of mathematical problem that earlier it would hardly have been practicable to tackle. At the same time – and here, I think, is the parallel with the way in which new theories and new applications grow up in the natural sciences alongside new instruments – has come a realization that there are problems of business and public administration that will yield to the use of mathematical methods of a relatively advanced kind. When a computer is available, problems can be formulated and equations solved to provide answers as good as and sometimes better than will normally be reached on a rule of thumb basis or by the intuition of those with long practical experience – and this as part of a standard routine that, once established, can be operated with accuracy and speed by men untrained in the field of knowledge to which the problem belongs.

This is a revolution: the invasion of the field of business decisions by the powerful methods of modern mathematics aided, where necessary, by the new instrument. The applications of these techniques are, I suppose, relatively few as yet, though they are by no means of negligible importance. But they will grow in number. I will try to list some of these, though I must emphasize my relative mathematical ignorance and acknowledge the help of my mathematical colleagues.

There is the use of probability theory and calculus, associated, as in all the applications, with simple economic concepts, in optimizing the amount of stock that a business holds, balancing the costs of holding stock – money and space tied up, and risks of damage, deterioration, and so on – against the damage to goodwill that would be caused by running out of stock and the lower costs of an even production flow during the year as compared with an uneven one.

There is the use of probability theory and calculus in queueing theory – an application relevant where there are bottlenecks, for example, in transport, or in production, or in communication networks, where it is necessary to balance the cost of waiting time against the cost of the additional equipment that would reduce the wait.

There are programming methods, based on matrix algebra, for determining the best mix of materials in a given product as the prices of materials vary; or the best blend in the refining of oil products as the selling prices vary; or for minimizing transport costs, for example, from variously dispersed collieries to different coke ovens or power stations; or for determining the optimum mix of outputs of a textile mill, as prices vary; or for so cutting paper rolls as to minimize the waste at the end of a given roll.

The Computer and Mathematics

What is the characteristic of these methods is that a solution had somehow to be reached before a mathematical method was available; now the optimization can be turned into a routine. The operational researcher, as it is convenient to call him, having established the theoretical model which suits the problem, can turn the solution over to less highly paid staff, who can keep it running until a new theoretical model is required in the light of changed conditions; and within the limits which the problem allows it will be known that as good a solution as is available has been obtained.

I do not want to mislead you. The computer is not always necessary for the solution of problems of operational research, even when they are posed in a mathematically sophisticated form. Actuaries have long managed without digital computers, though they are now taking to them as ducks take to water. Relatively simple actuarial calculations that can be solved without computers are increasingly being applied to capital budgeting problems. There is a class of problems in which statistical sampling methods, based on probability theory, are used. These have been applied successfully in business without computer facilities. They are such problems as the quality control of manufactured products, market research, certain aspects of auditing, the determining of maintenance costs of fleets of lorries, and so on. But there are many formulations for the solution of which a computer is essential; and the rapidity of advance in these methods has been, and will continue to be in some degree, dependent upon the growth of computer technique – a growth to which, at present, it is impossible to foresee any limit. In what direction these techniques will lead, and how fast, I cannot predict. But it seems to me that the signs of rapid development are present. The Americans with their usual vigour and interest in new ideas are driving ahead fast, and there is no lack of financial support in the United States for the work of colleges and research institutes in this field. The Russians are on the same track and will follow the trail with equal vigour and determination. The period when a business man could afford to be completely ignorant, not only of the manipulation but of the meaning and significance of such matters as calculus, probability, vectors, and the like, is almost here.

Future of Operational Research

Do not mistake me, I do not suggest that every decision, every problem in business, can today, or will, even within the next ten years, be solved by the application of higher mathematics. The range of application, as I have already indicated, is still small, though it is growing. Many of the problems of business are far too complex, there are far too many variables and far too complicated a network of relationships, to yield to existing mathematical procedures (though even in such cases a problem may yield to the use of simulation methods on a computer). But the appetite of the mathematicians and the operational research men will not easily be satisfied, and I am convinced that there will be a rapid expansion in the fields of useful application.

I do not want to pretend that there are no difficulties and that everything in this particular garden is as it should be. There have been and will be failures. In the early stages these could be expected to exceed in number the successes. This has always been so. It would have been unwise to condemn the idea of air travel on the basis of the quality and capacity of the aeroplane of 1910 – though I am sure that many did so. Or again it would be foolish to discount the future of the rocket as a result of the failures in Florida. It is the successes that count. By the same token there will be – there are – charlatans about who will and do make claims that they cannot justify. O.R. is O.K., if I may coin a phrase. The hangers-on will rush in. As usual, their failures will be wrongly taken by some as a sign that the whole subject is a sham.

Logic of Decisions

We must, however, not only think of techniques that are advanced in the mathematical sense. When all is said and done, to use mathematical methods is simply to apply logical methods of thought to certain types of problem. Mathematics is no more than a branch of logic that takes over where the symbols that we call words become too clumsy for the occasion. If some business problems are susceptible of solution by the application of certain advanced logical methods, may not others be better handled than at present by the use of simpler logical tools?

But, you will say, this is exactly what happens already. The business man applies logic to his problems. I am afraid that this is only a half-truth. I have no doubt at all that, given the way in which a business problem is formulated, and given the facts and relationships that are known and the assumptions about the facts and relationships that are less clearly known, most people in business are likely to reach a conclusion and make their decision by a logical chain of reasoning, for man is undoubtedly a logical animal. But the rub lies in the words 'given the way in which a problem is formulated'. The marshalling of knowledge before a decision is made can be done in many ways.

Anyone who has worked on operational research problems will, if he is competent and honest, confirm that in a certain sense the mathematics is the least part of the job. The really difficult problem is to set down clearly the circumstances, the aim in view, and the constraints or limitations within which the solution must be sought. These must be chosen so that they are relevant to the problem. This process is common to the solution of all business problems. But when the process that is to follow is a formal mathematical one, in which each piece of information must be fitted into some kind of standard pattern, there is little room for vagueness or sloppiness in the setting of the problem. The rigorous nature of the process that is to follow imposes its own discipline of thought.

I do not wish to suggest that the use of mathematical methods ensures the good sense and relevance of the selection of facts, the assumptions made, and the formulae used. Nothing could be further from the truth. There is no substitute for a basic understanding of the nature of business enterprise, its environment and its major aims. Some study of the economics of business enterprise is, I think, an essential concomitant of such work. The merit of the techniques of operational research is, I think, that the need for such a study becomes rapidly apparent when they are used, at any rate to a sensible man, as it does not always when a more haphazard, traditional, hit and miss method of decision making is employed.

Need for Systematic Decision Making

We must all know of the business committee in which some decision on the purchase of this or that piece of equipment is debated. How many of these discussions are preceded by the preparation of a systematic study showing the results expected to follow from alternative courses of action? How many really large decisions are made on little more than hunch? How many boards of directors even trouble to have calculated, however roughly, the rate of return that their business is earning on the current value of the resources they control? How many even realize that such a calculation is relevant? – more perhaps now than before Mr Chambers and his board made their recent bid, so fortunate for the shareholders of Courtaulds; but still very far from all – perhaps not even most. How many boards even realize that the very concept of profit as it is measured by accounts is – and must be in the last analysis – vague and ambiguous; clear enough in terms of accounting procedures, but clothed in uncertainty in its economic and financial implications? Do not misunderstand me here. I am well aware that few business problems have a unique solution. The future is uncertain and hazy. Errors are inevitable. It will often be seen, *ex post facto*, even when the most brilliant men are concerned, that a different course of action would have produced better results. But there is no need, for this reason, deliberately to cultivate ignorance. Carefully chosen hypothetical examples based on likely assumptions and worked out, before the event, to show the results in terms of cash flows over time, can throw light on almost any business problem – and sometimes expose an unsuspected major pitfall in a proposed course of action.

It is indeed, as I have already said, true that a critical, careful and systematic approach towards decisions, attempting to put numerical values upon the results of these, need not only arise as a by-product of advanced mathematical work. It is, however, a reproach, both to men in business, and I think also to many university economists in this country who have held themselves aloof from business,

that there is far too much woolliness in business decision making and far too little thinking in figures, or at any rate using figures as an aid to thought in a way that can at least avoid the silliest of mistakes.

You may reply that my criticisms do not apply to some businesses. This is true. I am not here concerned with such businesses. High quality men will produce high quality work, wherever they are. Such men will find, like *le bourgeois gentilhomme* who found he had been talking prose for forty years, that they have been doing operational research since they went into business. But I am concerned with the others who need guidance. This, after all, is what education is for.

Mathematical Training for Business

It will now I think be apparent in what direction my mind is turning. You will not be surprised when I say that in my view the time has come for young men and women who wish to prepare themselves for more senior posts in the management stream of business – and of public bodies – to think seriously whether they should not provide themselves with a better mathematical education than has hitherto been considered necessary for such posts; and for schools and colleges to consider what preparations they should now be making to meet this need.

It may seem that the need is not yet pressing; and it is true that there is as yet no apparent abnormal demand for the delivered product. There is all the more reason to be prepared, for education of this kind cannot be produced at a snap of the fingers. It is the job of educationalists to be thinking ahead. The higher education of a young person of 18 today is not designed – or should not be designed – for the business needs of today. It is to the needs of 1975 that we should be looking.

I am not thinking of specialists in mathematical and statistical work – though we shall need plenty of these – but of those who in their early days in business will specialize in such activities as marketing, purchasing, advertising, secretarial work, accounting, and so on. To some extent work in these fields already has an obvious mathematical or statistical basis as in marketing, in which sampling techniques are relevant, or in secretarial work where the application of quality control methods to such activities as invoicing is growing. I have already given my view that many more such applications of mathematics will be found in the years to come. But it is not merely in order to appreciate the significance of certain sections of their work that these young people will need a sounder basis in mathematics, desirable though that is. I have already implied that the use of operational research methods, even when applied to simple problems (and a business problem may be quite difficult to handle, even though no more than simple arithmetic is involved in the numerical work) can be of value in inculcating a systematic, careful and critical approach to business problems. Such an approach is desirable at all levels of business. It is most desirable in those who have reached the levels of middle and higher management. To understand these methods, some basis in mathematics is necessary.

The Accountant and Mathematics

My own subject, accounting, is in a special position in this respect. Accountants are already recognized as working in the field of numbers, and it is characteristic of the layman's attitude that he regards the accountant as a mathematician. Most of you will know that this is far from being the truth. It is a well-known saying in the profession that for success no more than an elementary knowledge of mathematics is needed – certainly no more is necessary than can be obtained in a course leading to mathematics at the ordinary level in the General Certificate of Education. I can assure you that this certificate can be obtained in the subject of mathematics by those whose range of knowledge and competence in the field is extremely limited.

Yet I believe that today the accountant, of all people, has most to gain by adding to his repertoire a reasonable competence in certain branches of higher mathematics – and by this I mean mathematics not necessarily much higher than would be relevant at the advanced level of the General Certificate of Education, though perhaps differently biased. Indeed, unless he does so soon, and moreover learns something of the way the mathematics can be applied to business problems, it is I think very likely that a substantial part of what is at present regarded as a legitimate activity for professional accountants – that broadly summed up by the words management consultancy – will pass to others. The statisticians and operational researchers tend at present to be limited in their approach. Their expertise tends to be mathematical rather than economic and financial, and to do their job they often have to work with those, such as economists and accountants, who understand these matters. But this may not last. These people will I think rapidly acquire an appetite for all aspects of management advisory work, and are unlikely in the longer run to limit themselves to the more technical side of their study. The less ready are accountants to make themselves competent in the new field, or at least to fit themselves to formulate problems in such a way that they can be handed over to the technical mathematicians and mathematical statisticians, the more likely is it that the work will pass to the latter. All the applications that I have given above – sampling, mathematical programming, queueing theory, stock control – are relevant to accountants' work.

Unless the accountants in industry are prepared to give themselves an understanding – though I emphasize not necessarily full professional expertise – of this subject, they may, I fear, find themselves in the longer run restricted to what is essentially high level book-keeping – provided the computer operators allow them to keep that side of the business – and to a *quasi* legal role, advising on such matters as income

tax and, except where a company may choose to employ specialist economist staff for the purpose, financing methods.

But to return to the educational side, whether one is thinking of accounting or of other business specialisms, there is no doubt that the study of business subjects too often tends to be approached in a rigid, uncritical and very often, I am afraid, sloppy and logically woolly way. No more proof of this is necessary than a perusal of some of the textbooks in use. Intellectually speaking many of these have no merits. There are, of course, honourable exceptions. But the study of our group of subjects has, intellectually speaking, and in general, sunk far below that of the equivalent on the science side, such as the various branches of engineering. It is true that a great deal of the work in the field of economics – which let me remind you should play a similar part in relation to business and Government to that of physics in relation to engineering, providing fundamental theoretical concepts – is of an intellectually satisfactory kind; unfortunately too many academic economists have fallen into the opposite sin, that of scholasticism – failure to keep their subject alive and to make relevant its theorems by close contact with the world of business (though I am happy to say that there are now some signs of change in this respect). The relevance of industrial sociology – a most interesting and important subject – to the side of business problems concerned with human relations has hardly been appreciated yet in this country. In general, business as an intellectual activity is a Cinderella and a pretty dull Cinderella at that. The situation is strikingly different from that which reigned in Renaissance Italy, and I have no doubt in Babylon and the other cities of Akkad and Sumer.

Role of Mathematics

It is my belief that the growth and importance of mathematics and mathematical statistical work in business will provide one of the stimuli that will put business studies once more on an intellectual par with their fellow sciences, and that this stimulus will extend from the mathematical work itself to the work in those parts of business studies that are not in themselves directly concerned with mathematics. To continue my metaphor, I see mathematics in the role of a fairy godmother for Cinderella.

Perhaps I may say in parentheses, since we are concerned with commercial education, that if this is to happen, a considerable number of promising young people of high intellectual calibre will have to be attracted to the teaching and academic study of these subjects, not only mathematics and statistics, but industrial and commercial economics, accounting and industrial sociology. It will not be enough to rely on the very small number of high-grade men and women who happen to like such work, and will for this reason accept monetary disadvantages in order to do it. Unless this is recognized we cannot expect much improvement. If the country wants high-grade business men it must pay for high-grade business teachers.

New Development in Accounting Education

Perhaps I may be permitted to refer finally to a development at my own college in the University of London, The London School of Economics and Political Science. Some of us who are concerned particularly with the teaching of accounting are so convinced of the need to raise the mathematical skills of our own graduates that we have, with the collaboration of our mathematical friends, introduced into the first year of the university course in economics which is followed by those who wish to specialize on the accounting side, a compulsory mathematics course. This is designed to allow our students, including those who have only reached ordinary level in mathematics in the General Certificate of Education, to bring themselves up to a standard which will permit them later, if they so wish, to study at least the principles of some of the new management mathematics.

Those who wish to can pursue these studies further in their second and third years. Those who do not will at least have a basis upon which they can build later should they experience the need to do so, after they have left the University. In some degree we regard ourselves as pioneers in this work.

I do not pretend that there have been no difficulties. That even the most elementary mathematical teaching in some of our schools leaves much to be desired is becoming very apparent to us – the raw material we get from the schools varies a great deal in the degree to which it has been processed; and I am afraid some of it has been spoilt. And, of course, we make mistakes ourselves. We shall, however, persevere and adapt our courses, so far as we are able, to meet these problems.

It is my own firm conviction that a vastly greater number of our young people would, if only they were properly taught, find little difficulty, and indeed substantial pleasure, in the acquisition of appropriate mathematical skills and that the time will come when it will be an exceptional business man who has no facility in thinking in figures.

INCOME AND THE *H. C. Edey*
VALUATION OF STOCK-IN-TRADE

IT is possible to make at least one valid generalisation on the valuation of stock-in-trade for income tax purposes. It is that no consistent principle can be found in the Income Tax Acts or in the decisions of the courts as a firm foundation for the valuation. It is true that it has long been generally accepted, on the basis of judicial decision, that in ascertaining the *quantum* of profit to be assessed to tax the following fundamental rule is to be observed: namely, that the ordinary principles of commercial accounting are to be followed except to the extent that they conflict with specific rules laid down by the Income Tax Acts. Reference was again made to this general principle in *Ostime* v. *Duple Motor Bodies, Ltd.*,[1] though it is not clear how far the decision in that case must be regarded as depending thereon. The Income Tax Acts are silent with respect to the method to be followed in stock valuation in a continuing business; hence, applying the principle, one might expect that any generally accepted accounting practice with respect to stock valuation would be acceptable. But *Patrick* v. *Broadstone Mills, Ltd.*[2] and *Minister of National Revenue* v. *Anaconda American Brass, Ltd.*[3] show that the courts are not prepared to follow this principle in all cases, and are prepared to reject methods of stock valuation that are fully acceptable for the purposes, for example, of presentation of accounts under the Companies Act.

It is, perhaps, worthwhile looking a little more deeply into the possible reason for this contradiction. At the root of the problem lies the fact that the Income Tax Acts do not provide a general definition of taxable income or profit. It might seem at first that this apparent deficiency in the statutes is not significant. If, indeed, one believed that annual profit was in some sense an objective phenomenon, one might well take the view that careful search was bound to disclose the appropriate formula, in the same way that a scientist by looking deeply into the nature of the real world is able sometimes to produce a formula describing, within very close approximations, a natural phenomenon, such as the propagation of light. But this is not the case. The terms "profit" and "income" are in fact used in our language to indicate a whole range of ideas. It is true that all these ideas have something in common. They all imply in some sense the receipt of a benefit during a given period of time. But there the common element ends. In fact, the systematic use of any one of the many concepts of income arises only because thereby a convenient

---

1 [1961] 1 W.L.R. 739 (H.L.).
2 [1954] 1 All E.R. 163 (C.A.).
3 [1956] A.C. 85 (P.C.).

social purpose is fulfilled; and for different social purposes it is convenient to use different concepts. There is no reason why the concept used for a particular social purpose should necessarily be appropriate for a different purpose.

If, for example, we look at the measurement of income as it is carried out by accountants for the purpose of company accounts, or for the purpose of a partnership deed, we are, I think, bound to conclude that the measurement is in essence designed to assist a group of parties, bound together in mutual contract, to settle, on a fairly rough and ready, approximate basis, on the division among themselves of certain accretions to their joint property. People come together in companies or partnerships with the object of receiving some return over and above the ultimate recovery of their initial investment. It became apparent long ago that in deciding how much of the return should be shared out annually among company members or partners, it was necessary to have a set of rules that could be applied without undue expenditure of time, and without an unduly subjective element of estimation entering into the calculation. In this way the ordinary rules of profit calculation, used in the financial accounts of companies and partnerships, arose. They were, and are, rough rules; but they are useful as a basis of a year-to-year sharing-out operation, and, if all parties concerned accept them, no serious injustice is done. When the introduction of general limited liability gave rise to the need for company law to set some limit on distributions to owners, in the interests of creditors, the courts decided that the same rules, applied in good faith, were appropriate for the determination of divisible profit.

It has always been realised that these rules are too rough to allow their use on occasions when substantial changes in the relative rights of partners or company members are about to take place. When a partnership dissolves, a new partner is taken, or a change is made in the profit-sharing ratios of partners, the balance sheet valuations (changes in which, over time, measure the accounting profit, after adjustment for capital paid in or withdrawn) are reconsidered carefully with an eye to the economic reality, as reflected by the market.[4] Similarly, when company reconstructions take place that involve a change in the relative rights of shareholders, it is usual to seek the advice of financial experts who are likely to be familiar with the current market situation. The asset valuations which arose from the application of normal accounting principles are abandoned on such occasions.

It follows from this that the profit which would be obtained in the

---

[4] It is true that partnership agreements may lay down a rule of thumb method for the valuation of partnership interests on such occasions. This does not affect the principle that different rules of balance sheet valuation are appropriate.

case of a partnership by taking the difference between the initial investment and the final valuation on dissolution (after allowing as usual for additional money paid in or money withdrawn by the owners) might be a different figure from that shown by summing over the same period the annual balances on the profit and loss accounts as prepared on conventional accounting lines. The same kind of comparison can be made by considering the life of a company from its beginning to the date of liquidation or of radical reconstruction accompanied by a revaluation of all the assets. This in itself is sufficient evidence for the proposition that profit, and the corresponding valuations that are made in the process of profit calculation, must be defined in relation to the particular purpose for which the figures are required.

Even from the point of view of management accounting, there is no clear cut concept of profit available. It is common to use the profit figure that emerges from application of one or other of the normal accounting conventions as a rough measure of management success. But one has only to look carefully at how such figures are computed to realise with what caution they should be used. The major defect from which all the conventional figures suffer is their inability to reflect changes in the business potential. From the point of view of the management of the business, or the shareholders whom that management represents, the value of the business interest usually depends upon the ability of the directors to make good use in the future of the assets at their disposal. Any important change in their capacity to produce a future flow of dividends is of fundamental significance in assessing the value of the shareholders' interest. A succession of good reported profits, accompanied by good dividends, over a period of years, counts for nothing with respect to the future of the company if the factors that produced these dividends have disappeared. Yet these changes in the capacity of a business to produce dividends—which we may call changes in the goodwill of the business—are incapable of measurement by the normal accounting processes. It is inevitable that this should be so, for their assessment is subjective, and requires a good knowledge of the business itself.

There are other defects in the use of conventional accounting profit calculations for management purposes that can be eliminated by taking a wider view of the conventions that are appropriate. For example, a particular business might have improved its economic position as the result of a shrewd policy of investment in such fixed assets as freehold land and buildings. If it was not the main function of the company to trade in real property, the normal conventions would prevent the rise in value of its fixed assets from appearing as part of the profit reported to the shareholders. Yet from the point of view of the assessment of the management's competence, and from the point of view of judging whether the company has been successful, the calculation of the profit resulting from the rise in value of these assets may be of critical significance. Here there is a clear divergence between what may be of relevance for management purposes—which may justify the preparation of special management accounts—and what is regarded as appropriate for company law purposes.

If we consider stock-in-trade, it is the saleable value of the stock at any given time that is really significant from the point of view of the management; some accounts prepared for management purposes do in fact record stock on the basis of its expected realisable value. Here again there is a difference between the information appropriate for management and what would normally be regarded as appropriate for company accounts.

When we turn to the income tax law we are concerned, not with the guidance of management, or the relations of joint or common owners among themselves, but with the relation between, on the one hand, a group of people having a legal interest in any accretions to the value of their business and, on the other hand, the State, which has a special interest in the same accretions. The interest of the State is based on the need to achieve certain social ends by economic means. If a tax system could be constructed *de novo*, one might therefore expect the calculation of profit or income for the purpose of that system to be based on a careful consideration of these ends and means. For example, the effect of applying tax to profit as defined in a certain way would, one might expect, be considered with respect to its effect on business activity, on investment, on employment, and so on. There is no reason to suppose that the concept of profit arrived at after such consideration would necessarily coincide with that adopted by accountants for the rough-and-ready purposes discussed above, even assuming that the latter could be subsumed under one general principle (which is far from being the case in fact).

However, the Income Tax Acts were not constructed in this way. They are based essentially on an Act of 1803, and their present structure owes its existence in the main to a continued process of expedient tinkering over a period of more than a century. It is true that the rules have been reviewed by more than one Royal Commission. But this has not yet led to the laying down of any general principle for the calculation of profit or income. In fact, the Revenue authorities, and the courts, have in the main been prepared to accept the rule-of-thumb approximations used by accountants for other purposes. This approach is embodied in the general principle of law referred to above, to which lip-service is still paid, namely, that the ordinary principles of commercial accounting shall prevail except when the statutes say otherwise. The principle actually applied is however rather different. It is that the ordinary principles of commercial accounting shall be applied except when the courts decide that they shall not be applied (as in the *Broadstone Mills* case). That the courts would interfere with the ordinary principles of commercial accounting was inevitable. A rough-and-ready method of sharing property accretions may work well enough when all those concerned have roughly the same interest. But when one-half of those concerned stand to gain heavily if the share of the other half can be reduced by altering the rules, something must give way.

It might be assumed that the divergence between accounting profit calculated for the purpose of income taxation and accounting profit calculated for other purposes, though important, need not prevent the development of a general principle of profit calculation for tax purposes and hence of a principle for the valuation, *inter alia,* of stock-in-trade. It might be argued that behind the normal accounting principles which are acceptable for tax purposes, there can be found some rather general, yet definable and usable, concept of profit that has emerged over a long period as the result of the combination of accounting practice with judicial decisions. The difficulty of finding such a concept can be illustrated by considering normal accounting practice.

If we look at an accounting textbook, we find that the usual definition of profit runs in some such terms as: " That surplus which remains after the maintenance of capital." But we are seldom told what is meant by the " capital " that is to be maintained; and consideration shows the difficulty of attaching a precise significance to the term. It might, for example, be argued that by capital here is meant the total capital value of the whole undertaking as measured in an actual or hypothetical market. To take this as the criterion, however, would imply that each year a reassessment was made of the capital value at the beginning of the year, so that at the end of the year one could determine how much cash could be distributed without encroaching upon that capital value. This clearly is not a procedure that is normally envisaged in business.

An alternative definition might be that capital is the sum of the individual market values of the separate assets, less the amount of the liabilities. But again it is common knowledge that no attempt is made annually to reappraise the values of all the individual assets of a business in order to decide how much of that value has been maintained at the end of the year. The practical difficulties of doing so are obvious.

It might be said that the maintenance of capital implies the maintenance of a given level of dividend-paying capacity. If this were so, the annual assessment of profit would require an assessment of this capacity, implying the preparation of a financial budget for the future. Clearly this procedure does not form part of the conventional profit calculation.

It cannot be argued consistently that maintenance of capital should be defined by assessing capital through the application of normal accounting conventions, since this leads us into a circular argument. If we are trying to establish the rationale of the conventions by establishing some principle for which they are valid—and this is our object here—we cannot invoke these conventions for the purpose of setting up the principle.

I have so far refrained from mentioning the rather special problem to which so much attention has been devoted in recent years, the question of whether capital, however it be defined, should be measured in terms of constant price levels or in money terms. This, too, is a matter that must be considered if a principle is to be established.

Thus however hard we try we are unable to detect a usable general principle of profit calculation lying behind the existing conventional accounting procedures, other than the principle of reasonable compromise in given circumstances.[5] I do not think that the figures produced by applying decisions of the Revenue court to these procedures fit any better into a standard theory that can be used to settle all problems. This follows from the fact that, on the whole, the decisions of the courts, *e.g.*, on matters of stock valuation, have merely specified the set of existing accounting conventions that are to be used in particular cases, or in general.

Dicta in the *Duple* case give perhaps the best rationale of the procedure that is in fact followed by the court. Lord Reid said: "The most I can do is to try to bring common sense to bear on the elements of the problem involved," and again: "It appears to me that we must . . . simply ask what, in all the circumstances of a particular business, is a figure which fairly represents the cost of stock-in-trade and work in progress."[6] If we apply these two statements,

---

5 It may be said that even a reasonable compromise implies the existence of some concept of profit and capital maintenance, however vaguely formulated. This is no doubt true. I would find it difficult, however, to detect behind the day-to-day approximations used in practice, any general idea of profit more definite than that of a very rough indicator of the rise in the dividend-earning capacity and therefore, in given circumstances, in the marketable capital value of the undertaking (after allowing for money paid in or withdrawn by the owners during the period), so far as this is due to the normal business activities, and, in particular, excluding changes in the value of the undertaking's goodwill, or arising from changes in the general level of interest rates and yields or in the dividend yield thought appropriate for the undertaking in question.

6 At pp. 753 and 754–755.

we arrive at the kind of rough and ready approach which has always, I believe, lain at the base of the ordinary accounting conventions, namely, that of setting up a working rule that will be acceptable to both parties. Since, however, in matters of taxation the interests of the two parties conflict greatly, and since businesses differ a great deal, some form of arbitration procedure is necessary; this is provided by the Revenue court. Whatever may be the legal point of view, this seems to be a reasonable interpretation of the function of the court with respect to many of the problems of profit measurement. If this is so, we cannot expect the decisions of the court to be susceptible to over-close logical analysis in the sense that it is possible to fit them into any but the most general pattern of principle.

Nor does it necessarily follow that if any general principle of income determination were to be laid down by Parliament, this would in fact lead to a better situation; for despite what I have said above about piecemeal tinkering with the statutes, an attempt to set up a profit concept otherwise than by what would amount to piecemeal improvement of existing rules (*e.g.*, by making available again the use of LIFO) would lead to difficulties. For example, Parliament might decide that, since the object of income tax is to assess burden broadly in terms of capacity to pay, profit should be calculated by making an overall valuation of all assets annually and taking the difference between the valuations at the beginning and end of the year (allowing as usual for capital movements into and out of the business). This would be a consistent and theoretically clear-cut principle; but that it would raise very severe difficulties in practical application I need hardly point out. Any general principle of this type seems likely to lead to similar difficulties.

It may be argued that to accept Lord Reid's dicta as the basis for the determination of income is inconsistent with a view of income tax legislation as an economic tool to be used in such a way as will best further national economic policy. To measure income on the basis of arriving at a reasonable and fair method suitable for a given type of business, is not, it may be said, to adopt the criterion of national economic good. There are perhaps two points to be considered here. In the first place, and this is perhaps the more important point, it is doubtful, for the reason already given, whether any approach is possible that does not leave a good deal of freedom to the courts in interpretation unless a set of rules for profit calculation is laid down so rigid that it is likely to produce serious and irremediable injustice in certain contexts. Even so, such a set of rules would have to be formulated in very great detail, to meet most foreseeable situations, and would be likely to impose, in certain cases at least, a considerable amount of clerical work that would not otherwise be undertaken. It is most desirable that businesses should not be prevented from calculating such magnitudes as the value of stock-in-trade on the basis of the rule of thumb or statistical estimates that they think most useful for management purposes. An income tax system that forces a business to invest heavily in clerical labour or mechanical and electronic aids merely in order to achieve apparent precision in tax assessment, is undesirable; quite enough national resources are already absorbed in the administration of the tax system. The possibility of reasonable flexibility provided by the present system of judicial decision is less restrictive in fact, from a point of view of economic policy, than might at first be thought. Judicial decisions which conflict seriously with broad economic aims can be set aside on an *ad hoc* basis in the annual Finance Act. This process of marginal adjustment is not necessarily a bad one, provided it is subject to continuing critical review and provided access to the courts is not too expensive: desiderata to which, perhaps, more attention should be paid. It is, however, desirable in the interests of clear thought that the fundamental basis of the judicial decisions should be made clear. There can be little advantage in claiming that, for example, the assessment of the appropriate value of stock-in-trade is based on some fundamental principle of " accuracy " in profit determination (as was suggested in the *Broadstone Mills* case). It is better to make it clear that the judges, when they decide these cases, are being asked to make an assessment in the terms described by Lord Reid.

When it is accepted that the estimation of profit for income tax purposes is not a matter of adhering to a clear-cut principle, but rather of arriving at a reasonable compromise, the various methods of valuation that are used in practice appear in a new light. It becomes apparent that arguments about the relevance of including an element of overhead cost in the stock valuation, of including factory overhead cost but not general administrative overhead cost, and so on, are sterile. None of the different methods that are acceptable at present to the Inland Revenue, or that are acceptable if the Recommendations of the Council of the Institute of Chartered Accountants are taken as the criterion, conform to any particular principle other than that (with one limited exception—the valuation in certain limited cases of stock at net selling price) they all produce a " cost " figure below the ultimate expected selling price and to this extent conform to the principle that " profit shall not be realised." They are all reasonable, but arbitrary, practical approximations.

If this is recognised, life becomes much easier. Instead of the search for some absolute criterion, stock valuation can be based for management purposes on that criterion which seems most likely to provide the management with useful information—which may differ for different managements; and if this particular criterion conflicts, as it occasionally may, with those set by the income tax law or by the practice of company accounting, an alternative calculation can be made for the purpose of these on the basis of the simplest and cheapest procedure available.[7]

---

[7] So far as financial accounting is concerned I would, however, argue that the rules of stock valuation at present acceptable to most accountants are in fact unduly restrictive. It may well be that in certain instances better information would be given to shareholders if stock were valued on a realisation basis at all times. However, this is a controversial matter and has no direct relevance to income tax problems.

Business Valuation, Goodwill and the Super-Profit Method*

By H. C. Edey

Reader in Accounting,
London School of Economics

The super-profit formula

The purpose of this essay is to examine the significance and usefulness of the procedure known as the super-profit method of valuing business goodwill.

Goodwill in the economic sense is another word for organisation. Its value is derived from the economic benefits that a going concern may enjoy, as compared with a new one, from (a) established relations in all the markets in which it is accustomed to deal—not only in its sales markets, but also in the markets for all the goods and services it buys, including the labour market, the markets in which it buys its raw materials, the market for finance, and so on; (b) established relations with government departments and other non-commercial bodies with which it has negotiations; and (c) the personal relationships that grow up among people working together in a business, and the fund of knowledge and the habits that are built up, all of which will in favourable circumstances make for smoother and more effective working than could be expected in a new business. These things cannot be separated from the business and sold as can such assets as plant and machinery.

The formula for calculating the value of a business by this method, as it is generally stated, can be written:

$$V = A + \frac{P - rA}{j}$$

where:

V is the value to be found [1];

A is the value of the net tangible assets;

P is the expected annual return;

r is the normal annual rate of return appropriate to the business, expressed as a fraction (that is, 10 per cent. is written ·1 or 1/10);

---

* Based on an article in *Accountancy*, January and February, 1957.
[1] But see p. 210 below for the case where V is less than A.

$P - rA$ is the super-profit;

j is the appropriate rate for capitalisation of the super-profit, also expressed as a fraction;

$\dfrac{P - rA}{j}$ is the value of the goodwill, which we may write as G.

We shall now discuss possible interpretations of this formula.[2]

The net tangible assets

The tangible assets are those assets that could be sold separately.[3]

For the time being we shall avoid the complication introduced by the existence of loan capital or preference shares by assuming that apart from current liabilities the business to be valued is financed entirely by equity capital.

We shall assume initially that the value of the tangible assets is defined as their estimated saleable value as individual assets in the best market available. To arrive at the net value, the amount of the current liabilities is deducted, so that A is an estimate of the break-up value of the business. Later, the alternative assumption of basing the value of the tangible assets on their market replacement cost will be examined.[4]

The dividend expectations

The annual return, P, expected from the business will be taken, for our purpose, as an estimate of the annual dividend distribution that can be maintained in the future by the use of the assets, organisational structure and management that are to be handed over to the purchaser. The assets in question, so far as these could be sold separately, are those of which the value is included in A.[5]

The future level of dividends will depend partly upon whether new capital is paid into the business at a later date. This possibility must be taken into account in any valuation. This point is usually ignored in texts and here we shall simplify the problem by assuming that no further capital is to be paid in.

Another determinant of the level of dividends after any given point of time is the level of dividends before that time. The lower,

---

[2] One of our problems is the vagueness of textual discussions of this method of valuation. This makes it necessary for us to consider what interpretations, if any, are likely to make this method a useful valuation procedure.

[3] We shall later make certain qualifications to this definition.

[4] Original cost valuations cannot be relevant. I assume this need not be discussed.

[5] Income from assets which are not to change hands, or which are to be valued separately from the business (*e.g.*, marketable securities), must be excluded from the estimate.

for example, earlier dividends are in the period after the valuation, the higher should later dividends be, for the lower level of earlier dividends will leave more resources in the business and these should add to earnings: restricting dividends has the same effect as paying additional capital into the business. This, too, is a question that is usually ignored in texts; again we shall simplify the problem by assuming that the business will be so run as to maintain dividends at a maximum constant level.[6]

These simplifying assumptions can be made because we are concerned, not with problems of valuation in general, but with relative merits of a particular valuation procedure. We shall show that even on simplified assumptions such as these, the super-profit method is not a very useful tool of valuation. Textbook expositions of the method do not explain how the formula could be adapted to deal with more complicated cases; but the argument that follows suggests that in such cases the method is not likely to be more satisfactory than in simple cases.

An important feature of our definition of P is that we have not identified it with profit. The future dividend level is the fundamental concept, for it is the dividend distribution that determines what can be spent by the owner or owners of the business; the profit reported for a given period is at best a rough indicator of the dividend stream to follow.[7] A series of dividends are cash receipts: a profit figure is only an accounting measurement of a highly approximate character.[8]

The normal rate of return

We now turn to r, the normal annual rate of return appropriate to the business.

Some textual discussion of the super-profit method seems to require that r be defined as the long-run rate of return an investor would expect to receive on an investment equal in amount to A, in a business of the type that is being valued, having regard to current market yields on other possible investments, and on the

---

[6] In principle, that pattern of dividend payments, capital investment (and capital repayments if any) will be planned which maximises (so far as can be seen) the value of V.

[7] Or, possibly, in exceptional circumstances, of the liquidation value later: a dividend in liquidation is a special case of a future dividend, and is equally important as a factor in the valuation.

[8] It is, we suspect, because the usual discussions of valuation in accounting textbooks and treatises have been based on the explicit or implicit assumption that profits will be fully distributed, so that they are identical with dividends, that profit is often spoken of as the fundamental factor in valuation. The valuers have really been setting a value on expected future dividends; but they have described this process as a capitalisation of profit. It is true that undistributed funds may be realised by selling the business interest; but this is only because the immediate or ultimate buyer expects dividends sooner or later.

assumption that A is the break-up value of the business. Presumably r will then be above the current market yield on irredeemable Government stocks.[9] It will presumably be less than the average rate which an investor would require on his whole investment in the business where this is greater than the break-up value A, since the risk can be presumed to be less: if the investment does not exceed the break-up value, the ultimate loss, should the venture prove unsuccessful, may well be less than if it does, even though the possibility exists that bad management will dissipate the whole of the assets.

Some idea of current rates of return in different kinds of business can be obtained from published financial data, the rate in each case being expressed as the ratio of the current dividend to the market value of the relevant security. However, these statistics can at best be no more than rough-and-ready guides, even for valuations not based on the super-profit method. In the first place the conditions of one business are seldom reproduced closely in a second: a rate of return that an investor would think appropriate for one business may well be inappropriate for another; but there is no way of determining the adjustment necessary to the first rate in order to approximate the second: this is for the individual investor. This affects all valuation methods and is not peculiar to the one we are discussing.

Secondly, the observed ratio between a current dividend and the market value of the share does not tell us the relation that is generally expected by the market to exist between *future* dividends and that price. This can only be estimated, and the estimates of different investors will vary. Hence no unique measure of the expected rates of return upon market prices for other investments is available; a valuer must be content with rather general impressions and must in the final analysis make up his own mind what rate is appropriate.[10] This, too, is a problem common to all valuations, whether by the super-profit method or otherwise.

---

[9] Strictly speaking these should be described as stocks redeemable only at the discretion of the Government: " one-way-option " or " undated " stocks, such as 2½ per cent. Consols.

[10] This raises an interesting question. In the conventional theoretical economic model we assume that a valuation is carried out by capitalising a given estimated future flow of cash receipts at a given rate of interest. In passing from this model to the world of experience, both the capitalised flow and the capitalisation rate acquire a certain fuzziness, in that it seems an investor or a valuer is likely to apply, consciously or unconsciously, explicitly or implicitly, a correction for uncertainty to both. He may cut down his first estimate of the dividend flow in order " to be on the safe side "; and then he may increase the first estimate of the right capitalisation rate for the same reason, or perhaps reduce it because the future of the company seems rosy. There is thus a functional relationship between the estimates of the dividend flow and of the capitalisation rate.

Finally, there is the problem that the market prices of investments cannot be identified with the net tangible assets of the super-profit method. The market prices of other investments include, for each other investment examined, the value of goodwill—the amount which we are attempting to measure in relation to the business to be valued. The reported yields on other securities—in each case the ratio of dividend to market price—cannot therefore be identified with *r* in our formula, which is the rate the investor would think appropriate on that part of the purchase-price invested which is equal to the saleable value, *A*, of the net tangible assets. This problem arises only when we are using the super-profit method.

This is a serious difficulty, for even in principle it does not seem possible to calculate the value of the equivalent of *r*, as we are at present defining it, for other investments. The values of the net tangible assets of other investments can perhaps be found, even though there are practical difficulties; but it is not possible thence to arrive at a dividend to net tangible asset ratio, since we cannot determine what part of the dividend is return on net tangible assets and what part is return on goodwill. The most we can do is ascertain this ratio for any investments whose market value is known not to exceed the saleable value of the net tangible assets. Hence, even if it cannot be said that this difficulty renders our interpretation of the super-profit method invalid, it certainly raises doubts. It would be surprising if those who have used the method have in fact had access to the figures of *r*, as we have defined it, for alternative investments. If these cannot be obtained we are left with little objective guidance in assessing *r* for the investment to be valued.

It can indeed be argued that all *ex ante* assessments of economic values are subjective; and that such an assessment of *r* need not involve a greater subjective element than the *ex ante* assessment of any capitalisation rate, that is, of any minimum required return. There is, however, a difference between *r*, as defined above, and an average capitalisation rate expressing the relation required between expected dividends and the total amount invested. In principle, whether the latter has been received can be checked *ex post* if we consider the whole life of the business. There seems no way of checking *r*, even *ex post*, since this involves the splitting of the dividends received into a part attributable to use of the net tangible assets and a part attributable to goodwill.

However, let us assume that this definition of *r* is acceptable as a procedure that a prospective investor may find useful.

Capitalisation of the super-profit

We have now provisionally defined A and r. From these we obtain the product rA. This is, by definition, the annual dividend which would satisfy the investor on the assumption that he invested a sum A in the purchase of the business. The quantity $P - rA$ is the super-profit. It will pay the investor, when he calculates his maximum offer price for the business, to add to the sum A any amount up to the present value he sets on $P - rA$. This addition is the value of the goodwill. The formula assumes that he capitalises $P - rA$ at a rate j, so that the value of the goodwill is

$$\frac{P - rA}{j} = G.$$

We now have to consider, therefore, what meaning should be attached to j.

Again there is little help in the texts. Given the above interpretation of r, we may reasonably assume that the investor would set j sufficiently above r to reflect the greater possibility of loss in buying an expectation of future dividends unbacked by saleable tangible asset values. One would also expect j to be assessed having regard to alternative investment opportunities. It is only possible to calculate the value of j for a similar business opportunity, however, after the value of r has been determined for that opportunity, for until that is done we do not know how much of the dividend on that other investment is super-profit; if then we estimate the value of A for that investment, the value of j can be obtained from our formula (by inserting the known market value as V and solving for j). But, as we have noted, r is in general unknown for other investments. It seems then that all we can say of j is that it is assessed by the potential investor as some figure higher than r and higher than the average minimum rate of return he would accept on the total investment.

Alternative definitions of r

These difficulties are reduced if we define r as the market yield on undated Government stocks or the average market yield on debentures or preference shares, or some approximation to this; rA would then represent a fixed interest return available to the investor if the net tangible assets were disinvested. This would still leave the problem of calculating j for other possible investments in order to assess the alternatives available. In principle, however, this would be possible, as we have just seen, by estimating the value of A for each other investment; since we know V, its market value, and r is now given, j can be calculated from our formula.

This definition has the advantage of precision. It also gives a fairly clear-cut meaning to rA, as the fixed interest return that could be obtained by investing the break-up value of the business: if P is not greater than this there is certainly no point in continuing the business. On the other hand, it may still not be worthwhile to continue the business even though P is greater than rA: something better than a fixed interest rate is to be expected from an equity investment, even when fully represented by tangible assets. Furthermore, there is the practical difficulty in assessing the value of j, where r is a low rate, that (especially where the assets happen to be very specific so that A is low) the numerical value of $P - rA$ may be high, and a relatively small, possibly arbitrary, alteration in j may make a large difference to G, and therefore to V.

A third possible interpretation would be to take j as equal to r, both being defined as the estimated market rate of return appropriate to the whole investment being valued, including the value of goodwill. This would be to define r and j as we should define the capitalisation rate used when the method of valuation is the direct capitalisation of expected dividends.[11] In the simplified case we are discussing this method is described by the formula

$$V = \frac{P}{r}$$

where P has the meaning given above. If r and j are so defined, the two formulae are algebraically identical since

$$A + \frac{P - rA}{j}$$
$$= A + \frac{P - rA}{r}$$
$$= \frac{rA + P - rA}{r}$$
$$= \frac{P}{r} .$$

This interpretation raises no difficulties in ascertaining r (and therefore j) that would not arise in a valuation by direct capitalisation, at a single rate, of the future expected net cash flow.

On the other hand, the first possibility we have discussed, namely that r should be rather below this rate and j rather above

---

[11] I shall call this the *dividend capitalisation* method.

it, has the attraction that it draws specific attention to the greater uncertainty that probably attaches to the " top slice " of the value. It is true that there is less guidance from market data in the assessment of r and j; but after all the assessment of a direct capitalisation rate rests to a large extent on personal temperament and judgment. Certainly yields on other securities that at least look as if they were direct capitalisation rates are published daily, while the equivalents of r and j are not. But as we have pointed out above, the former are not true alternative yields to that obtainable on the business to be valued: they are at best only rough guides or indicators.

Significance of break-up value

It may be helpful at this point to take a numerical example. In a given business let the net tangible asset valuation, A, be £1,000, let the value of the expected maintainable dividend, P, be £120 per annum, let the value of r be 10 per cent. per annum and let j be 20 per cent. per annum. Then we have

$$V = 1,000 + \frac{120 - \cdot 1 \times 1,000}{\cdot 2}$$

$$= 1,000 + \frac{20}{\cdot 2}$$

$$= 1,100 \ [12]$$

The first point we note is that the use of the formula demands the calculation of the break-up value of the business, and thus draws attention to this figure and to its relation to the total value of the business. The break-up value is an important figure for three reasons. First it is the minimum value of the business. A seller would be foolish to sell at a lower figure; and it would always be worthwhile to buy a business at a figure below its break-up value (allowing, of course, a tolerance for the uncertainty of a break-up estimate). Secondly, as has already been implied in the above discussion of r, the break-up value is of significance in relation to the risk of investment, in that it gives some indication of the possible salvage value if the worst comes to the worst. True, bad management or misfortune may result in this salvage value being dissipated as time goes on; but at least this value is available when the investment is first made. Finally, the break-up value

[12] This gives the same valuation as would have been obtained from the direct capitalisation of the expected dividend at a capitalisation rate of about 11 per cent. Let i be the dividend capitalisation rate. Then

$$i = \frac{120}{1,100}$$

$$= 10 \cdot 9 \text{ per cent. approximately.}$$

gives the minimum liquidity available to the owner, subject again to the size of any losses incurred after the investment is made.

Net tangible assets and goodwill: further considerations

At this point, however, we must introduce a qualification. This arises from the difficulty of defining the tangible assets clearly. Among the assets that could often be sold separately from the business as a whole we must include such things as patents, unpatented knowledge, and the like, which are probably specific to the type of business being valued, but might be bought by another business in the same line. If our concept of A as the break-up value of the business is to be preserved, we must include in A an assessment of the value of such assets. There is no doubt, however, that both textbooks and practical valuers tend to regard the value of such assets as too doubtful for inclusion in A, and regard their value as part of the value of G. This may not be unreasonable, in that it restricts the break-up value to be included in A to that part of the net realisable value concerning which there is less doubt. It does, however, mean that our definition of the tangible assets will not always hold. Possibly it would be better to avoid the use of the term " tangible assets " in this context and merely define A as the best estimate of the current break-up value of the business that can be made.

The next point to be noted is that an excess of the total business value over the break-up value, given by a positive value of

$$\frac{P - rA}{j} = G$$

can be due to several causes. The business may possess goodwill as it is defined on page 201 above: that is, it is expected to produce a higher dividend stream than a new business similar in all other respects because the former is well organised. Secondly, the tangible assets may be specific, so that their break-up value included in A is significantly lower than their replacement value, even when new. If this is the case we cannot regard G as the value of goodwill only; it may include an element of value attributable to the contribution of the specific assets (though it will normally not be possible to say how much). If no break-up value has been assigned to such assets as patents and the possession of confidential knowledge (as is likely in view of the uncertainty of such valuations), G will include the value of these. G will also include the value, if any, of any other advantages that cannot be assigned a break-up value, such as the possession of a non-transferable licence, the services of particularly valuable staff at salaries favourable to the business, and the advantages of favourable location where these are not reflected fully in the rental paid.[13] Finally *G* will include any value derived from absence of competition.[14]

Clearly there are many possible factors operating here, the relative contributions of which will not be given by the formula and indeed, in general, will not be susceptible of estimation. The significance to be attached to *G* will vary with the relative importance attached to these factors. It may be argued that, as the division of the value *V* into two elements, *A* and *G*, may draw explicit attention to the break-up value, so it also draws explicit attention to the need to explain *G* and therefore to the possible effect on future returns of the presence or absence of these factors.

It is possible for the value of *G* to be negative where the value of *P* is less than the return, at the chosen rate of interest *r*, on *A*. This is an indication that the value invested in the assets can be put to better use by liquidating the business and investing elsewhere, at any rate in the view of the purchaser or valuer who assesses *A* and *r*. In this case the valuation must not be taken as *V* but as *A*, provided that *A* is the full break-up value.

Temporary super-profits

A special case arises when the value of *P* is likely to fall after a given period of time.[15] The business may enjoy profitable advantages that are expected to disappear at some foreseeable time in the future, such as the services of men or property in return for a payment below what will be demanded in the longer term (for example, when the contract under which the services were enjoyed terminates), or the temporary enjoyment of absence of competition.

In the numerical example above, the tangible asset valuation was £1,000, the net maintainable dividend was £120, *r* was 10 per cent. per annum and *j* was 20 per cent. per annum. These figures gave a super-profit of £20 which, capitalised at 20 per cent. per annum, gave the goodwill a value of £100. Now suppose,

---

[13] Where the site is owned, however, the value of location would presumably be included in *A* as part of the value of land and premises.

[14] Strictly we should say, not that the value of each of these things will be included in *G*, but that *G* will be greater or less as these factors are present or absent. This is because the value of *G* is partly determined by the values of *r* and *j*; and as we have seen different definitions of these are possible; and moreover the numerical assessments, given the definitions, may contain a substantial subjective element.

[15] This possibility is mentioned because it receives a good deal of attention in texts dealing with the super-profit method. Possible explanations of this may be found in Appendices I and II.

instead, that after six years the total profit was expected to fall from £120 to £115 because the lease of the premises occupied by the business would then have expired, and the competitive rental that would then have to be paid would be £5 higher than at present, so that the super-profit would be £20 for six years, then falling to £15. The longer term super-profit of £15 should presumably be capitalised separately from the £5, which will be received for only six years. The valuation would then be given, in £'s, by:

$$V = 1,000 + \frac{115 - \cdot 1 \times 1,000}{\cdot 2} + 5 \times \left[\frac{1 - \dfrac{1}{(1 \cdot 2)^6}}{\cdot 2} \right]$$

$$= 1,000 + 75 + 17$$

$$= 1,092$$

the term in square brackets being the present value of a terminable six-year annuity of £5 per annum.[16]

However, had the direct capitalisation of dividends method been used the same problem could have been dealt with quite simply by capitalising separately (a) the net maintainable profit of £115, and (b) the six-year annuity of £5. The super-profit formula seems to offer no particular advantage in this situation.

Replacement cost of net tangible assets

Earlier we deferred consideration of the possible significance of the super-profit method where A is defined not as the break-up value, but as the replacement value of the net tangible assets, that is, the estimated cost of replacing the tangible assets in their condition at the date of the valuation,[17] less liabilities. At first glance it might seem that significance could be attached to A, so defined, as the maximum value that a purchaser should pay for the business, since for this amount he could acquire a similar collection of assets and liabilities. If, for example, the replacement cost of tangible assets is £500 and the capitalised value of super-profit is, say, £100, giving a total of £600, the correct value of the business, it may be said, is nevertheless £500, for no one is likely to pay more for a business than the cost of creating a similar one.

However, this argument conceals a fallacy. An upper limit to the value of a business is indeed set by the fact that no sensible

---

[16] The actuarial symbol for this term is a_n. Values for this can be found, for different periods and rates of interest, in actuarial tables.

[17] In the case of assets of a specific type, for which there is no good second-hand value, this concept can be interpreted as the current cost of new assets of the same kind less an allowance for depreciation calculated on the replacement value.

purchaser would pay more for it than the amount he would need
to set up a similar business yielding the same expected return,
less an allowance for the extra trouble and risk and for the amount
in the early years by which the dividends would probably fall
short of the required level. It is indeed desirable, in principle,
to estimate the full cost of creating a similar business to that being
valued in order to set an upper limit on the value V.[18] But this
upper limit is, in general, a different figure from the replacement
value of the tangible assets *less* the liabilities.

In the first place, the productive methods that would be used
if a new business were established may well be different from that
of the business being valued. New and improved assets and
methods may be available. Secondly, it can happen that mistakes
were made in the business to be valued that would be avoided
in another business: the wrong assets may have been acquired.
Thirdly, the upper limit includes, in principle, outlay that would
not be covered by the valuation of the tangible assets. In order to
set up a similar business it may well be necessary to spend money
on such matters as development of productive methods and
markets, and very likely to accept a zero dividend in the early years
of the business, or a dividend below the estimated longer term
competitive rate. It is, indeed, the fact that such expenditure or
sacrifices have been made that may account for the emergence
of valuable goodwill, in the sense of an excess of V over the
value of the net tangible assets.

We must, I think, conclude that where A is defined as the
replacement cost of the net tangible assets it is difficult to attach
such significance to the super-profit method as to make it a
useful valuation method.

Capital gearing

We must now consider the problem of capital gearing. Where
there are prior interests in the form of loan capital or preference
shares, some expositions of the super-profit method suggest
that the value of the equity interest can be arrived at by first
finding a value for V that includes the value of the prior interests,
i.e., by estimating V as if the business were financed wholly

---

18 This procedure is valid, even if the potential purchaser is not in a position to
set up a business for himself, for it gives the maximum figure that a potential
competitor would have to spend in order to enter the trade or industry. It
would obviously be dangerous to pay substantially more than this sum for an
established business merely because earnings were in excess of a market rate of
return thereon, in view of the possibility of competition likely to be induced by
such a level of earnings. Of course, if it was not possible to reproduce the
business (*e.g.*, because it possessed a legal monopoly) the replacement cost in
this sense would become infinite.

by equity capital, and then deducting from the value of V so found the liquidation value of any loan or preference capital. Interest and dividends on such loan and preference capital are, in consequence, not deducted in computing P. This method ignores two relevant facts.

First, the total value of a business financed wholly by equity capital is not necessarily the same as that of the same business financed partly by fixed interest or dividend capital. It is a matter of experience that it may be possible to raise the total value of a business by altering its capital structure. Indeed the concept of an optimum gearing that will give the maximum value to a particular business is one that reflects experience. For some business interests, where uncertainty is high, the optimum gearing may be zero. But, in general, some element of gearing can be expected to raise the total value. Hence a valuation that ignores the effect of gearing may be less than the possible maximum.

Secondly, the current market value of such prior interests as debentures and preference shares is not necessarily equal to their liquidation value unless, indeed, liquidation is expected to take place in the near future. It may in fact be greater or less, depending upon the interest or dividend expectations, the degree of uncertainty attached to these, and current market rates of interest, such interests normally being valued by the dividend capitalisation method.

It seems therefore that if the super-profit method is to be relevant it must be applied to the equity interest and it must be assumed that the optimum capital gearing possible will be adopted,[19] so that V, A, P, r and j all relate to the equity interest, not the whole business (except where these are the same). In the calculation of the break-up value, A, the amounts payable on liquidation to the holders of prior rights must be deducted. P must be defined as the dividend that can be paid on the equity interest after meeting interest or dividends on loan or preference capital. The total value of the business must then be reached by aggregating V with the value found separately for the loan and/or preference capital.[20]

[19] Where the interest to be valued is not a controlling interest in the business, the owner will not be able to affect the gearing; even so, market forces, such as the threat of take-over bids, may sometimes bring about an adjustment where this is possible. The possibility of change in the capital gearing will, of course, depend in all cases upon the existing capital structure and upon who holds any prior interests. In some cases it might be worthwhile to offer existing holders of loan or preference capital a consideration for a change in their rights.

[20] This implies, in principle, a trial and error process. It may be necessary to estimate the effect, on the overall value, of different possible capital structures, as it is necessary to estimate the effect of different possible business policies. That gearing and policy will be assumed, within the range of possibility, that give the maximum overall value to the business.

Usefulness of the super-profit method

What has been said above suggests that the super-profit method of valuation has little to commend it, even when it is possible to give a significant interpretation to the formula.

It is true that if A is computed as the break-up value of the equity, the formula does draw express attention to the greater uncertainty that may attach to any excess value. This will not always be of great practical significance, but it is undoubtedly a factor which most valuers would wish to consider. There seems no particular advantage in using the super-profit formula, however, in order to gain this advantage. It is just as effective to carry out the valuation using the direct dividend capital-isation formula and to estimate separately the break-up value of the equity as the lower limit to the valuation. Similarly, the upper limit can be obtained from an estimate of the replace-ment value of the business as a whole, including in this figure an allowance for any estimated extra outlay or lower dividends likely during the early years of a new business.

Certain legal valuations are required to take goodwill into account.[21] This requirement is a way of drawing attention expressly to the fact that the full value of the business is required, not merely the value of the net tangible assets. Such a require-ment does not, however, imply that a specific valuation of good-will need be made by using the super-profit method. A valuation by the capitalisation of expected dividends will necessarily include the value of goodwill (which can be obtained separately, if desired, by subtracting the assessed value of the net tangible assets).

Our discussion has been based on the assumption of simpler conditions than will normally be met in practice. In particular a valuation must take into account the possibility of a varying dividend pattern over time (the most usual expectation being a more or less steadily rising dividend), the possibility of additional capital payments into the business by the future owner or owners, and the possibility of special capital distributions. The super-profit formula is not well adapted to deal with these complications. It may be argued that they are not usually taken expressly into account in the dividend capitalisation formula. It is true that in the analysis of investment opportunities on the organised securities market the usual starting point for discussion is the simple formula

$$V = \frac{P}{i}$$

[21] See, for example, section 59, Finance Act, 1940.

where P is the current dividend (or possibly an estimate of next year's dividend) and i is given the heavy task, not only of representing the return on alternative opportunities, but of reflecting all the hopes and fears of the investor or his adviser, including the expectations of rises (or falls) in the dividend, of calls for more capital and the possibilities of return of capital. Those, however, who wish to take expressly into account the logical implications of the points we have mentioned, can do so, without departing from the direct dividend capitalisation principle, by substituting for the above formula the more general formula for the present value of any future cash stream, positive or negative:

$$V = \frac{P_1}{(1 + i)} + \frac{P_2}{(1 + i)^2} + \frac{P_3}{(1 + i)^3} + \cdots$$

where the P's are the estimated net cash receipts, considered separately, for each future year 1, 2, 3, . . . ; the receipts may be negative in years when the owner pays in funds, and may include both dividends and capital repayments; i is a rate of return which reflects current alternatives foregone. This formula can be made even more general by giving i a time suffix, that is, by assigning to each separate year its appropriate rate of interest.

This concludes our survey. In the two appendices that follow we shall discuss, respectively, a possible theoretical basis for the super-profit method, and the application of the method to the valuation of professional practices.

APPENDIX I

Theoretical Basis for the Super-Profit Method

In my view the super-profit formula represents a brave but unsuccessful attempt to apply certain concepts of abstract economic theory to an important business problem. It can be given significance in the following way. Assume a world with conditions approaching those of perfect competition. Assume that resources have little specificity, and that there is little technical change. The saleable value of an asset approximates closely its replacement value. Rates of return on investment and interest rates tend to a standard level.

We can then define A as the market value of the business assets and r as the standard rate of return. In such conditions, profits (equal to dividends) will deviate little from the standard rate of return on the market value of the assets; that is, P will usually approximate to rA. The existence of super-profit will be exceptional. Should P be found to exceed rA, this will imply a disequilibrium that is unlikely to persist. The present value of the super-profit will therefore be that of a short series of receipts capitalised at rate r. If we set j equal to $\dfrac{1}{a_n}$, this valuation of the super-profit can be represented by the simple capitalisation formula

$$\frac{P - rA}{j}$$

instead of the more usual form $(P - rA)\, a_n$, (a_n being the present value of an annuity of 1 for n years at $100\, r$ per cent.)

APPENDIX II

The Value of Professional Practices

It is typical of professional practices that the earnings from them are largely due to the personal qualities and exertions of the practitioner. The assets used in such a practice are likely to be relatively few and low in value in relation to net earnings as compared with trading and manufacturing businesses. Profit is fairly clearly defined.

An incoming practitioner buying a practice from a retiring practitioner will in general be prepared to pay the market value of the practice assets, corresponding to A in the super-profit formula, and a further sum in consideration of the fact that he will probably enjoy the full benefit of the connection his predecessor has built up instead of having to build up his own practice over a period of some years. This corresponds to G, the value of goodwill, in the super-profit formula.

Suppose we take the average net profit which the outgoing practitioner has been able to withdraw annually from the practice in recent years as P in our formula, and rA as the return attributable to the investment in the practice assets; r in this case might reasonably be the overdraft rate of interest. $P - rA$ is then the net personal earnings. Suppose, too, we assume

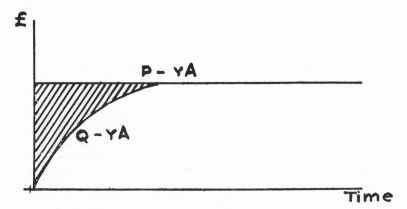

that the incoming practitioner would have been able to build up his net fees to P in three or four years if he had started a new practice. If he acquires the established practice as a going concern the net fees will be at this figure from the beginning.[22] Let us now plot the level of $P - rA$ on a graph, of which the y axis measures money value and the x axis time from the date of purchase. On the same graph we plot a curve $Q - rA$ which we assume measures the net fees, Q, that the new practitioner would earn if he started his own practice, less rA, the interest on the money he would in that case have to invest in second-hand assets like those in use in the existing practice. We then have the pattern shown by the diagram on page 216.

The shaded portion shows the maximum the new practitioner would be prepared to pay for the goodwill of the practice, subject to a discounting factor to bring it to a present value. If the present value of the shaded portion $P - Q$ turned out to be roughly equal to three times $P - rA$, the value of the practice would be given by the formula

$$V = A + \frac{P - rA}{j}$$

where j was $33\frac{1}{3}$ per cent.

This is not an unreasonable approach to professional practice valuation, provided that the full significance of each term in the formula is borne in mind in assessing the value to be assigned to it. If one can assume there is some uniformity in the time it takes to build up a practice to its normal level, we might expect j to take a fairly standard value.[23] On balance, however, it would seem simpler, and less likely to lead to error, to recognise the problem as simply that of determining the present value of an annuity of the difference between the net fees to be expected in the practice and the net fees that would be earned by an average practitioner in a new practice.

The use of the super-profit formula may be explicable historically in terms of this approximation for the professional firm, however.

---

[22] If the outgoing practitioner has specially outstanding personal qualities it may of course be that part of his fees will be permanently lost as soon as he goes. We should then take P net of this loss.

[23] Another approximation would be the simpler formula:
$$V = A + nP$$
where n was chosen to make the value nP equal to $\frac{P - rA}{\cdot 33}$. This would explain the rough-and-ready method of valuing practice goodwill on the basis of n years' purchase of net fees; we can assume that n too might be fairly uniform as between different practices.

COMPANY ACCOUNTS IN BRITAIN: THE JENKINS REPORT

HAROLD C. EDEY*

ONE hundred years ago the Parliament of the United Kingdom enacted the Companies Act of 1862. This Act was [to] be, for nearly half a century, the main [sta]tute for the regulation of British com[pa]nies; and in the Act's provisions—or in [wh]at was lacking in those provisions—the [str]ong individualism and laissez-faire [spi]rit of latter 19th century Britain were [ma]nifest. For the Act contained no manda[tor]y provisions with respect to accounts or [au]dit: these were matters of private con[tra]ct, to be left to the stockholders of Vic[tor]ian Britain. Such requirements had ap[pe]ared in the earlier statute of 1844 which [fir]st introduced into Britain the principle [of] incorporation by registration, though [va]gueness and lack of enforcement provis[ions] took the teeth out of them. They had [be]en abandoned in 1856 (though special [ac]counting legislation continued to be ap[pli]ed to public utilities, insurance com[pan]ies and banks throughout the remain[de]r of the century).

It was not until 1908 that the first major [ste]p was taken on a path that was to lead [to] regulation far more detailed and effec[tiv]e than would have been dreamed of by [th]e 19th century business men (though, [ev]en to-day, perhaps less rigorous and far [rea]ching than that applied by the federal [sec]urities legislation of the United States). [Ei]ght years earlier, compulsory auditing [ha]d been re-introduced, and now the prin[cip]le of public registration of balance [sh]eets and the specification, even if in [ra]ther general terms, of their contents, was [es]tablished.

[T]he 1908 legislation followed the report [of] a Board of Trade Departmental Com[mi]ttee—the Loreburn Committee. From then onwards it may be said that a regular pattern in British company law amendment was established. Once in every fifteen to twenty years a Departmental Committee takes evidence, cogitates, and reports on the state of the company law; and an amending statute follows. (The pattern of reports is broken, it is true, in 1918; but the Wrenbury Committee's report of that year was not followed by legislation.)

The Companies Act of 1928 (followed by a consolidating Act in 1929) was the next major enactment; this followed the *Greene Report*. The 1928 Act introduced a considerable stiffening into the accounting requirements; and was the first to refer specifically to the income (profit and loss) account. It was, incidentally, also the first Act to recognise the need for special rules with respect to holding companies, though the preparation of consolidated accounts was not to be required for another twenty years.

The next major reform took effect in 1948, following the *Cohen Report* of 1945. Accounts began to take a modern form; and the British company law requirements could now be compared on not too unfavourable terms with those of the S.E.C.

Now, seventeen years after the Cohen Report, has come the *Jenkins Report*.

Much of the Report is concerned with the general law. And even in that part concerned with accounting, some of the recom-

---

* H. C. Edey is Professor of Accounting in the University of London. He is co-author of a book on national income and social accounting as well as articles in various accounting and other journals and in books of readings.
This article and the one following were solicited as book reviews by Stephen A. Zeff and are placed here in order to keep all the material in this issue on the Jenkins report in one place.

mendations deal with technical points that have special relevance to British circumstances only. Here I shall try to sketch in, and comment upon, some of the discussion and recommendations that are particularly controversial, or seem likely especially to interest American accountants.

The flow of take-over bids in this country in the last sixteen years has highlighted sharply the need for good balance sheet figures of the values of all readily saleable and chargeable assets, and especially real property. The Report's reaction to this is disappointing. Most accountants and economists would agree with the Report in believing that an attempt to assess the current saleable value of such a specific asset as, say, a steel plant, is usually not likely to yield a useful figure. But as one moves towards less specific assets, a reasonable attempt to attach a current market valuation becomes increasingly worthwhile. The Jenkins Committee were prepared to agree that the current values of some fixed assets could be important enough to warrant the directors reporting them; but they were not prepared to impose a duty to this effect. Nor did they— as they might well have done, and as was suggested in the evidence they took— recommend that directors should be required to report the insured value of each group of assets: a figure that, while not perfect for the purpose, would at least provide useful supporting evidence of the company's current economic and financial state.

Generally, the Committee's attitude on this question suggests they had not, as a body, grasped properly one of the fundamental assumptions of economic life in the western world: that it is the directors' duty to make the best possible use of the equity entrusted to them. They say: "The directors' duty is to manage the company's business . . . it would be unreasonable to impose upon them the legal responsibility

to make periodical investigations—even these were of significance to the sha holders—into the possible alternative u to which the company's land and buildi might be put and what the site value mi be worth . . . " But why not? This is deed an extraordinary statement for company law committee in a capita country.

On the other hand the Commit recognise—and here they are surely ri if balance sheets are to reflect econor reality, as the S.E.C. has I think be wrong—that it may be legitimate for dir tors to revalue fixed assets; they wis recommend that when this has been do the balance sheet should state when, whom, and what basis.

It seems likely in fact, that the Comn tee were swayed more by practical diffic ties than by principle, for on the valuat of investments they are on the side of angels. They recommend that the agg gate market value should be stated for investments (other than in subsidiari which would normally be consolidated) which a satisfactory stock exchange quo tion is available; and that where no quo tion is available, the directors should eit give their own estimate of value (wh would commit them to a stated opinion) state in some detail the reporting co pany's share of the aggregate income a dividends of the companies whose sto comprise the investments. It is remarka that the Committee then go on to reco mend that if the above information given (e.g. as a note), the directors sho be allowed if they wish to write down book value of the investments by amount of any profits on realisation: it is if the Committee said "Provided you g the true position *somewhere* in the ann report you can make the book value in balance sheet as useless as you like."

On stock inventories, the main reco mendation is good. The choice of invent valuation base may affect significantly the time pattern of profit reporting. The Report says: ' . . . shareholders ought to be concisely but adequately informed as to the basis used.'

The Committee's views on the reporting of surplus (for which 'reserves' is now a term of art in British company accounting) are linked to its views on the definition of profit. In British circumstances this issue has a dual significance. It reflects the view given to stockholders of the company's economic progress and prospects; but as British law limits distributions involving the release of assets to members, the question 'What is distributable profit?' has a further significance. The Committee's general view is that the statutes should not lay down any 'code of precise rules', the only satisfactory general rule being that already generally accepted (and based on judicial precedent) that 'profits must be ascertained by reference to the normal standards of commercial prudence.'

This gives, however, a rather more simplified view of the present law than one might think on a single reading of the Report. Although no set of precise rules exists with respect to distributable profit, there is a set of precedents built up over many years that forms part of the intellectual stock in trade of all British public accountants. These precedents do in fact, if not in form, constitute a rough code, though not one without ambiguities and inconsistencies. Aware of this, the Committee has made certain recommendations that, if adopted, would go some way towards removing the ambiguities. For example, it is a moot point (although some British accountants do not realise this) whether a British company can legally distribute a profit arising from the revaluation of unrealised fixed assets. The Report comes down unequivocally against this.

When, however, the Committee turn to the balance sheet classification of reserves

('surplus' in the U.S.A.), it recommends the abolition of the distinction hitherto made between revenue (or distributable) reserves, and capital (or non-distributable) reserves, on the grounds that there are no precise statutory rules to aid the directors in making up their minds. Since the directors are bound to make the distinction for the purpose of paying dividends, and since the balance sheet must *in some way* indicate the distinction if it is to comply with the overriding requirement to show a 'true and fair view,' the Committee's view is odd, to say the least. It could perhaps be rationalised on the basis of a desire to leave room for experiment in balance sheet design; but this point is not made in the Report.

One of the major innovations called for in the Report with respect to the income account is that the figure of sales turnover should be disclosed. This has been urged for many years by leading British economists, and by some accountants; the 19th century concern for privacy in business has in this instance lingered on well into the second half of the 20th century. The walls now seem to be crumbling however, though even now, and in the face of the American example, the Report vacillates, and is prepared to exempt from such a requirement companies whose directors are satisfied that disclosure would be harmful and make a statement to that effect in the accounts. (It should be said that some important British companies have made this disclosure voluntarily for years, not in all cases because they wanted a listing in America.)

On the general question of adjustments for price level changes, the Report endorses the historical cost basis; but nevertheless goes as far as to agree that the law should not insist on a uniform application of this principle in all circumstances. Moreover, it asserts that accounts prepared on the historical cost basis may need to be accompanied by supplementary information in order to give shareholders the 'true and fair view' required by the Act. I believe that, though this seems rather cagey, it is an important step forward, for the 'true and fair view' provision is an overriding requirement of the Act. Henceforward no accountant can say unequivocally that price level adjustments are irrelevant: he must indeed address his mind to the problem.

A point of some interest to an American audience arises on the wording of the statutory audit report. In 1948 the old, fairly short, form of report was replaced by a more lengthy one, which requires the auditor to state, among other things, whether proper books of account have been kept. The Report must also refer to a number of other specific matters that would form part of the normal work of a proper audit. The Committee has accepted on this issue the view of the principal professional account-ing bodies. This is to the effect that the es-sential duty resting upon British company auditors is to report whether in their view the accounts present a true and fair view and that an unqualified report might well be confined to a statement to that effect. They say, with some force, that if an auditor is not satisfied on any matter and a qualification becomes necessary, it will be more obvious to readers in a short report.

Generally, the accounting recommenda-tions of this report can be regarded as an attempt to add marginal improvements to existing legislation, rather than as a plan of radical change. Many of the improvements will be valuable. The general impression that the report gives is of a Committee that, as a whole, possessed a high technical competence in law and accounting, but substantially lower one in economic policy.

ACCOUNTING PRINCIPLES AND
BUSINESS REALITY

by

H. C. EDEY, B.Com., F.C.A.
(Professor of Accounting in the University of London)

I The Objects of Financial Accounting

1. It is perhaps not always remembered that financial accounts fulfil more than one purpose. Consider the most important part of financial accounting: that concerned with company accounts. Of the numerous reasons for preparing annual company accounts, we can distinguish four major ones:

(1) To provide a working basis for the annual share-out among shareholders.

(2) To provide a basis on which, after suitable adjustments, the annual income and profits tax assessments can be made.

(3) To provide shareholders, and others with financial claims on the company, with an indication of the business prospects of the company and the relative success of the directors.

(4) To indicate to owners what remuneration and perquisites have been enjoyed by the directors.

The fourth object differs from the other three in that no economic estimation of profit is involved, and I shall not discuss it further here.

2. The other three objects have in common the calculation or estimation of a figure called 'profit'. The purposes served by the calculation have, however, a significant effect on the way it is approached and, I would argue, on the accounting principles that are appropriate. Whatever their ultimate rationale, the rules relating to distributable profit and to taxable profit are now more or less tightly drawn. The desire to avoid uncertainty in their application has played a great part in their development. On the other hand, the idea of profit as a guide to shareholders and other interested parties must, if it is to be of much use, be a business (or if you prefer it an economic) concept: a more flexible approach is required.

3. In my view the idea of the annual accounting report as a statistical aid to financial management has not yet been properly disentangled from the much older idea of the annual accounts as a simple check on directors' honesty *vis-à-vis* their shareholders,

3

and as a rough guide to the equitable distribution of annual dividends with an eye on the interests of various classes of shareholders and of creditors.

4. Indeed, I think that there have been occasions when changes in accounting methods intended to improve the information given to shareholders (or to management) have been prevented because auditors have taken the view that they conflict with the rules for profit calculation generally assumed to be imposed by the judicial decisions on dividend law. Whether auditors are always right on such occasions does not matter here, since the point I wish to make is that such considerations are not necessarily relevant to business needs.

5. Furthermore, I believe that tax law has an influence on company accounting practice, in that it may inhibit a change of method that would commend itself on other grounds. Accounting principles (e.g. of stock valuation) that will do for company law purposes may be unacceptable by the Revenue courts. For example, in the cases of *Patrick and Broadstone Mills Ltd* ([1954] 1 All E.R. 163 (C.A.)), and *Minister of National Revenue v. Anaconda American Brass Ltd* ([1956] A.C. 85 (P.C.)), the base stock and LIFO methods of stock valuation were held to be invalid for income tax computations. The balance has, for the time being at least, been restored by the decision in *Ostime v. Duple Motor Bodies Ltd* ([1961] 2 All E.R. 167 (H.L.)), allowing valuation by direct costing. But no one knows in which direction the decision in such cases will go. Most accountants would hesitate before introducing a modification in accounting procedures if this meant that in future there was a risk that two sets of figures would be required, one for the Revenue and one for the annual report: duplication is not without cost.

6. The conventions on which financial accounts are prepared – the normal accounting principles – have grown up as the result of a historical process. They were originally needed in order to provide workable rules by which the maximum dividends appropriate to the situation could be approximately gauged. They were, I suggest, no more than a sensible, rule of thumb, way of solving a particular problem. The old auditing cases show that this is how the judges understood them. It is doubtful whether in the days when they developed they were ever intended to provide precise measures of the degree of business success. Clearly there was no intention that they should do this for shareholders, for as you know directors had, at any rate until the *Royal Mail* case, no compunction in reporting profit net of significant undisclosed

4

contingency reserves, not necessarily based on any careful consideration of future known liabilities. Secret appropriations to reserve were perfectly respectable.

7. The *Royal Mail* case, the Institute's *Recommendations* and the Act of 1948 may be thought to have changed all that. But is the change as big as was thought? The Recommendations and the 1948 Act have done good. But this should not obscure the fact that financial accounting statements and business reality can still be far apart. Indeed, although there is still room for improvement in financial accounts – for example, with respect to valuation methods – I think there are reasons for believing that we may be nearing the end of fruitful development in the traditional form of accounting report. In order to show what I mean I shall now turn to the question of business aims and in particular the nature of the investment process.

II The Nature of Investment

8. Business considered as an economic activity is essentially a process of investment: purchasing power is parted with in the expectation of receiving greater purchasing power in the future. On this view, we must agree, I think, that the owners of business are, *so far as economic decisions are concerned*, interested ultimately only in the amount of purchasing power committed to the investment, the future flow of cash receipts (dividends) they may expect to receive, and the potential liquidity in the form of available cash which the investment will give them at all future times. In short they are interested in the relation of the financial input of the investment to the financial output. Nothing else is of economic interest to them. I have been careful to avoid saying that nothing else is of interest: the adjective 'economic' is of great importance. Non-pecuniary considerations probably enter to a greater or a less degree into most investment decisions. But this does not concern us here; our problems are those that arise when allowance has been made for all such matters.

9. You will notice that I have spoken of dividends and of liquidity and not of profit. This is quite deliberate; much of what I have to say turns on this point, that – in the end – it is money that buys things and not figures of profit.

10. Some formulations would suggest that the economic interest of shareholders lies simply in the relation of a single expected pattern of future dividends to the resources initially at risk; but this is not enough: liquidity must be brought in too.

5

It is because liquidity may be of importance that writers on the valuation of securities lay so much emphasis on 'marketability' – an important determinant of the liquidity of such investments. The question may be just as important in relation to an internal management decision: 'If something goes wrong or we need more finance suddenly, how much could we realise by discontinuing this process ?' It would, indeed, be possible to make a classification of shareholders such that the classes constituted a range, at one end of which lay shareholders whose interests were almost entirely confined to future dividends, with little concern for liquidity, and at the other end those whose sole interest lay in the liquidity they could withdraw from the investment in the near or more distant future: at one end would be the purely 'income-conscious' person, at the other the purely 'capital-value conscious' person. In between we should find the majority who are interested in varying degrees in both.

11. One can perhaps simplify the picture by regarding potential liquidity as nothing more than a possible alternative cash receipt flow. One can then think of any given investor as making his plans in terms of a standard 'most probable' dividend expectation – perhaps continuing for an indefinite period into the future – but with an eye on the possibility, should his general financial position require it, of stopping this flow at any point in time and accepting in lieu, a single, final cash receipt; or, where part of the investment was realised, of accepting a specially large cash receipt plus, thenceforth, a smaller flow. In its most obvious form this appears as the possibility of selling part or whole of a quoted investment, thus obtaining liquidity at the point of time of the sale and sacrificing any further dividend flow from the part sold. An owner-manager may be able to raise liquidity for personal use in this way by selling off part of his ownership claim, e.g. by selling equity shares, and he must take this possibility into account in his overall plans. When he is considering investing resources in any particular activity to be carried on as part of the business, he is faced with the same kind of pattern in his internal planning: he must (assuming, of course, that he is attempting to make a systematic appraisal) consider the possible contribution to the net cash flow yielded by the new expenditure – the dividends to the whole enterprise from this particular investment, if you like – and also the possible net realisation receipt if he decides at any time to terminate the activity and liquidate the assets he is using. If any activity is not expected to be of indefinite duration, one component of the flow of cash released by the activity will be that realised in its final winding-up. A board managing a company on behalf of shareholders is in a similar position, though one must assume in their case that in choosing between opportunities they are

basing their decisions on what they consider will best suit the shareholders rather than themselves.

12. Thus, when we get down to the kernel of the matter, there is a structural similarity between the arithmetical pattern that describes the economic aspect of an investment in a security – say an ordinary share of an industrial company – and that which describes any industrial investment project, such as the outlay made by a chemical manufacturing company on a new plant. From this two things follow. First, that whatever formal calculation procedure is used in evaluating the one, will be relevant to the other. It is, for example, the view of some financial controllers, of economists and, I may say, of academic accountants, that the use of discounted net worth calculations (or their arithmetical equivalents in the form of annuity or compounding calculations) is the best approach at present available to the task of making clear the logical implications of investment: of the significance of assumptions that have to be made about future cash flows and initial sums invested. (See Appendix 1 for a note on the rationale of this method and an illustration.) Such methods are equally appropriate, whether one is a member of a financial committee concerned with the economic justification of a new chemical plant or a new power station, or the investment manager of a pension fund.

13. Second, the general principles guiding the preparation and presentation of the arithmetical information on which the decision is based, and the figures which are later used to check (so far as is ever possible) whether the outcome of the decision tallies with that planned, should be the same, whatever the form of the investment. These principles should be related to the criteria on which the investment decision is based. There are, of course, considerable differences in detail between one investment decision and another, and between internal management investment decisions and decisions to invest in this or that stock or share. But – and this is what is important in getting to the root of things and in setting up a systematic general framework for one's thinking – the formal pattern is the same: the relevant magnitudes are the initial amount at risk, the future flow of cash released and available for other uses, and the amount of cash that could be disinvested (by sale or otherwise) should the need arise, at any point of time, however uncertain may be the assessment of all these.

14. I have referred to investment projects in terms of the relation of future cash flows to an initial money outlay. There are occasions when the word 'cash' may not be entirely apposite,

7

because an initial investment, a dividend, or a final liquidation payment, are made in kind. We can, however, assume that in such cases the value transferred is a cash equivalent, obtained by taking the current realisable value. An important example of this arises when we consider the initial investment. Economic activity is a continuous process of re-investment. If we take any activity we choose – a large business group, a division within that group, a single plant in the division, a stock exchange security – each represents, to its owner, locked up purchasing power that could be released by a process of realisation. This realisation can be sale to some other person, or transfer to some other use by the same owner. In either case the decision to continue the use of an asset in its existing employment is equivalent to a decision to invest in that employment the money value the asset could realise, whether this would be in the form of a direct cash receipt or of saving the necessity for laying out cash elsewhere.

15. Thus, to go on holding a share involves (subject to the cost of using the market) the same considerations as to buy the share. The justification of the continued use of an asset in terms of future contribution, whether in the positive form of surplus cash outflow created by the asset or of saving in cash inflow otherwise needed, is just as desirable in the interests of economic efficiency as a similar justification for new money invested. True, there are many situations where this justification is so obvious – where the effect of withdrawal of the asset would cut the cash flow by so much – that no detailed study is needed. One does not have to make a special calculation to justify the continued use of the rails of the London–Birmingham railway line. But one does – or should – have to justify the continued operation of the whole line and, therefore, the retention of the economic resources invested in it.

III The Investment Plan as a Budget

16. You will have noticed that in specifying the financial figures that seem relevant for investment decisions – whether taken inside a company, or by a shareholder buying an interest in a company – it has not been necessary to bring in directly the concept of accounting profit. What has been said so far calls, rather, for a set – or sets – of cash budgets. Any given investment project can be characterised by a budget of the overall cash account for that activity, showing the estimated amount of the cash absorbed initially by the investment activity and the flow of cash 'dividends' released thereafter.

8

17. Thus, for a cash outlay of say £1,000 used in a particular way, the net cash flow shown by the long-term cash budget might be as follows (in £s):

$$-1,000, +100, +110, +120 \dots +600$$

where the minus sign indicates cash initially absorbed by the activity (say a new plant) and the plus signs indicate cash released each year thereafter. Such a series might be finite, or might be assumed to extend into the indefinite future. The first step in the process of investment choice could take the form of calculating a series of this type, as the outcome that was assumed to be most probable. The discounting procedure of Appendix I could be applied to this. Other possible patterns might be calculated, based on alternative assumptions about the future course of events. It is in this way, indeed, that the liquidity question could be introduced. For example, one possibility considered might be that a need for cash elsewhere in the enterprise would call for the liquidation of the investment at the end of the third year. The cash flow series could be re-calculated on the new assumptions. An estimate would have to be made of the cash that would be released in such a contingency. If this amount was set at, say, £900 in addition to the £120 expected in the third year in any case, the new series would be:

$$-1,000, +100, +110, +1,020$$

This procedure could be repeated for other assumptions. This brings out, incidentally, that the liquidity question can be regarded as a matter of setting out in figures (on paper, or perhaps more vaguely in one's mind), on the appropriate assumptions, those particular cash flow series which correspond to cases in which the investment, or part of the investment, is assumed to have a shorter life than what is considered the most probable case.

18. In principle, investment choice requires the study of an indefinitely large set of such patterns for each proposed activity. As the number of possibilities is usually very large, and as the estimation of the cash flow from any investment is often very difficult and frequently has to be based on very shaky foundations, investment choice looks a difficult process; and so it is. This explains why in practice so many rules of thumb have to be used. Nevertheless, the kind of pattern I have indicated is relevant, for though all possibilities can never be explored – a large part of good decision-making being indeed the ability to pick the small number of alternatives that are worth looking at – a logical pattern of thought, bringing in the financial realities, is needed for those that are considered.

9

19. You will perceive that in this example I have skated over many of the problems of investment choice. I think, however, that I can be excused, for the problems I have avoided are not concerned with the main point I wish to make, namely that the ultimate economic reality of investment planning is concerned with cash flows – it is as a consideration for the provision of cash that interest and dividends are paid, and it is cash that is needed for the payments. This does not, of course, mean that investment planning can be done on the basis of a single year's cash budget: this is not a question of using a receipts and payments account for one year instead of a profit and loss account for one year. When I speak of cash flows and cash budgets it is to the whole series of annual budgets, as far into the future as it seems worth while going, that I am referring.

20. When one discusses this kind of procedure the following type of objection is often made: 'How can one look so far into the future? Surely, to suggest that one can estimate the cash flow ten years hence resulting from a given investment now is to be quite unrealistic.' This objection must be met, for though I think it to be irrelevant, the thought prompting it is not unreasonable. It is quite true that there are great uncertainties in estimating – or guessing – so far ahead. But this does not excuse management from asking questions of the form: '*If* we make this investment, and *if* the results in terms of future cash flow are such and such, will it have been justified and to what extent?' and following up the posing of a series of such questions by posing a second kind of question of the type: 'Do the answers to the first set of questions suggest that the investment should be undertaken when we weigh up as best we can the probabilities of the correctness of the assumptions on which they are based?' It is by posing questions of this type that the systematic methods of the natural sciences can be made to pay off in business. Posing and answering the questions sometimes requires simple arithmetical studies. Sometimes more elaborate models are necessary. The fact is that most investments can only hope to pay for themselves over a period of years: whatever one may think about the difficulties of forecasting the future, the decision to put money into any long-term project implies the taking of a long-term view, whether one admits it or not. There is no excuse for doing it haphazardly. (It may, incidentally, be noted that the preparation of a profit and loss account usually involves assumptions of the same type about the long-term future. Any depreciation calculation involves assumptions about the useful life of an asset and its residual value.)

21. These considerations suggest that for the investor, whether he be owner-manager or minority shareholder, the type of ac-

counting statement that would be most useful would be a cash forecast; a statement setting out the components of the long-run cash budget. The statement would, necessarily, show the dividends it was hoped to pay, and would give details of further finance to be raised in the future. If budgets are good for management, why should they not be for shareholders ? If this seems fanciful, let me say that much of the work of investment analysts is essentially an attempt to sketch in an outline of such a budget for each company they examine, even though the figures they produce necessarily fall far short of a complete picture. The art of interpreting financial accounts is, indeed, in large part that of building up in one's mind, by detective work and intuition, a picture of the future cash flow, while incidentally forming gradually an opinion on the general quality of the direction and management.

22. Nor is the suggestion that shareholders be given a forecast of future dividends without precedent: as you know such a forecast forms, to the extent of the next dividend, a normal part of the information provided by the board of directors in a prospectus. Though I am sure that there would be much opposition to the introduction of a legal requirement that information of this kind should be made available to shareholders as a normal rule, and though there are clearly difficulties, I think that a case can be made out for it. Certainly it would, at any rate so far as larger companies are concerned, fit in with current ideas of the need to co-ordinate the plans of different companies in the interests of the economy as a whole. It has been proposed for the nationalised industries.

23. If, then, the fundamental information needed to enable investors to manage their portfolios takes the form of long-run forecasts of the cash flows of the companies in question, of what use are published accounts in their present form? Let us start by considering what these accounts purport to show, taking the profit and loss account first.

IV Investment Planning and Profit Reports

24. It is generally stated or implied in accounting textbooks that the profit and loss account shows the amount that could be distributed by way of dividend while 'maintaining capital intact'. The concept of maintaining capital intact is unfortunately not a precisely formulated one. It conveys the general idea of money benefits derived from ownership of a particular interest. It does not, however, as Professor R. S. Edwards pointed out twenty-five years ago, give us an unequivocal general rule for assessing the amount in question. If one ignores niceties, there seem to be two

main ways in which one could interpret capital maintenance. First it could mean maintaining the maximum, constant, level at which the distributions of the current year and of each future year could be held. With this concept, reported profit in a given year would be the maximum amount that could be distributed in that year while maintaining future distributions at the same level. Or capital maintenance could mean maintaining the total value, in some sense, of the concern as a whole. Furthermore, each of these concepts could be interpreted in terms of money value or in terms of purchasing power with some sort of price index adjustment to allow for changes in the value of money. As I wish to concentrate on the more general question I shall assume for the sake of discussion here that the price level problem does not arise. This does no harm, as most of what I have to say applies whether price level adjustments are made or not.

25. When we examine the idea of maintaining capital as expressed by the maintenance of the level at which future annual distributions could be held, we are bound to accept that it does not provide a satisfactory general statement of existing practice, even though we may have some suspicions that it comes nearer to describing the idea of profit in the minds of some directors than any other. It should be noted, incidentally, that to adopt this definition would imply a readiness to accept general provisions for the maintenance of dividend earning power – provisions not necessarily linked to the original cost of an asset or indeed to any particular asset – as profit and loss account debits. (I do not say that this is necessarily unsound.)

26. We now turn to the alternative definition of capital maintenance: as the maintenance in some sense of the capital value of the undertaking as a whole. If capital value has a business meaning it must, I think, refer to the amount that someone thinks the entity valued is worth to buy, or alternatively (if that someone is an owner) the minimum amount which he would accept if he sold – his reserve price. How far does this fit in with present practice? It is clear that it does not in any exact sense. We all know that balance sheets do not purport to measure such a value and that accounting profit does not purport to measure the increase (after, of course, adjustment for money paid in or withdrawn by the owners) in such a value.

27. I am afraid this leads only to the conclusion that accounting profit as at present understood has no exact business meaning; a not surprising conclusion perhaps when we bear in mind the different results that are given by different valuation methods that lie within the bounds of generally accepted accounting principles.

28. At this point I shall turn again to the budgeting aspect, for it is from this point of view that the relevance of annual profit as a business concept is perhaps most clearly seen. Most businesses are expected to continue indefinitely and, for the reasons I have given, one would expect their basic financial plans to be in terms of anticipated cash flows over a relatively long period. A business is, however, faced with the need to take decisions on what to produce and in what quantity, on how to produce it, on pricing, and so on. These are usually considered in the framework of an annual plan. When long-term plans have been made, the plan for a given year rests upon some kind of general assumption about the pattern of cash flow in succeeding years. The assumption (expressed or implied) may be, for example, that some or all of the succeeding years will be similar financially to this year. In the arithmetic of the financial planning of any given investment the assumption appears in the form of a figure for the amount of the invested money value which will (it is hoped) be collected during the year in question. The residue is the 'value' to be set on the asset or group of assets at the end of the year, to be recovered in later years.

29. In order to examine the problem further, let us concentrate on one asset in a business, treating this asset as if it had its own set of accounts. Consider a business investment in a new plant. If the investment in the plant is to be justified, a contribution must be obtained over the life of the plant, in the form of cash receipts less operating outlays, sufficient to cover the initial money value invested plus the rate of return considered appropriate (which will be assessed in the light of the cost of capital and of other investment opportunities). But as a practical expedient it is convenient to convert the plans into annual equivalents. Suppose that the plant costs £100,000, that its life is initially estimated to be ten years, that the annual rate of return to be earned to justify the investment is 10 per cent, and that the net cash contribution earned from year to year seems likely to be constant over its life. Using the method described in Appendix I, we find the required level of the annual contribution as the annuity which will just recover the initial capital value over the whole period together with interest at 10 per cent per annum on the amount outstanding from time to time. Tables give this to be about £16,300. (We assume for convenience that each annual contribution comes in as cash at the end of each year.) Suppose that the plant is bought and the contributions earned are as hoped. In the first year, of the £16,300 contribution, £10,000 is budgeted 'profit' or return on the investment (this being 10 per cent of £100,000); and £6,300 is recovered in capital value, leaving £93,700 to be recovered in the later years. The latter figure could be entered in a budgeted

balance sheet as the value of the asset at the end of the first year, and the planning profit and loss account for the plant would show:

		£
Net operating revenue	.. .. ..	16,300
Less Depreciation (capital recovery)	..	6,300
Profit	.. ..	£10,000

The budgeted balance sheet would be as follows:

		£
Plant at cost	.. ..	100,000
Less Depreciation	.. .. ..	6,300
		93,700
Liquid funds	.. ..	16,300
		£110,000

		£
Capital invested in project ..	.. ..	100,000
Profit not yet withdrawn ..	.. ..	10,000
		£110,000

If, in the succeeding year, the original assumption continued to be justified, a £16,300 contribution would again be earned. Of this, £9,400 would be needed to return 10 per cent on the capital value of the plant at the beginning of the second year; the remaining £6,900 would represent recovery of capital value. The asset value at the end of the second year would be £86,800. If the original assumptions held, the capital value would, by the arithmetic of compound interest, be completely recovered by the end of the tenth year. (The arithmetic is that for the annuity method of depreciation.) We assume the residual value is zero.

30. I have given this example to illustrate the theoretical link, in a simplified case, between investment planning and budgeted annual profit calculations. The latter are inherent in the budgeting process; but they – and the intervening budgeted balance sheets – emerge as the result of assumptions (normal planning assumptions, appropriate in any capital budgeting committee) about the whole course of the investment and about the rate of return to be earned. It is, as you know, a maxim of good control that the form of accounting reports should follow that of the budgets which preceded them and on which they report. What has been said about the budgeted accounts applies, *mutatis mutandis*, to the

actual accounting reports, provided these are drawn up on the basis of the planning model and assumptions: if the results by some stroke of chance exactly match the budgets, the accounts will contain the same figures. Note that the profit for the first year can only be calculated after assumptions have been made about the cash flow over the whole succeeding nine years. There is no question of profit being objectively determined by the past. From the point of view of the management (and therefore, one may argue, of an investor) the basic data are those of the long run cash forecast. Note also that the profit figure does not tell one about the future unless one knows the assumptions on which it is drafted.

31. The next step is to consider the effect of a change in the assumptions during the course of the investment. Suppose that in the above example it was decided, at the end of the first year, that the original assumptions must be permanently revised. Let us say that the annual cash contribution earned by the asset will henceforth only be £12,000, and will run only for eight more years. Stated in the form of a cash budget this needs no further explanation. From a planning point of view there is no need to think any more about the originally budgeted figures. What is now important is whether the new pattern of return is worth while having regard to the money that could be obtained by disposing of the plant now: a new investment type of decision must be made. Let us suppose the net disposal value of the plant is set at £40,000: much lower than original cost or the earlier budgeted balance sheet value (because, we will suppose, the plant is very specialised). We will assume again that 10 per cent per annum must be earned to justify the investment (or, to be precise, to justify not dis-investing). Compound interest tables tell us that the annuity which will recover £40,000 with interest at 10 per cent per annum over eight years is about £7,500. As this will be more than covered by the expected annual contribution, the decision is taken to retain the plant. The implied value of the asset is now about £64,000. (This is the actuarial present value that is equivalent, at 10 per cent per annum, to an eight-year annuity of £12,000; £64,000 is the capital value which an annuity of £12,000 will just recover over eight years and give a 10 per cent per annum return on the unrecovered balance from year to year.) From a business point of view there has been, at the end of year one, a drop in value from £93,700 to £64,000: unexpected depreciation of £30,000. Again, the assessed capital value depends upon the expected future cash stream. The profit and loss account for year one is now:

				£
Net operating revenue	..	..	..	16,300
Less Depreciation	..	..	..	36,000
Loss	..	..	..	..	−*£19,700*

The balance sheet is as follows:

				£
Plant at cost	. .	. .	. .	100,000
Less Depreciation		. .	. .	36,000
				64,000
Liquid funds	. .	. .	. .	16,300
				£80,300
Capital invested in project		. .	. .	100,000
Less Loss	. .	. .	. .	19,700
				£80,300

One is tempted to say that most of the heavy depreciation is a special 'capital loss', to be omitted from the profit and loss account. But we are interested in the reality of the business: in the year in question, the board, on their own reckoning, have lost the company £20,000.

32. Now consider a conventionally prepared financial account for the project. This would, at the end of year one before it was found that the expectations must be revised, probably give the following information, assuming that, as is likely in practice, straight line depreciation was applied:

				£
Net operating revenue	. .	. .	. .	16,300
Depreciation . .	. .	. .	. .	10,000
Profit	. .	. .	. .	£6,300

				£
Plant at cost	. .	. .	. .	100,000
Less Depreciation		. .	. .	10,000
				90,000
Liquid funds	. .	. .	. .	16,300
				£106,300

				£
Capital invested in project		. .	. .	100,000
Profit not yet withdrawn	. .	. .	. .	6,300
				£106,300

This tells a story that has some resemblance to the planning figures used by the management. It suggests profitable operation. It is very far from giving an accurate picture of the true rate of return on the investment *on the assumptions adopted by the management*. It shows a rate of return on capital of only 6·3 per cent against 10 per cent in the management's own accounts. It is, in effect, telling the financial story on a different, and in this case more conservative, set of assumptions. What are these assumptions? The reader of the accounts cannot tell. He may deduce, by a little detective work, that a further life of nine years is assumed for the plant (even this information might be difficult to find in a real life case). He does not know on what rate of return the management are planning. In short the account merely gives a rather vague, general idea of how things are going. We may note that if all goes according to the original plan throughout the life of the plant, the later financial accounts will show a growth in the rate of return on the investment in the plant, whereas the planning assumptions are that it will remain constant.

33. How do the conventional accounting reports appear when the directors revise their expectations? The total cash recovery from year two to year nine will now be £96,000: £6,000 in excess of the book value of the asset in the financial accounts after deducting one year's straight-line depreciation. Hence I do not think we can assume that the asset will be revalued at the end of year one, though we cannot be sure of this. It is possible, though not certain, that the annual depreciation provision will be amended for the shorter life of the asset, the annual straight-line provision of £10,000 being adjusted to approximately £11,100 over nine years. It is also possible, though I think unlikely, that the directors will revalue the asset by writing it down to the figure justified by their planning assumptions. Let us compare the profit figures that will result from three alternative assumptions:

(1) that no change will be made in the depreciation provision;

(2) that the depreciation provision will be adjusted to a nine-year basis;

(3) that the asset will be revalued on the basis of the new planning assumptions and straight-line depreciation thenceforth written off on the new value over the revised life;

with:

(4) the profit figure that will result from using the arithmetic appropriate to our planning assumptions, that is, revising the asset valuation and depreciating on the annuity basis.

17

34. For convenience of comparison let us assume that no profit is distributed in any of the four cases, and that profit ploughed back, together with depreciation provisions, will earn interest in some other investment at 10 per cent per annum. We shall assume that planning expectations as revised at the end of year one are fulfilled exactly. The detailed figures are given in Appendix II. The final profit figures (in £s with minor rounding-off adjustments) are as follows:

Case 1. Asset not revalued and straight-line depreciation not revised
6,300 3,600 5,000 6,500 8,100 10,000 12,000 14,200 6,600

Case 2. Asset not revalued but straight-line depreciation revised
5,200 2,500 3,900 5,400 7,000 8,900 10,900 13,100 15,400

Case 3. Asset revalued and straight-line depreciation revised accordingly
−19,700 5,600 7,000 8,500 10,100 12,000 14,000 16,200 18,600

Case 4. Asset revalued and depreciation based on planning assumptions revised accordingly
−19,700 8,000 8,800 9,700 10,600 11,800 13,000 14,300 15,800

35. The differences in pattern corresponding to the different assumptions speak for themselves. When no adjustment is made in year one to reflect the significant drop in expected returns (as in cases 1 and 2) the profit reported for the first year is materially larger than that for the next two years. In particular the accounts suggest that a substantial distribution would be justified in the first year. The first series also produces a sharp drop in profit in the final year, a drop that does not correspond with the business facts. The other two series both bring out the setback in year one clearly, and thenceforth give the correct trends, though only the fourth series, with depreciation calculated on the annuity basis, reports in a form that corresponds with the investment assumptions and shows a return on capital in accordance with those assumptions when the investment goes according to plan. Perhaps the most significant point is that in year one in particular none of the series can be interpreted without a statement about the future expected cash flows.

36. It will be noted from the figures in Appendix II that over all the years the totals of the profits for the four cases are the same. This happens in this simplified example because we have assumed that no dividends are distributed (i.e. that dividend behaviour is not affected by the accounts) and because we have taken the

whole life of a single investment project. In real life the pattern of the profit reports may affect behaviour; moreover, business is a continuing process, and with different bases of profit calculation, reported profits may continue to differ in total over a lengthening series of years as well as from year to year.

37. I do not think that we can be very satisfied with principles that can produce such varying results, all of which are 'right'. It is sometimes said that such variations are not of great significance, for 'they will all come out in the wash'. In a large number of transactions, it may be said, the figures will tend to even out. I do not think that other professions would be prepared to accept such arguments: there is no evidence that such discrepancies do even out, and we are in fact ignorant about the effects on actual company reports of varying bases of profit calculation, both in the short and in the long period.

38. I do not wish to suggest that a mere change in the depreciation conventions selected, or the more frequent reconsideration by directors of depreciation provisions (and other matters such as the stock valuation), would be enough to put financial accounting statements as we now understand them on an entirely satisfactory footing. I think that the time is ripe for what is in some respects a more radical step, though one that need not cause a break in existing audit practice. For whatever conventions are used, however the acceptable accounting principles are amended, the traditional accounting forms of report – profit and loss account and balance sheet – must, I suspect, remain indifferent guides to action.

39. The main line for improvement lies, I believe, in the provision of financial information independently of the formal accounts, unshackled by the legal requirements that attach to them. It is for this reason that I think we should welcome and do our best to develop the important suggestion in paragraph 334 of the *Jenkins Report*, that accounts may need to be accompanied by supplementary information in order to give shareholders the true and fair view required by the Companies Act. It is true that this statement related specifically to limitations of historical cost as a basis for asset valuation; but this public recognition that formal accounting statements may require supplementation if business needs are to be satisfied may prove to be the first step on a path leading to a major development in financial practice. Once this principle is accepted the way is open for a movement towards providing shareholders (and of course managements) with the fundamental data of financial decisions: estimates of the

realisable value locked up in their companies' assets (needed to provide the basis for an assessment of the rate of return of dividends on the value of resources absorbed, and as an aid in the assessment of the company's current liquidity); forecasts of the future cash flows in the form, for example, of flow of funds budgets; and, we may hope, an interpretation of both by the management, more systematic and business-like, less amateurish, than what is too often found today in directors' reports and chairmen's statements.

40. In the following paragraphs I shall try to give you some idea of what I have in mind when I refer to estimates of realisable value and more systematic interpretation. I shall not say more about flow of funds budgets, for the concept is clear enough.

V Supplementary Information in Annual Reports

41. The take-over bid movement has taught us how important it is to tell shareholders what their company's assets are worth in the market. Saleable values of the less specialised kinds of assets – such as land and buildings – are an important factor in the liquidity position of the company, affecting its ability to raise cash quickly by sale, by mortgage, or sale and re-lease. When such assets form the major part of the undertaking's resources, the comparison of their realisable value (along with that of the other assets) with the flow of dividends produced and expected to be produced by the directors is a specially important part of the financial control. If the dividends are significantly low in relation to the realisable value, the time may have come to change the nature or methods of the business – or the directors: this is the kind of situation that attracts the take-over bidder.

42. It would, perhaps, be unduly expensive to have, for example, real property valued independently every year. Perhaps once in five or even seven years would be enough. In the intervening period the directors could report the approximate values they were assuming to guide their own decisions.

43. It is often argued, rightly, that the estimation of saleable value is difficult; and that wide margins of error are likely to arise. It would no doubt be right to warn shareholders that such valuations were no more than approximations. This is not, however, a reason for withholding such information as is available. One should not be frightened of approximations.

44. If the assets are specialised they may have a low saleable value in relation to their value in the business for which they were designed (provided it is profitable). In this case the realisation value has less significance. It can, however, be argued that share-holders – and creditors – should know what assets are not realis-able by sale, or available for charge, except at figures substantially lower than the balance sheet valuation, and should have some idea, however approximate, of the order of magnitudes involved.

45. The realisable values of assets are relevant in assessing potential liquidity, chargeable capacity, and the minimum return that should be earned. In the longer run, however, a business is not viable unless it can provide an adequate return on the finance needed to replace its assets. In interpreting the report, a financial analyst will wish, therefore, to relate dividends paid and expected to be paid to the net asset valuation on a replacement basis. The assessment of the latter figure raises difficulties, mainly arising from the fact that, in general, assets are not replaced in their existing form. As usual, therefore, we have to accept an approxi-mation. The simplest method is to take some estimate of the replacement value of existing assets. Perhaps the most direct way of obtaining an indication of this, for many assets, is to report their declared value for the purpose of fire insurance (a practice that I understand is being increasingly adopted in Holland). This is not wholly satisfactory, but precise figures are less important than figures which are reasonable indicators of the orders of magnitude involved. It is when the asset values are *grossly* out of line with business reality that balance sheets become seriously misleading.

46. It is a poor argument to say that shareholders could be confused or misled by such figures. This is undoubtedly true; but the answer is to provide reasoned explanations, in clear English, when necessary.

47. It will be generally agreed that the gearing of the financial structure of a company is of significance in an assessment of the possible effects of illiquidity, and of the degree of risk attached to investment in its shares and debentures. Financial gearing is often understood merely in the sense of the relation between fixed interest and dividends and the equity share of profit. The amounts of fixed interest and dividends are, of course, disclosed under the existing legal requirements. Bank overdrafts, and short-term loans, may also contribute to the gearing, however, and interest paid on these is not usually disclosed. The balance sheet may show that such loans exist: it certainly will not tell us what level they may

21

have reached during the year. There seems a good case for the disclosure of all interest paid, and not only that on longer term liabilities.

48. A more subtle kind of gearing may exist in the form of long-term contracts for the payment of lease rentals, royalties, and so on. Such contracts are obligations that must be honoured whatever the state of business; they have corresponding significance for liquidity and risk. I would argue that the shareholders should know of their existence and of the amounts involved when these are material.

49. An important factor in the assessment of a company's financial stability is the extent to which it may be called upon at short notice to repay existing finance, and the extent to which it has call on further finance. The balance sheet in its present form may give some indication of the first, though only as at a given moment of time. It does not on the other hand tell the reader the amount, for example, of agreed overdraft facilities that are available. A summary of any special financial commitments likely to arise during the ensuing year, and of new finance arranged, would be a helpful addition to the present form of report. Boards or their chairmen do in fact tend to give general information on such matters in their reports or speeches. It would be better, however, to give a summary of the main financing changes expected in the year to come, in the form of a statement of the anticipated receipts and payments.

50. If, as I have suggested, the profit figure reported for a given year, or even for each of a series of years, is in itself an uncertain indicator of the business prospects of the company, and if the most direct solution – the provision of a forecast in some detail of future cash flows – is ruled out, it becomes particularly important that the directors should draw the attention of shareholders to situations in which they think that recent profit reports are particularly poor indicators of the future. It is not possible to provide an exhaustive list of the situations in which such a statement might be appropriate, but the following are examples:

(*a*) Permanent changes in sales market conditions.

(*b*) Loss of important contracts.

(*c*) Important technological changes, bringing present equipment significantly nearer to obsolescence.

(*d*) Situations in which continued and significant additional expenditure on research, development or advertising are likely to be needed to maintain present sales figures or to prevent expenses from rising.

(*e*) The extent of additional finance that will probably be needed to maintain the existing volume of output as prices rise, presented each year as a supplement to the expenses shown (unless depreciation and cost of sales in the legal accounts already reflect this).

It is true that directors' reports and chairmen's statements often touch on such matters. But the comments are usually general and non-quantitative, and are often vague. Unless such statements are accompanied, year by year, by estimates in the form of the change in the annual cash flow expected to result, or the increase in finance needed, they are of unnecessarily limited value. Of course, such estimates cannot be precise, but they can indicate orders of magnitude.

51. In the absence of cash forecasts, it may be difficult or impossible to judge how successive years' profits are affected by the arbitrary apportionment of a cost or revenue to one year rather than another. The following are examples:

(*a*) The effect of a fall in price of raw material stocks below cost may vary considerably as between one year and the next, depending upon whether stock is valued at replacement cost or at net realisation value.

(*b*) Methods of reporting the profit on hire-purchase business vary, and can influence significantly the relation of one year's profit to that of succeeding years.

(*c*) A policy of writing off the cost of heavy production re-tooling in a given year can alter the pattern of reported profit significantly as compared with depreciating the cost over several years.

Some help is given to the reader of accounts if the method used in each case is explained, though one cannot assume that this will always be the case at present. The reader is not, however, able to judge the full significance of what is happening unless he is told the order of magnitude of the amounts involved. There seems no good reason why directors should not analyse profit in substantially more detail in order to bring out the full significance of the figures in such situations. They would expect this in management accounts prepared for them: why should not the shareholder be told too?

23

52. You may well feel after reading the previous paragraphs that I am inconsistent in asking for simplicity in presentation. However, there is, I think, no inconsistency, for I would not have these detailed explanations or analyses in the body of the accounting report. They could, I think, well be relegated to a separate board pamphlet that would not necessarily be sent to all shareholders: it could be restricted to those who asked for it. By using this device the accounts themselves could be considerably simplified. The major aim in this process of simplification should be, I think, to make the logical pattern of the account clearer to the intelligent layman by avoiding unnecessary jargon (some may be unavoidable) and adopting a simple narrative form of account. In particular one may hope that the present nonsensical division of free reserves into numerous sub-headings would be abandoned. In general it should, I suggest, be accepted that the choice of appropriate technical names for particular items, though of some relevance in achieving standardisation of terms, is not a substitute for description in good, clear English.

53. Two arguments that have been repeatedly put forward for more than one hundred years when pleas have been made for more information in accounts are:

(1) That competitors will learn too much, to the damage of the business that provides the information.

(2) That shareholders will be misled by the additional information they are given.

Both arguments are in my opinion of doubtful validity. As to the first, the disclosure works for everyone: If A. sees what B. is doing, B. also sees what A. is doing; and it is by no means obvious that it is against the public interest to make businesses aware what their neighbours are doing. The second argument has in my view even less to commend it. Non-expert shareholders can always read the financial Press or call on expert advice; and the deliberate withholding of knowledge is inconsistent with the basic principles of a free society.

54. Another argument that might be used is that some of the information I have described is not available to all directors. The answer to this is simple. If they have not the information, they are lacking in data they should possess in order to make their own management decisions. It would be as well that shareholders should know this.

55. On the other hand, it may reasonably be doubted whether the supplementary information I have mentioned could all be subject to audit. Some of it certainly could – for example the more

detailed analysis of profit earned on hire-purchase transactions –
but it would be more difficult to audit effectively directors'
estimates of the longer term effect of particular changes in business
conditions. I see, however, no great difficulty in separating audited
from non-audited figures: this is already achieved in prospectuses.
It would not be easy to legislate for all these matters; but I do not
see why they should not gradually become an accepted feature
of good company reporting.

56. Finally it may be said that much of the information I have
mentioned is of a very rough and approximate nature, tainted by
uncertainty. There is no doubt that this is the case. But in this it
differs in no way from the data on which nearly all human decisions are made. We have to accept the best information we can
get, poor though it may be. It may indeed be said that one of the
accountant's most useful functions is to find satisfactory methods
– principles if you like – for the approximate representation of
business reality.

APPENDIX I

The Use of Compound Interest and Annuity Formulae in Investment Choice

1. The use of these formulae is based on the fact that any investment (or capital expenditure) absorbs valuable resources that could have been used in some other way to produce an alternative cash flow. An investment is therefore only justified if the flow of cash it releases (that can be used for some other purpose) is enough to return the original money invested and in addition earn interest on the amount not yet recovered at as good a rate as can be earned in another investment of equal risk. In other words, the formulae can be used to express the maximum amount which can be spent on an investment such that the expected annual net cash return will just: (*a*) recover the amount invested, together with (*b*) interest at the selected target rate from year to year on the amount not yet recovered. Investment choice does not indeed depend on these calculations alone: a qualitative weighting has to be introduced, by judgement, for varying risks and other non-measurable factors. The calculations we are discussing are, however, a necessary step in the logic of choice – in assessing the quantitative implications of varying assumptions.

2. The nature of the calculations can be illustrated by taking a simplified example. Suppose that the problem is to find the maximum initial outlay (investment) justified on the assumption that the outlay will produce an expected net annual cash inflow (assumed as an approximation to arise on the last day of each year) of £1,000, over a period of three years. It is assumed that a rate of interest of 7 per cent per annum can be earned throughout the period on money invested in the best alternative way with the same degree of risk.

Let: the maximum initial outlay justified be C;

the annual percentage rate of interest to be earned be $100r = 7$;

the number of years be $n = 3$;

the net annual cash contribution be $d = £1,000$.

Then, in £s, $C = d[1/(1+r) + 1/(1+r)^2 + 1/(1+r)^3]$

or substituting figures:

$$C = 1,000 \, (1/1 \cdot 07 + 1/1 \cdot 07^2 + 1/1 \cdot 07^3)$$
$$= 2,624 \cdot 3 \text{ (from tables)}$$

This may be called the actuarial present worth or value.

27

Proof

	£
Initial outlay	2,624·3
Add interest at 7 per cent for year 1	183·7
	2,808·0
Cash received at end of year 1	1,000·0
Leaving outstanding at beginning of year 2 ..	1,808·0
Add interest at 7 per cent for year 2	126·6
	1,934·6
Cash received at end of year 2	1,000·0
Leaving outstanding at beginning of year 3 ..	934·6
Add interest at 7 per cent for year 3	65·4
	1,000·0
Cash received at end of year 3	1,000·0

3. Thus the annual return will justify an initial investment of £2,624, being just sufficient to recover this initial investment and provide interest at the required rate on the unrecovered amount from year to year.

4. The same principle can be applied where the annual expected receipt varies in amount over time, using the above formula, with d varying in each year.

Alternative formulation

5. Suppose the problem was to find the minimum annual net cash contribution receivable over three years which would justify an initial investment of £2,624, given a required interest rate of 7 per cent p.a. If d is the annual contribution (or 'annuity') we have, in £s:

$$d = 2,624/(1/1·07 + 1/1·07^2 + 1/1·07^3)$$
$$= 1,000.$$

6. Here the assumption we are making is that if £2,624 was available it would be possible by investing in another way to create a flow of £1,000 payable at the end of each of three years. Hence no lower annual receipt is acceptable in the investment being studied.

Recovery of part of capital value at end of period

7. If part of the initial value will be recovered at the end of the period the calculation can be split into two parts. Suppose that the proposed investment was £4,624 and that in the use envisaged £2,000 was expected to be recovered (e.g. in scrap or second-hand value) at the end of the period. The calculation proceeds as before for the non-recoverable part of the initial investment, £2,624. This leaves the second, recoverable, part, £2,000. The annual receipt required in respect of this part is merely interest at the assumed rate of 7 per cent, or £140. Hence we have:

Initial investment £	*Receivable at end* £	*Minimum annual receipt* £
2,624	—	1,000
2,000	2,000	140
£4,624	£2,000	£1,140

8. If we want, instead, to calculate the present worth of the items in the second and third columns, we proceed as follows, in £s:

$$\text{Present worth} = 1{,}140\ \left(1/1{\cdot}07 + 1/1{\cdot}07^2 + 1/1{\cdot}07^3\right) + 2{,}000/1{\cdot}07^3$$
$$= 4{,}624$$

the truth of which can be checked from 7 per cent tables.

APPENDIX II

Year	Net Operating Revenue (Cash Flow)	Interest on Surplus Funds at 10 per cent p.a.	Total Revenue	Depreciation				Net Profit				Total Capital invested at End of Year on Planning Assumptions*
				Case 1	Case 2	Case 3	Case 4	Case 1	Case 2	Case 3	Case 4	
1	16,300	—	16,300	10,000	11,100	36,000	36,000	6,300	5,200	-19,700	-19,700	80,300
2	12,000	1,600	13,600	10,000	11,100	8,000	5,600	3,600	2,500	5,600	8,000	88,300
3	12,000	3,000	15,000	10,000	11,100	8,000	6,200	5,000	3,900	7,000	8,800	97,100
4	12,000	4,500	16,500	10,000	11,100	8,000	6,800	6,500	5,400	8,500	9,700	106,800
5	12,000	6,100	18,100	10,000	11,100	8,000	7,500	8,100	7,000	10,100	10,600	117,400
6	12,000	8,000	20,000	10,000	11,100	8,000	8,200	10,000	8,900	12,000	11,800	129,200
7	12,000	10,000	22,000	10,000	11,100	8,000	9,000	12,000	10,900	14,000	13,000	142,200
8	12,000	12,200	24,200	10,000	11,100	8,000	9,900	14,200	13,100	16,200	14,300	156,500
9	12,000	14,600	26,600	20,000	11,200	8,000	10,800	6,600	15,400	18,600	15,800	172,300
Total	112,300	60,000	172,300	100,000	100,000	100,000	100,000	72,300	72,300	72,300	72,300	172,300

*The total capital invested at the end of each year on the planning assumptions is: the balance sheet valuation of the asset at the beginning of the preceding year, *less* the depreciation for the year, *plus* the total of retained profit to date, *plus* accumulated depreciation to date, in each instance using Case 4 figures.

It will be noticed that (subject to minor differences due to rounding-off) the net profit for Case 4 is, from years 2 to 9, equivalent to 10 per cent on the total capital invested at the end of the previous year.

THE PRINCIPLES AND AIMS OF BUDGETARY CONTROL

Professor H. C. EDEY
Department of Accounting, The London School of Economics and Political Science

---

General nature of control

Control cannot properly be separated from planning. Unless you know where you want to go you cannot say how far you have strayed from your path. There are, no doubt, differences of opinion about the financial goals of business. Despite these, I think it can be assumed that for control purposes a business plan can be expressed in terms of three concepts: the initial endowment of resources; the potential flow of cash from the business to its owners from the beginning of the plan to some defined future date, or into the indefinite future; and the present value (to those owners) that is set upon that flow. The relation between the cash flow and the present value depends upon the other opportunities for investment available to the owners and the uncertainties of estimation. The relation is, for measurement purposes, expressed as a 'capitalization' or 'discount' rate. A financial objective can then be expressed in the form:

$$\text{Maximize } V - C$$

C being the initial investment – the value of the initial resources – and V being defined as follows:

$$V = \sum_{t=1}^{n} d_t (1 + r)^{-t}$$

where d_t is the cash flowing to the owner at time t, and r is the appropriate rate of discount in any given unit period ending at t, expressed as a rate per cent per unit period (t being an integer). The d's and r's are, of course, expectations.

Business planning then involves relating actions or sets of actions (which imply decisions) to possible values of d's and r's and, therefore, of V.

The general problem of control over the business activities as a whole can now be stated. It is to measure the changing value of V as the business moves through time and to relate this measurement to the figures that were planned earlier, with the objects of:

a   adjusting plans and decisions to the extent required by deviations from the initial assumptions and estimates;

b   improving future performance in planning and action by studying the causes of these deviations.

An important part of (b) is the experience gained of the performance of people; this involves establishing relations between financial measurements and personal responsibility, before and after the event. When we speak of 'costs' and 'revenues' it is to change in the set of cash flows, negative or positive, and to the equivalent in terms of the present value, that we should, I think, be referring —at any rate when we are concerned with management decisions as distinct from such legal matters as tax assessment and company law.

V is a function of the d's and r's. It should, therefore, be sufficient to control the values of these. I shall limit my discussion to the former.

The cash flow and long-run control

The rest of this paper will be concerned with the control of cash flow. The principle of control is to check actual results against the budget figures. But such a control cannot be left until after the event. You cannot wait twenty years, until a long-run plan is completed, in order to see what went wrong. It is like riding a bicycle: the corrections must be made as you go. This idea is familiar enough to engineers; but it raises formidable problems. Each year a re-budget for the succeeding years must be made to project the net cash flow and its major components in the light of the new conditions. These will, in general, differ from the old. At the same time, last year's figures are reported and compared with those in the original budget. These two operations cannot be divorced, unfortunately. It is easy enough to compare cash surpluses released this year with those projected for this year. A good deal can be done by way of detailed study of what went wrong. But what happened this year is nearly always inextricably linked with what will happen in later years. The causal links run over our conventional time divisions. The inter-temporal relationships can range from the obvious to the very subtle. A short-fall of cash this year may be due to the disruption of a production programme or even mere failure to send a bill to debtors. There may be no long-run effects. On the other hand, an excess of cash over budget in year 1 might be brought about by a policy of making inferior products: this could have a negative effect on cash flows for years into the future. The problem is to find out when such a cause-and-effect chain exists, and to evaluate it.

Apart from such interrelationships, the long-run budget must be adjusted for those changes in the assumptions on which the original figures were based that have become apparent during the current year, whether these changes arise out of the technical, economic, social or political environments, or arise from decisions within the business, such as may result from changes in staff or policy, or simply from growth in knowledge. There does not seem to be any standard procedure by which this kind of problem can be tackled. The important thing seems to be: to be aware of its existence and in particular to provide for as thorough a continued monitoring of the assumptions on which the long-run plan is based as is practicable. This suggests the desirability of establishing check-lists of the important assumptions underlining the long-run projections so that the budgets can be examined periodically for continued validity in the light of current conditions. The check-lists will cover, in addition to the appropriate rate of discount for valuing the cash flow and future rates of interest for borrowing, which may affect the choice of plans and the overall optimization decisions, such matters as the external economic conditions that affect the relative prices of inputs and outputs, the aggregate demand for outputs and inputs, the tax law, the physical environment, internal know-how and organizational arrangements.

The planning procedures, whether these be rule of thumb and trial and error, or more subtle operational research methods, must be applied to the new conditions in the light of the main objectives so that a new expected cash flow can be projected. We can then, in principle, compare the cash flows of the current year and of all future years: as originally projected; and as now re-budgeted; and search for the causes of the variances. I believe such principles will be applied in the control procedures of the future, though I have no doubt that the monitoring and re-budgeting will be by computer program and will be continuous throughout the year. At present the procedure is crude and empirical and often neglected.

The accounting reports

Accounting procedures must be considered here for they are used widely as a substitute for, or in conjunction with, the type of procedure I have just outlined. At first glance the figures the accountant provides seem to avoid the problems I have indicated, for they can relate to a single year and they appear to provide directly for the comparison of the V's of our model, budgeted and actual, without the necessity for breaking-down the formulation into the d stream and the discounting rates r. This is done by substituting for our total value V, an alternative figure for the interest of the residual owners, which we may call

V', found by classifying all the business resources, positive and negative, into discrete classes ('assets' and 'liabilities'), recording value changes in these on the basis of standardized rules, and summing the results algebraically. The change in V' from any management action or succession of actions —such as the conduct of the whole enterprise for a year—is very far from being the same figure as the corresponding change in V from the same action, as the management will assess it. There are two reasons: the standard accounting procedures (the ultimate foundation of which must be sought in legal rules) are not closely related to future expectations—yet as we have seen the present and the future cannot, in general, be separated; asset changes which are recorded do not usually include any residual change in the value of the undertaking, such as may be due to improvements or deteriorations in the general conditions, internal or external, under which the firm operates. What we call accounting profit is no more than the measured change, from one date to the next, in the value V', after deducting or adding, as the case may require, payments made between the firm and its owners. The major limitation of this figure as a measure of success and as a control figure is now, I hope, apparent.

Short-run control

We are far from solving satisfactorily the problem of long-run control, whether we are considering the control of the whole firm and the assessment of the effectiveness of top management, or the control of capital budgets (which by definition involve the long-run) and the effectiveness of those responsible for these budgets. The position with respect to short-run control—control in which we concentrate our attention mainly on the cash flow in the current year and the near future—is somewhat happier.

Few businesses can claim financial success on the basis of one year's results; but the space of one year is ample for such an adverse deviation from plan as can be very serious for the future of the business or even completely disastrous, for example, through failure to foresee cash deficits, or careless use of resources. The control of the operations of a given year forms an important part—indeed a major part—of the longer-run control, in that changes in the assumptions that have been made for the purpose of the longer-run plans can be thrown up by the short-run control methods, thus contributing to the completion of the check-lists which I have already mentioned.

Standard costing and flexible budgets

The basic control tools used by modern accountants are standards and flexible budgets. The standard control systems described in text books are usually extremely simple in their essential ideas, but often unduly intricate arithmetically in that instead of a few simple indicators being produced, reports contain a mass of figures the interpretation of which may well distract attention from more fundamental questions. We are not clever enough yet to use any but very simple costing systems. The really important elements, as I see them, in standard costing (or standard profit control, as it might be better to call it) can be stated quite shortly. First, we have the laying down clearly of specifications of the operation or process whose cost we wish to control, in terms of operational layouts, material usage, labour requirements and so on, the money value equivalent of these being arrived at by applying to the physical quantities appropriate price or wage rates, or such other standard money amounts per period of time as are believed to reflect in a satisfactory way the use of resources.

Another essential element of the system is the continuous monitoring of the standards once they have been established. There is no reason why this monitoring should not sometimes be carried out by some kind of sampling process—there is, I believe, much scope for the application of systematic sampling methods in the field of cost accounting. It will be better sometimes to monitor easily measurable physical quantities (such as labour hours) together with the assumptions by which these have been converted into value (for example, the wage rate structure and the mix of labour categories used on a particular job), than to attempt to work out in full the value equivalents.

Another fundamental of control by standards is that only significant variances from standards are reported, so that the management do not have their time wasted by voluminous reports about everything. Finally, the variances must be reported as soon as they happen, when it is easiest to interpret them and to apply the lessons learnt.

The term 'flexible budget' is usually applied to expense standards relating to the whole activity of a given section of the business for a given period, whereas standard costs and revenues usually relate to a particular operation or process, or unit of output. As the name implies, such a budget is not so much a single standard as a set of standards, each relevant for a particular level of activity. It expresses, therefore, the 'cost function' for the activity under specified conditions: the variation in total cost as the level of activity changes.

Both of these devices, by breaking down the components of cost into detailed classifications, e.g. according to function and responsibility, and by the various inputs purchased and used, can provide for the analysis of variances between actual and budgeted figures in ways that can be extremely illuminating.

Contributions and allocations

A major development in management accounting in recent years, that affects the setting of standards and the construction of flexible budgets (though it has relevance also for long-run control), has been the acceptance of what may be called the 'contribution approach' to planning and control. The essence of this approach is that, in any choice between alternative actions, attention should be directed towards an assessment of the variation in the economic position of the enterprise caused by choosing one action rather than the other, and not to mere book-keeping figures. In terms of my decision model, this means that the essential consideration is the difference in V that will result from the decision, or, if we assume all the r's unchanged, in the values of the d's—the cash flow: rather than the difference in V', the conventional accounting valuation, or in conventional sub-decisions of V'. The irrelevance of so-called 'allocations' of overhead cost in choosing between production of product X or product Y is gradually becoming accepted. The old concepts of the 'total cost' of a product made up of prime cost plus an overhead allocation, and of 'overhead absorption', are giving way to the concepts of the avoidable cost involved in any given decision and of the total contribution towards non-allocable expenses and profit. The really difficult problem arises from the interdependence of most of the activities of business. I have already discussed interdependence through time. Similar, though somewhat less intractable (and unavoidable, even in much short-run control), is the problem of interdependence between activities in the same period. Budgetary control involves, among other things, the relating of variations in cost or revenue to changes, or possible changes, in plans, with the object of helping to determine whether the latter are justified. The cost and revenue standards and flexible budgets, and their relationships to the reported results, give first approximation answers. But neither standards nor budgets can be correct unless we can assume that the conditions for which they are valid hold, and that no change elsewhere in the business has affected the assumptions on which they are based. Standards and budgets can only be valid under a limited range of conditions: and it is in most circumstances impossible to specify these fully. Allowances must be made for this in the interpretation of reports of variances. This, it seems, must often be a matter of judgement.

Control by responsibility

We usually want to test the relationships between particular financial outcomes and the men responsible for particular functions. A special case of this is the control over the outcome of the whole business which reflects the capacity of management. This kind of control is, as I have already said, only effective to the extent that we can effect-ively take long-run considerations into account, or rule them out.

The time interdependence problem can be re-duced by reducing the responsibility of the person concerned to specified actions within a given period. It is possible to impose very precise financial limits on action, for example, by specify-ing what he can spend under each of a stated set of heads and by defining in detail what resources he is to end the period with. It is much more difficult to define sufficiently precisely the way a man is to exercise his function—the quality of his work. And control of this kind can only operate by limiting severely his freedom of choice, with all the consequential effects in damping incentive and encouraging conformity.

At the other end of the spectrum is the exercise of control at the most general level by placing resources of stated value under the control of the manager responsible for a function and merely requiring him to produce a specified cash flow. The problem of control here is exactly that which arises in the control of the actions of top manage-ment: normally the time interdependences make any short-run financial assessment almost ir-relevant in itself. In practice the control must usually lie somewhere between these extremes. A target may be set of the long-run type indicated by the decision model; but the manager must also get his annual budgets approved in detail, which implies that the short-run cash flows are under fairly close supervision, as is the general structure of his assets and liabilities.

The interdependences inside the business further complicate the issue. We are all familiar with the problem that arises when A's budget is overspent, but the fault is B's or C's. Good sense and judge-ment are needed.

Where the interdependences are serious, a solution may be sought by the use of transfer pricing: if A's division provides services to other parts of the business, or sells or buys goods to or from them, a price may be set upon these, to be taken into account in the financial results of both sides. Such arrangements may be effective in reducing the amount of detail control, emphasis being switched to aggregate results. The trouble with such arrangements is that they can, through the incentives they give to the managers concerned, easily lead to non-optimal results when considered in relation to their effect on the whole business. However, some managements might consider the advantage in terms of liveliness gained by these methods to more than compensate for any loss that might be avoided with more detailed control. It may be noted that the accountant's conventional end-period valuations are a kind of inter-period transfer pricing, the manager selling, so to speak, his resources to the new period at the accountant's valuations. Like other transfer prices, their care-less use can easily lead to non-optimal actions.

Conclusion
It is evident that financial control is still very much an art. The good control method is perhaps that which promotes awareness of the problems involved.

The Nature of Profit

Harold Edey

Recent discrepancies in profit figures reported by different managements with regard to the same transactions have led to increasing advocacy of the view that the rules of computation of company profits should be standardised, and further, that the bases used and assumptions made in particular cases should be stated, so that those who rely on the figures can draw their own conclusions.

The case for disclosure of basic methods and assumptions seems indeed unanswerable. However, in the discussion that has taken place there have been indications of a belief in some quarters that a method of accounting can be found – perhaps by suitable research – that, if applied in any given case, will produce a unique and objectively determined 'correct' or 'true' figure of profit. It is the aim of this paper (which contains little that is new) to show that this belief is fallacious and to suggest that thought and effort on the reform of company accounts would be better directed towards defining and improving the quality of the various pieces of information that they contain, on which useful analysis can be based, than in attempting to establish a formula for the calculation of 'true' profit.

The uses of profit statements

Profit calculation is not based on a law of nature. It is a human activity, carried out for a human purpose. The method used, and the kind of assumptions on which the calculation is based, should be determined by the end desired. The first step in a discussion of the bases of profit calculation is, therefore, to ask why the measurement is wanted. If an aim or aims can be clearly established, the next step is to consider what kind of figures, and how calculated, are likely to achieve these aims. The rules of calculation – the accounting procedures – that seem likely to do the best job can then be formulated.

However, it does not follow that all the objects desired can in fact be achieved. Some of the disappointment with accounting statements that at present exists is almost certainly due to expecting more of them than they can in their nature give. The onus is therefore upon accountants to be clear in their own minds about the meaning of their profit statements, and to draw attention with force and clarity to the nature, significance and limitations of their figures.

The accounting aims to be considered here are those that arise out of the company-shareholder relationship. The objects of company accounts are from time to time said, explicitly or by implication, to fall under one or other of the following heads: to enable shareholders or other investors to form a realistic view of the value of a company's shares – this may be called the 'share valuation' aim; to enable investors to judge the efficiency of the directors – the 'measure of management success' aim; to provide shareholders with an account of stewardship and determine how much can properly be distributed in dividend – the 'stewardship' aim. These aims to some extent overlap, but it is helpful to distinguish them for the purpose of discussion.

It is not necessary to decide whether company accounts are for shareholders only or for all investors, since all shareholders are investors and they (or their financial advisors) can be presumed to need the kind of information that other investors also want. In this paper the word 'investor' will do service for both. Moreover, discussion of the basis of profit calculation has as much relevance to profit forecasts, which may be intended for investors other than the present shareholders of the company concerned, as to statements for past periods.

Share valuation

As any reader of the financial press knows, daily use

is made of figures of reported profit, alone or as an element of a price-earnings ratio, as evidence in deciding the value which it is suggested buyers or sellers should place on the shares of the company concerned. The way in which these matters are presented in the press, in stockbrokers' circulars, and the like suggests that some analysts at least assume that past profit reports have – or can have – a strong predictive value with respect to future benefits from holding the shares in question. There is, so far as I know, no empirical evidence that this is true in general. (Perhaps the best negative evidence is the relative scarcity of millionaire accountants.) This paper, however, is concerned with the rational basis for such a belief. To examine this it is necessary to start by considering what it is that determines the market behaviour of investors.

The price which a person is willing to offer or accept for a share in a stock exchange transaction or in a private deal normally depends, so far as the attributes of the share are concerned, upon his expectation of benefits which the share is likely to yield in future, and upon the degree of certainty with which he holds that expectation. The benefits expected normally comprise one or more of the following: a flow of dividends; a dividend in liquidation or a receipt in a capital reduction; the proceeds of a sale when the investment is finally realised. The benefits expected under one or more of these heads, taken together, comprise the cash flow which the investor hopes for from his investment. (The benefits may, of course, be subject to tax, depending upon the tax status of the investor; but this is a separate question.) Insofar as such a cash flow includes future proceeds of realisation, its amount will depend upon someone's expectations of further benefits, as estimated at the time of realisation. It may appear at first therefore that the value of a share can depend, so far as the benefits from holding it are concerned, on nothing more substantial than a chain of expected future realisable values, so that the share value is held up, so to speak, by its own bootstraps. It is true that for a time the capital value of a share can be held up by speculation alone unsupported by realistic dividend expectations, in the sense that the price which a buyer is willing to pay depends upon the belief that others will later buy at a higher price. But in the longer run capital value will not be maintained unless there is a reasonable hope of dividends or capital distributions, as more than one investor has learned to his cost. Expectations of future distributions are therefore the ultimate source of share values.

Insofar therefore as an investor or an investment analyst is acting rationally in regarding the profit figure reported in the company's accounts as a predictor of share value, logic seems to require – unless perhaps he is concerned merely with short-run price rises which may depend upon the way other people interpret profit figures – that it is because this figure is thought by him to indicate in some way the level of future distributions by the company or changes in the capacity of the company to make such distributions. It is necessary therefore to consider how far this is or can be the case.

In the longer run, the ability of a management to provide dividends or to build up to an ultimate capital return – that is, to provide sooner or later a flow of money or a lump sum payment of money to the shareholder – rests upon the management's ability to generate cash receipts in excess of cash outgoings. This is evidently not necessarily true in any one given year or even over a given number of years, since cash that has been raised by issuing further shares, by borrowing, by realising assets or from previous business operations can, provided the profit and loss appropriation account still has a credit balance, be used to pay current dividends. This is so even at a time when very much larger cash amounts are being spent on extending capital equipment, on development, on expanding working capital, and so on.

If, in the latter case, the expenditure is successful, the fact will be evidenced in due course by a rise in the annual rate of inflow of cash from operations, providing finance for raising of dividends so that they are commensurate with the earlier rise in the amount of the shareholders' resources committed. The profit and loss account will at some time begin to reflect the higher revenue. At this stage the process can be repeated, and so on. In practice the process may be more continuous, with new commitments being made before earlier ones bring in the full annual flow of cash expected from them.

Things may however go wrong. Cash incomings may remain obstinately below outgoings, or be so little above them as to provide an inadequate return on money that could, had an earlier expansion not been undertaken, have been diverted to the shareholders' pockets; or to the extent that the money was borrowed, be inadequate for repayment or at least to justify the risk imposed by the borrowing on the shareholders. In such a case the annual profit figures will, sooner or later, begin to reflect the worsened situation, in that they will fail to rise to an extent justified by earlier capital expenditure and growth in working capital, and may even fall. Sooner or later dividends will fall or fail to rise as originally intended. On the other hand the cash flow may in due course exceed expectations, and the profit figure and dividends rise accordingly.

All this is, of course, commonplace to accountants.

What is crucial, and has received less consideration, is the point of time at which success or failure begins to show in a clear way in the profit figure. This is as important for good news as for bad news, as may be seen by considering the point of view of shareholders who sell their shares.

An extreme example often clarifies a point. One of the worst types of financial failure arises when it is found, from one day to the next, that stock inventories and debtors cannot hope to realise more than a small fraction of their balance sheet worth. It is quite possible for such a situation to be preceded by a series of favourable – perhaps extremely favourable – annual profits, so that the profit figure itself is far from suggesting that cash flows to the company – and thence dividends and share values – are in danger. This message can only get through to the profit and loss account by management anticipation of what is going to happen, leading to the creation· of the necessary provisions. The current profit report cannot be better than the management's own anticipations. Hopefully in such an extreme situation there will be evidence on which the auditors can judge that the management are being unduly optimistic, or careless, or fraudulent. This does not alter the fact that the quality of the profit figure as an indicator depends upon someone's opinion with respect to the future – in this case the short-run future; and different people will hold different opinions, with differing degrees of confidence; and they may arrive at conclusions at different points of time.

What is true in the extreme case and in the short run is equally true in the more normal case and in the longer run. The company's flow of cash in the future – on which the future dividend flow and the value of the shares depends – is bound up with the use of the existing set of resources, real, money and human. The only way in which the current reported profit can reflect the future is through the effect on it of someone's expectations of the results of this use – normally the management's since the figure appears in their account. As a matter of book-keeping this happens through the recording of changes in the balance sheet figure of the resources – the 'net asset value' – in the light of those expectations.

To a limited extent present practices and conventions allow this to happen, and indeed require it. If, for example, it has become clear to management that a fixed asset is unable to contribute a return in future that will cover at least its current book value it is (or should be) written down. The profit falls accordingly (if the loss is debited to current profit and not to reserve) and the message is given. If the management are on the ball in their accounting there need be little time lag between the rise of the new

opinion on the asset's value and the effect in the shareholders' accounts. The example suggests, however, how limited is the scope of the present profit and loss account in this respect. If an expected fall in future cash flows can be related to a particular asset and is such that the asset will not recover its book value, the effect can be recorded. But none of the following happenings will, in the general way, be reflected in any provision or in the profit balance: (a) a change in expectations with respect to a particular asset that does not bring the present value of that asset below its balance sheet value; (b) a change in expectations that reduces the present value of an asset that has not been recorded in the balance sheet at all, though hitherto it has been thought to have significant earning capacity; this includes a loss in general earning capacity that does not call for a reduction in the value at which particular assets are recorded in the balance sheet, that is to say, a fall in the present value of goodwill; (c) a change in expectations that raises the present value of a particular asset, or the net assets as a whole including goodwill, above the conventionally acceptable figure for balance sheet purposes.

The kernel of the matter is that a profit figure that reflected changes in future cash flows, and therefore growth (or decay) in the business sense (as distinct from the purely book-keeping sense), would have to be based on an assessment of those very flows – that is to say, on a budget forecast of the cash account of the company for some shorter or longer period. On the basis of this the shareholder could assess for himself the present value of the company's shares. A comparison of the assessment of current value with a similar one made at the beginning of the accounting period would lead to a statement of 'profit'. This would be to assess profit on the basis of an annual valuation of the company (or its shares) as a whole, with all that that implies. Profit in this sense would not be calculated prior to the valuation process, but on the contrary would emerge from it, and would have little relation to profit in the ordinary accounting sense.

This is not to say that annual accounts in their present form, and based on the present type of assumptions, have no relevance in judgement of future cash flows or of share values. A consideration of the basic information needs in the process of share valuation does, however, demonstrate the severe, and to a considerable extent, arbitrary, limitations of the profit figure as at present conceived – limitations that would persist even if rules of procedure were completely standardised – as an indicator of future growth; and it shows too the dangers in the present extensive and loose use of figures of earnings per share and price-earnings ratios.

It is not even the case that the figure of profit in the annual accounts can be assumed to be a reliable indicator in the sense of always moving up (or down) when a careful management assessment suggests an improvement (or worsening) in future expected dividend flows. It is easy to construct examples to demonstrate this point.

Profit as a measure of management success

It may be said that the usefulness of the profit figure to investors depends upon its quality as test of past management success, rather than upon any ability to predict or suggest the future. This may appear at first a more hopeful line of enquiry, if only because so much accounting literature has insisted upon the objectivity or 'factual' nature of accounting profit as an historical record. It is certainly possible to pick very simple cases where the profit calculation can be made objective and meaningful. The financial success of a once-for-all venture can be demonstrated by totalling the cash payments to and from the owners over the life of the venture; the net difference between these will equal the sum of recorded profits (inclusive of any adjustment on final liquidation). This indeed is true of any completed venture, however long its period; though as the period lengthens it becomes increasingly important, when interpreting the result, to apply price-index corrections so that amounts of cash paid in and cash returned at different dates are brought to a common purchasing power standard; and also to apply a compound interest rate of return test (a 'DCF' test) to allow for the fact that invested resources have an opportunity cost in terms of the interest or profit from other possible uses that have been foregone.

The objectivity disappears, however, as soon as the test has to be applied to a going concern in which a significant part of the cash flow to the owners, on which the test of efficiency depends, lies in the future. At the end of any accounting period there are, in most companies, substantial commitments to the future, the ultimate financial results of which will be decisive in assessing the success of the present management.

It would, of course, be possible to ignore all assets but cash in the closing balance sheet. This would reduce the convention of profit calculation for the business as a whole to the textbook method for very speculative ventures – write off all expenditure as it is incurred and take credit for revenue only when received in cash. This method would come nearer to producing objectivity (though provisions for liabilities would still have to be estimated), subject to the price-level and discount factor adjustments already referred to; but it would fail to distinguish between managements who had brought their companies to the threshold of a brilliant future from those who had done less well, and thus would fail in its basic object.

The existing conventions of profit measurement do provide for an assessment of sorts of the state to which the company has been brought by its directors at the end of any accounting period. As the preceding section has already shown, however, these procedures cannot, by their nature, provide the kind of assessment of the future that is needed for the purpose under discussion; and so far as they provide any indication of the future of the company, they are not objectively determined, but depend upon management opinion and upon the planning assumptions of management, whether these are explicitly formulated and written down or not (for assets that under one plan are reasonably expected to recover their original cost and more, may, under a different plan, be worth no more than scrap). The difficulty here is not a practical one, but is fundamental, arising out of the nature of the problem. A change in a company's capacity to earn positive cash flows may not be related to any change in the assets recorded in the balance sheet under the present type of convention, and the accepted procedures do not require mention of the director's views on this question. Yet it may be much more significant in judging their relative success than any reported change. The results will no doubt ultimately appear in the published accounts. But by the time that the change in the cash flows affects the accounts significantly, the knowledge of the change may have become available in other ways.

The estimation of future cash flows, including future expected dividends, or even of estimated changes in the value of the concern as a whole, based upon such estimates, seems the only way in which the theoretical measurement difficulty could be met; and since such assessments would be made by management (and are indeed being made by some managements as part of the normal process of management control), the test of management efficiency would be based upon subjective assessments made by the persons whose degree of success was being tested. There seems no way out of this difficulty.

It is tempting to believe that the problem of estimating the potential cash flows of the future, which determine the value which the directors have, so to speak, handed on to future years, could be met by a system of management audit, under which an independent management auditor would assess the correctness of the directors' views on this matter. 'Correctness' has, however, no place here, for there is no yardstick with which to measure: it is merely one man's views against another's. Such an approach also assumes that someone outside the central management can, in the general case, exercise as good judgement on these matters as members of that management – a view that will be rejected by many.

The conclusion seems to be that accounting profit reports based on anything like the present conventions are not, and probably cannot be more than rough and, generally speaking rather unreliable, gauges of management efficiency; moreover, so far as they do provide such a gauge, there will tend to be a time lag of unpredictable length before the profit figure reflects important changes in the company's circumstances – a lag that may be so great that outside events demonstrate management success or failure well before the accounts give a clear signal.

Stewardship

It is the received view in professional accounting circles that company accounts are accounts of stewardship. Under this view it is the directors' duty to report honestly and fairly to the shareholders what they have done with the shareholders' money. This duty to account extends to explaining what resources have been obtained by issuing capital or borrowing and how these have been used. In its simplest form such an account could well consist of nothing more than a summarised cash account together with a list of liabilities incurred and of real and monetary assets acquired, with no attempt at valuation and no attempt at profit measurement.

This is of course a narrow view of stewardship: it explains what has been done with the owners' resources, but does not show the result of the use. A more demanding idea of stewardship would call for a justification of the use made of shareholders' funds and a statement of the value created by their use. At the limit such a view would require an estimate of the value of the undertaking as a whole at balance sheet date. This comes back to the ideas already discussed in the preceding sections.

Somewhere in between these two extreme views of stewardship is the idea that has emerged and is used in practice. Under this the stewardship account gives from year to year an account of the ownership funds that have been raised and of the obligations that have been incurred, and conveys by means of rough and ready rule of thumb 'valuations' of assets some indication of the resources remaining under the control of the directors. In this account the 'values' shown in the balance sheet are clearly understood by accountants to lack any precise significance when taken as a whole. The most that can be said about them in general is that (if the accounts are properly drawn up)

the value of the net assets recorded is not more than will, in the directors' view, be recovered in future periods, though much more may be recovered. The year to year comparison of this net 'value' (with adjustment for owners' funds paid in or distributed), determines the figure reported as 'profit'.

The auditors report whether the accounts are true and fair. It follows from the foregoing that in this phrase the word 'true' should be read in its restricted sense of 'honest', while 'fair' should be read to mean that the usual rules accepted by accountants have been fairly applied. True and fair accounts are those that have been drawn up honestly and with a reasonable standard of care on the basis of conventions acceptable in current accounting practice, consistently applied. A re-wording of the standard form of audit report on some such lines as these might save much misunderstanding.

The idea of a precise indicator of, or even of a best guess at, the total economic and financial state of the company or of changes in this – the kind of indication that would interest an active investor – plays no part in the conception of company accounts that has led to their present form and nature. This conception was largely formed as the result of nineteenth century legal argument, arising in part from disputes between ordinary and preference shareholders as to the amount of dividends that should be distributed, and the argument was conducted within a narrow interpretation of stewardship. The aim of the judges in laying down the rules for dividend distribution that are now accepted, and on which the present conventions of profit calculation to a large extent depend, seems to have been to arrive at workable and honest solutions to a practical problem, solutions that would respect the rights of shareholders of different classes and of creditors. The judges did not concern themselves with any attempt to arrive at an accurate assessment of the company's current economic worth, or to assess the quality of directors' past performance.

Until 1929 there was no statutory requirement to present an annual profit and loss account, and until 1948 there was no requirement for full disclosure of profit. Until the early 'thirties the whole spirit of accounting practice, backed up by the law, was directed, so far as profit calculation was concerned, to seeing that it had been carried out honestly, under established legal rules, and that there was no over-reporting. It was accepted that 'commercial judgement' must enter largely into profit calculation. It was important that balance sheet asset values should not be over-stated or liabilities under-stated, but under-statement of net asset value was another matter: secret reserves were acceptable, even commendable.

A major shift of opinion took place as the result of

the *Royal Mail* case in 1931. It became accepted that the non-disclosure of profit might be as serious an evil as over-statement, especially if profit that would have been reported under the normal accounting procedures was concealed and reported in a later year in order to make things at that later date look better than in fact they were. This led in due course to the present rules regarding reserves and provisions which appeared in the law for the first time in the Companies Acts of 1947 and 1948, the way for these having been paved by the Recommendations on Accounting Principles issued for the first time by the Institute of Chartered Accountants in England and Wales in 1942.

These changes in the law and practice did not – and this is important – impinge on the basic procedures used in the calculation of profit. They merely meant that profit calculated under the practical rules of thumb that had been developed in the nineteenth century was to be fully disclosed. Secret reserves still existed and exist now: assets can be and commonly are recorded at values far below the value which would reasonably compensate the company concerned for losing them; goodwill seldom appears, however good the dividend-paying prospects of the company may be; profit certainly does not in general show the growth in the company's value as a business man would assess it in the process of deciding whether to sell or buy an interest in the company. Nor, for the reasons already discussed, could it do so on any objective basis.

This is not to say that company accounts are useless, and certainly not to say that any attempt at making them more useful is wasted effort. It is however right to assert more clearly, for the benefit of all who use such accounts, their fundamental and unavoidable limitations and at the same time to stress what they can do, and might do even better with some reform. The first and perhaps most important point to be made to the public at large is that no one figure or set of figures appearing in a set of accounts should lead to final conclusions. The function of the accounts is best conceived as that of raising in the minds of those who read and study them useful *conjectures* about the company's financial state and progress – conjectures which can be related to knowledge about the company obtained in other ways and which can lead to further enquiries. The study of accounts should lead to the formulation of questions rather than to answers. Least of all can a firm conclusion be drawn from a price-earnings ratio the denominator of which can, by its nature, be given no precise economic or business significance.

The kind of analysis that can lead to fruitful conjectures is based on the examination of such simple things as changes over time in ratios of current assets to current liabilities and in the respective proportions of stock, debtors and cash in current assets, the relation of loan capital to the total mortgageable value of assets (if it can be ascertained), the growth in sales value and in sales volume over time and changes in this rate of growth. The study of the various elements that make up the profit balance and of their relations to one another, to earlier figures and to various balance sheet figures are of much greater significance than the final balance itself.

It seems to follow from the above that reform and improvement in company accounting should be directed towards helping this kind of analysis by providing well-defined figures on which it can be based. Two matters seem of particular importance. The first is the urgent need to provide, on a systematic basis, information on the effect of inflation on the various elements of the profit figure, notably those relating to stock consumption and depreciation, and indeed more generally to move towards reporting in constant price level terms, even if this is only in the form of supplementary statements prepared on a reasonably standardised basis. The second is the need to move towards the provision, as a matter of course, of clear statements of the bases and assumptions on which the accounts have been prepared. The importance of establishing standard accounting practices lies in my opinion here, rather than in the will-of-the-wisp hope of producing figures of accounting profit that are both 'objective' and 'correct'.

The True and Fair View

Harold Edey, London School of Economics

Our present accounting methods come down to us from our nineteenth-century predecessors. The corporate form of enterprise for ordinary business was then new. Our predecessors had to decide how to settle, year by year, the size of the profit fund from which dividends might be paid. Their criterion of profit involved the measurement of the capital value of the enterprise. It is interesting to refer to the Great Western Railway's private Act of 1835. Dividends could be declared from the 'clear Profits' of the company, and 'no Dividends shall be made exceeding the net Amount of clear Profit at the time being in the Hands of the said Company, nor whereby the Capital of the said Company shall in any degree be reduced or impaired'.

The need to measure capital value made it necessary to establish rules or conventions for practical use. These developed as working rules of thumb, conservative in their effect, tending towards under-statement.

Judges were called upon from time to time to express views upon these methods. When they did so they tended to follow the accountants' practice, adding glosses and giving judicial blessings to methods that have hardened into the normal accounting practice that we all know today. I think we can infer that the nineteenth century judges and accountants were well aware that they were not setting up a foundation of absolute truth, but rather were establishing reasonable working rules, rough perhaps, but to be applied honestly and without bias.

Then, as now, it was accepted that within the general rules (or principles) so established there must be application of personal judgement – for example, to such matters as the value to be set upon stock in trade, or debtors, or the extent to which development expenditure should be capitalised.

Whether the words 'true and fair' were ever intended to suggest absolute accuracy it is not easy to say. It is, I suppose, possible that 'true' was once conceived in terms of an account of cash received and either spent or accounted for to the rightful owner, where absolute precision has meaning. The words have been used – though not always together in the same phrase – at least since the first half of the nineteenth century.

The Joint-Stock Companies Act of 1844 – the first statute providing for general incorporation by registration, and the forerunner of our present Companies Acts – required a 'full and fair' balance sheet to be presented to shareholders.

The Companies Clauses Act of 1845, intended to be applied to statutory companies, required the balance sheet to show a 'true statement' of property, etc.

Mandatory audit for registered companies was abandoned in 1856, but Table B of the Joint Stock Companies Act of that year, later to become Table A of the consolidating Act of 1862, which was to endure for over half a century, said 'The Auditors . . . in every . . . Report shall state whether in their opinion the Balance Sheet is a full and fair Balance Sheet . . . properly drawn up so as to exhibit a true and correct view of the state of the company's affairs.' The Railway Companies Act of 1867 referred to a 'full and true' statement of the financial condition of the company.

It is not surprising, in view of lawyers' love of precedent, that the words 'true' and 'fair' have persisted in the legislation. And it is clear that, however they may have begun, they are now used in the familiar phrase as a term of art – a technical term.

The difference between the naive interpretation and the legal one is well illustrated by the case of *Re Press Caps Ltd*, reported in the Chancery Law Reports of 1949 at page 434. The balance sheet value of freehold property differed by a very substantial sum from an accepted estimate of its saleable value. It was alleged that the balance sheet did not represent the true position – i.e. was not 'true'. The judges rejected this argument. Somervell, L. J., said that the basis used for showing the freehold property in the balance sheet (cost less depreciation) was common practice; it did not seem to him that there was anything misleading in the balance sheet in this respect.

But to the man in the street, and one must include, I think, the financial journalist in the street, the words 'true and fair' are likely to signify that the accounts give a true statement of facts. He will be likely to associate 'facts' with 'actual profit' and 'actual values'. He does not realise that 'profit' and 'value' are abstractions. Before they can be conceived at all in any precise way they must be defined in such a manner that the definition contains in itself, or implies clearly, a method of calculation that could be followed in practice. Different definitions may be required for different purposes. Taxable profit is not the same as profit for the purpose of dividend law. Both may differ from a definition set up in a particular partnership agreement. Profit for the economist is likely to be somewhat different from all these.

The 'true and fair view' is concerned with profit, and with balance sheet values, for the purpose of accounting to shareholders under the company law. Our troubles here stem from insisting upon an annual carve-up. The old merchant adventurers were better off in this respect. They invested in a ship or cargo. Three years later when it returned – if it returned – they could sell off the cargo in the market, sell the ship to a new venture, and pocket the money. The difference between this and the money first invested was profit. Since the money was likely to be in gold or silver coin as distinct from depreciated pound notes, the price index problem was not likely to worry them.

At any point of time the management of a modern business will have committed many hostages to fortune. However glamorous the growth in past dividends, the quality of the business at a given moment depends upon potential for future dividends or capital distributions.

This potential, indeed, is what the balance sheet values represent, in a humble way: they do not, of course, reflect the full value of the cash that is expected to be released in future; but they do show at least a part of this. The setting-up of balance sheet values depends, without question, upon views taken of the future. And so, therefore, by the rules of double entry (which only reflect a fact of life – that you can't have your cake and eat it) does the profit and loss balance.

Any attempt to do more than merely report past receipts and payments involves us in a view of the future, whether this is a direct estimation or guess of future cash flows – cash receipts and payments – or at very least an assumption that they will run at not less than a certain level. Without this there is no basis for judging the truth and fairness of the balance sheet asset and liability values, and of the profit reports.

Suggestions have been made that the problem of profit measurement can be met by throwing away the profit and loss account and adopting 'cash flow' reporting – or returning to the simple receipts and payments account.

This has indeed the merit of simplicity of concept. Everyone knows what cash is, and a cash balance can be measured precisely. A statement of a cash balance can be said to be 'true' in every sense of the word.

If everyone was prepared to wait until the final liquidation date for his share of profit, like the merchant adventurer, and did not want an earlier assessment of how things were going, beyond what past cash receipts and payments could tell him, the measurement problem would be reduced to calculating the loss of value of money when it was ultimately received, depending upon the life of the company.

If, however, evidence of success or failure are wanted before that time, or an earlier sharing out of the fruits of success are desired, it is less simple. The cash flow idea is simple in concept, and is one that I myself believe to be fundamental to management planning and control. But to tell the whole story the whole account is needed. The past receipts and payments are only half the story. The rest lies in the future. The substitution of cash flow reporting for normal accounting methods requires that the management's future budget be made available.

Someone familiar with the recent literature of financial management might be tempted to suggest a way in which a balance sheet could reflect fully, instead of only partially, the company's financial condition as seen by the management; and by which in consequence, by comparison of successive balance sheets, making due allowance for new capital paid in and dividends withdrawn, a better profit figure could be obtained. All that has to be done, he might say, is to draw up a budget showing the expected future cash flows to the shareholders, discount these, using as a discount rate the long run yield expected by the same shareholders (which would include an allowance for growth over time and for uncertainty), and the result is the balance sheet value of the enterprise at the time of the calculation. The annual increase (allowing for transactions with shareholders) is the profit.

The balance sheet would be magnificently simple. On the left-hand side would be two figures – capital and undistributed profit. On the right-hand side would be a single figure labelled 'net present value of undertaking'.

For some purposes this is by no means a foolish idea. Some kind of calculation like this must be made in valuing shares, whether as purchaser or as an expert advisor. Some managements approach their longer-run planning in this kind of way. There are, of course, formidable difficulties of estimation, and many assumptions have to be made. But this is unavoidable in business.

The real snag is that the guesses and estimates have to be made by management; and though it would certainly be interesting for shareholders to see the figures, they would hardly provide an objective test of stewardship.

The old-fashioned way of doing things – sometimes called the accrual method of accounting – does not avoid estimation and judgement by management. It does, by applying rules of the game, on a 'prudent and conservative' basis, limit the range within which the judgement is applied. The current view is that this range is at present somewhat too wide. But the price paid for the limitation of the area of judgement is a reduction in the significance of the figures, for certain aspects of the picture, which depend on estimates of the future, are excluded.

Accrual accounting is in fact an uneasy compromise between a wholly objective record of past cash receipts and payments, and a wholly subjective assessment of the current value of the enterprise, based on peering into the future. Like most compromises it has flaws. Since we probably have to live with it for a long time there is much to be said for bringing to public notice, very clearly indeed, the nature of the general concepts on which it is based, and the assumptions made and bases of calculation used in particular cases. This, as I see it, is one of the major reasons for formulating and promulgating well-defined standard accounting practices.

One of the difficulties with compromises is that the exact rules that are adopted are arbitrary and there is no theory or logical rule that can tell you where to draw the line. How far do you accrue profit on uncompleted contracts? How far should a portion of overhead cost be carried forward in the value of closing work-in-progress? The only test that can be applied is to ask which method is most convenient and useful, taking into account, and balancing the interests of all parties concerned.

This brings us back to the 'true and fair' concept. It would perhaps be clearer to the lay public if a form of words with a smaller range of possible meaning were adopted. A formula suggests itself when the Council statement on reports on profit forecasts is studied. A variant of this, adapted for the purpose of the audit report, might run on some such lines as follows:

In our opinion the balance sheet and profit and loss account are properly compiled on a basis consistent with accounting practices normally adopted by the company. These practices accord with accepted accounting standards [except in the following respects...]

Objectivity cannot be obtained with respect to all that appears in a set of accounts, only with respect to the manner in which they have been drafted.

OMEGA, The Int. Jl of Mgmt Sci., Vol. 2, No. 6, 1974

Some Aspects of Inflation and Published Accounts

HC EDEY

London School of Economics and Political Science

(Received June 1974; in revised form July 1974)

Company accounts are at present drafted in an uneasy compromise between different objectives. It is not yet generally appreciated that no single figure or set of figures can sum up the whole financial state of an enterprise. The basic tools of financial management are short and long-run cash projections and the reports of actual flows which monitor these. The problem in drafting annual accounts so that they will help shareholders and others to make decisions is that financial reality requires a look into the future and this in turn calls for subjective judgement. But the more realistic are the accounts in this sense, the less susceptible are they to objective audit. Inflation adds a further level of distortion, but the effects of this can be brought out in a relatively simple way by making corrections based on movements in a general index of prices. Although there are considerable practical difficulties it seems likely that a more fundamental improvement would be the introduction of a 'current value' or modified 'replacement cost' approach to ordinary accounting in addition to (but not in place of) the general index inflation correction.

Introduction

THE GENERAL case for requiring that the effects of changes in costs and prices be shown in published accounts rests on the view that if such accounts are to provide a basis for any kind of action involving the assessment of economic or financial alternatives, then the information in them should relate to prices and costs current at the time to which they refer.

How can this be done?

A number of suggested changes in current practice to meet this requirement has been made, some involving more fundamental reforms than do others.

In my view the best of those which are practicable in the short term, particuarly having regard to the need for a substantial and wide measure of agreement on method, is that set out in Exposure Draft 8 (ED8) of the Accounting Standards Steering Committee.[1] Briefly, this proposes that the information given in the ordinary accounts should be supplemented by an inflation accounting statement in which the ordinary figures are corrected by the application of an index measuring the fall in the general purchasing power of the pound (the retail price index). Thus the normal accounting conventions are used but are applied to transactions which have been re-priced in pounds sterling appropriate to the closing date of the accounting period.

The supplementary inflation statement can throw considerable light on financial results during inflation and can help to promote enquiry. It throws particular light on the effects of gearing and of holding monetary assets on the benefits of ownership. It also shows up the impact of corporation tax in conditions of inflation. One must accept that ED 8 has limited aims and that it does not attempt to deal with the more fundamental problem of how profit should be defined and how assets should be valued and liabilities assessed for the purpose of financial statements. It is concerned with inflation only—i.e. changes in the general price level—not with changes in relative prices and value, which can, of course, arise in the absence of inflation.

If published accounts are to be more useful than at present in making judgements about management performance and the prospects of the enterprise, information on current values of assets (in the sense of the outlay that would be imposed on the business by their loss if it were to be fully compensated), and the effect of these on costs and revenues, seems likely to be useful, at least in some instances. Such information would not be a substitute to the type of correction envisaged in ED 8 but a supplement to it. This is not a matter of correction for inflation. It arises from the fact that relative changes in prices and values are constantly occurring in business. Such changes would arise in the absence of inflation, though they may become larger and more frequent during a period of inflation.

There, are, however many difficulties and questions to be resolved, some of which are indicated below. It is in the nature of things that accounts of the type at present in use cannot in general, even when corrected for inflation, provide more than useful supporting information to back up other types of shareholder information. They certainly cannot sum up the state of an enterprise in a single unique and definitive figure, or set of figures. (The major instruments of planning and control for financial management should, in my mind, be the short and long term cash flow budgets controlled by follow-up reports of "actuals" and it is these, were it practicable to disclose them, that would best inform shareholders.)

---

[1]Accounting bodies in the British Isles collaborate through this Committee in formulating and issuing public statements which define standard procedures to be applied in the preparation of published accounts. *Exposure Draft* 8 has now become, in an amended form, *Provisional Statement of Standard Accounting Practice* 7.

The objectives of company accounts

Proposals for reform meet the serious difficulty that there is no general agreement on the basic objective that is aimed at in drawing up annual company accounts. At least three possible objectives suggest themselves:

1. To provide a statement of stewardship to the owners that is intended to show, in summary form, how their funds have been used, but not designed to give an indication of the management's business efficiency. (Such a statement would evidently not be sufficient to comply with the present company law.)

2. To provide, in addition to a bare stewardship report of the type described in 1, a conservatively based assessment of the maximum amount ("profit") that could prudently be distributed in dividend without damage to the company's creditors, and generally in compliance with the company law. Since such an assessment is based on a legal requirement, breach of which can involve penalties, a fairly high degree of standardisation of the accounting procedures used is desirable, in order to reduce uncertainty about the correctness of the result. Such an assessment also serves the purpose of providing a basis for tax assessment, which similarly demands a reasonable degree of certainty in the calculation.

3. To provide a reasonably precise assessment of the success of the management in producing a satisfactory return for the shareholders to date without sacrifice of future prospects. It is evident that an assessment of future prospects is an essential part of judging management success to date, since it is possible to make current results appear satisfactory by action which prejudices the future, and unsatisfactory current cash flows can mask a brilliant future. An account which could serve this purpose would also therefore serve that of providing information as a guide to investment decisions and for such public purposes as investigations under anti-trust or price control legislation.

Company accounts at present are widely assumed to serve all three of the above objectives. The conventions on which they are based, however, reflect something of an uneasy compromise between objectives 1 and 2 on the one hand, and objective 3 on the other. There is a wide misapprehension on this question. Many people assume that accounts are designed to serve objective 3, or at least that they should be.

Limitations of present accounting conventions in the absence of inflation

When considering the question of inflation and its effects on company accounts, it is helpful first to examine the uses and limitations of these documents in the context of the above objectives in the absence of inflation, i.e. in the absence of changes in the general price level, when the only changes in prices, costs and values are relative ones, and the value of money is constant.

For objective 1, simple stewardship accounts, an audited summary of cash receipts and payments, with a list of assets owned and of legal liabilities, would suffice. Such an objective would not be affected by inflation, since the accounts would presumably be intended only to indicate, when audited, the presence or absence of fraud and the cruder forms of negligence on the part of the directors.

Accounts on present-day lines seem to be fairly satisfactory instruments for achieving objective 2 provided the standards of accounting procedure and presentation are reasonably well-designed. The precise conventions to be used for this objective are to some extent a matter of public policy, since what is needed is a set of conventions that are susceptible of reasonably objective application, that is, where the area of subjective judgement is limited, and is as clearly specified as possible. Whether adjustments for general inflation should be applied is a matter calling for decision on the criteria to be adopted:

a. for deciding how the maximum legal distribution to shareholders by way of dividend is to be determined (if indeed any limit is in fact necessary beyond a general requirement that directors should not pay any dividend which could reasonably be expected to endanger the position of creditors); and

b. for settling the appropriate basis for corporation tax assessment insofar as this is determined by the accounting policies adopted by the company.

The considerations mentioned below in relation to objective 3 have some bearing also on measurements for objective 2, in relation to:

a. the limitations of the figures prepared (e.g. for tax purposes) under present-day conventions;

b. the problem posed by the increasing degree of subjectivity in assessment introduced by a move towards a more precise assessment of the economic results of the business operations;

c. the implications of adjustments respectively for inflation alone (as in ED 8) and for other price and value changes.

Objective 3 above related to the assessment of the economic achievement of management for the benefit of shareholders or other interested parties (such as the Monopolies Commission), and of the economic prospects of the company. Problems which pose themselves in this context, even when inflation is absent, and which are superimposed on those of inflation when the latter is present, are:

(1) What definition of profit, if any, will provide a satisfactory indicator? From the common-sense point of view of the man in the street, profit as a measure of management success is the increase in the value of the enterprise (or of his share in it) after allowing for dividends and for any new capital paid in. Since the value of the enterprise as a whole is in the end dependent upon the

future flow of surplus cash which it can generate, profit in this sense can only be ascertained by making an overall valuation of the enterprise at the beginning and end of each period. (There is an analogy here with the actuarial determination of the profit on a life-fund by the calculation of net present value.) If it were possible to adopt this concept of profit, the price-level problem, so far as it related to profit measurement, would reduce to bringing opening and closing valuations to the same price level by use of a general index of consumption prices. The practical difficulties in the way of developing such a definition for published accounts do not need to be stated here. The idea does, however, seem useful because it provides a clear conceptual base from which thinking can start. The problem would be to choose a set of accounting conventions which would provide a reasonable approximation to this ideal and which could be applied consistently in practice, assuming this to be desired. As already noted, an assessment of the company's future prospects is a necessary accompaniment of the assessment of the degree of management success.

(2) A definition of profit on the above lines thus requires an annual overall assessment of the enterprise's value, based necessarily on the judgment of management. It thus leads to the difficulty that the figure on which management is to be judged is itself based on highly subjective judgements by that management. The scope for audit would almost certainly be limited to reporting on the method used in the assessment.

(3) On the other hand, the present method of profit calculation has, in the absence of inflation, the following limitations in achieving the objective under discussion:

(i) Profit is obtained in effect (though accountants do not usually look at it in this way) by summing certain types of change over the year (with allowance for dividends paid out and new capital paid in) in the net assets listed in the balance sheets.

(ii) The calculations for (i) are based on standardised rules that preclude additions in value being brought in unless an asset has been converted into cash or a near-cash equivalent; but reductions in expected realisable value or value in use in the ordinary course of business are brought in. Hence the net accounting *change* in value of an asset over a year does not necessarily approximate, in size or even in direction, to the change that management judgement would accord to it: where management recognises in a given year a rise in value, the accounts can record a fall.

(iii) Value changes, even on a standardised basis, that cannot be identified with specific liabilities and provisions, or with recorded assets, do not enter into profit calculation at all.

B

(iv) It follows from (i), (ii) and (iii) that, even in the absence of inflation, accounting costs do not necessarily bear any consistent relationship to the current economic costs of operation in the sense of the sacrifice of current purchasing power, actual or in prospect, arising from business actions.

Inflation correction by general price index

In conditions of inflation, a new distortion is added in that the historic costs on which the accounting values and costs are based relate to different price-levels and hence to different amounts of purchasing power even where relative prices are constant. It is the purpose of inflation accounting of the type used in ED 8 to remove this distortion. In effect it adjusts all assets and liabilities by applying the change in the general price index since the date of acquisition, and then (a) writes monetary claims by and against the company down again to their face value in money (thus recording a net gain or loss to the equity interest due to having such claims), and (b) writes down any other assets if it is estimated that the inflation-corrected value will not be realised in the ordinary course of business in the short run (current assets) or long run (fixed assets).

The inflation-corrected figures are, therefore, still subject to the limitations outlined in (i)–(iv) above.

Adjustments to asset values and costs by reference to costs of replacement

A general price index correction applied, year by year, to the value of the equity interest in the company will thus show the amount of current value needed to maintain intact the original invested purchasing power (calculated from a given starting point).

In assessing the cost of using an asset, however (e.g. as cost of sales or depreciation), a figure related to its current replacement cost may give a better approximation of the current economic cost than if the valuation basis adopted is historic cost, or (where there is inflation) historic cost adjusted by a general price index. However, a number of problems arise:

(a) A suitable special index number or other indication of replacement cost must be found.

(b) A precise definition of what is meant by replacement is necessary. This, in principle, will depend upon the business context. In some situations no replacement is intended. In others the aim would be to replace the asset in question by a wholly different kind of investment, so that "replacement" can only refer to the cash flow stream produced by the replaced asset or to the service that the asset in question is providing. In some situations the replacing asset would be identical except in age to the one replaced. In others replacement cost seems to have little meaning unless it refers to the cost to the enterprise as a whole of replacing a specified increment of cash flow earned or of service or goods supplied, and the replacement cost of any one specified asset has little or no significance by itself.

Saleable values of individual assets

Reporting saleable value of individual assets may convey useful information in certain contexts. It is more likely to be significant in relation to assets of a non-specific character which enjoy a good market and have a value which is substantial in relation to the total resources of the company. In such a context a knowledge of realisable value may be a relevant factor in estimating whether the management are making economic use of the resources in their hands, and in judging the scope for raising further loan finance. On the other hand it is doubtful whether an estimation of the value of highly specialised fixed assets on a forced sale would in general be of much significance except perhaps to, say, a banker contemplating an advance of money to an enterprise on the verge of insolvency.

Conclusions

The foregoing considerations suggest that the major questions to be answered in the process of drawing up proposals for reform are the following:

(A) What alterations, if any, are required in present accounting conventions in the absence of inflation?

(B) Does the method of ED 8 (current purchasing power correction) combined with any changes arising under (A) provide an adequate method of correction for general inflation?

A number of detailed questions that arise in considering these points are:

(1) Should the capital contributed by equity shareholders, directly and through profit retentions, be measured in terms of constant consumer purchasing power, and therefore adjusted year by year by a general consumer price index, when judging whether a profit has been made, whatever the method used for valuing assets and calculating current costs? How far is the answer affected by the assumed accounting objective?

(2) Is original cost adjusted by a general price index (and then reduced by writing down to the estimated value of the asset in the ordinary course of business where this is less) a good substitute for a more accurate attempt at assessment of asset value for (a) balance sheet valuation and (b) calculation of profit? In other words, is the method of asset valuation used in ED 8 an adequate approximation method for both purposes? How far is the answer affected by the assumed objective?

(3) Should the question of balance sheet valuation be separated from that of profit calculation?

(4) Should directors be required to comment to shareholders if in their view the future prospects of the enterprise do not justify the balance sheet values *taken as a whole?* In such a case, should a specific provision be written into the accounts? Should such a provision reduce reported profit?

(5) Should a reasoned report be made in the contrary case to (4), i.e. where the directors' assessment of the value of the enterprise as a whole exceeds the balance sheet figure?

(6) How far can the sum of the estimated replacement cost of individual assets less an allowance for depreciation, where relevant, provide a good indication of the current value of the enterprise as a whole?

(7) Would the re-calculation of costs on the basis of the estimated replacement cost of individual assets used up or otherwise depreciated give a better indication of costs facing the company than present methods, or the method of ED 8?

(8) If a re-calculation of asset values on the basis of replacement cost were carried out annually, should the consequential excess (or deficit) of value over the value determined by applying a general consumer price index (as in ED 8) be regarded as current profit (or loss) for tax and other purposes?

(9) Would the reporting of the estimated replacement cost of individual assets be useful ancillary information, especially where the assets were of a non-specialised character, with a good market?

(10) Should the estimated net disposable value of fixed assets be reported to shareholders, as ancillary information?

(11) If replacement cost (adjusted for depreciation) is accepted as an appropriate concept in relation to asset valuation and cost estimation, should it be defined in relation to particular assets or in relation to the capacity to produce a particular mix of goods or services by the use of the complex of assets? If the latter, should it be defined in relation to the future cost of increments of production? Or should it relate to the replacement of the total production of the enterprise?

(12) If replacement cost (adjusted for depreciation) is accepted as an appropriate concept for asset valuation and cost estimation, how should the convention be modified to allow for situations where replacement would not be economic?

(13) Given that values and costs are related to a particular management policy (a decision by management to scrap an asset may represent a change in their view of its value to the business) should there be a requirement that management report, with some degree of precision, the main elements of their commercial strategy?

730

(14) Should liabilities be represented in the balance sheet at the current market value based on prevailing rates of interest? If so, should gains or losses arising from such adjustments be treated as profit or loss for tax or other purposes?

DEPRIVAL VALUE AND
FINANCIAL ACCOUNTING

Harold Edey

1

A major weakness of financial accounting is the absence of a clear relationship to management policy and plans.[1] Despite many efforts through the years to improve and adapt it, in essence it remains a mixed collection of rules of thumb, still strongly influenced by the nineteenth-century legal problems that it was originally designed to meet. The position of management is becoming increasingly like that of the captain of a ship who plans his voyages on an up-to-date Admiralty chart, steers his ship using the same chart and the navigational aids made available by modern technology, and is then required to report his progress to his owners by plotting it on a sixteenth-century map. It is, therefore, a major merit of the deprival value approach to asset valuation and profit calculation, introduced by Professor W. T. Baxter in his recent book on depreciation,[2] that its application in financial accounting could help to relate the latter more closely to information that is directly relevant for management action and therefore, presumably, of direct interest to those interested in the results of management.

In its simplest form, deprival value is a method of valuing an individual asset whose expected series of financial contributions, positive or negative, can be estimated reasonably closely and independently of other assets of the same concern. In Section 2, I shall demonstrate the idea of deprival value as I understand it, on the basis of this simplifying assumption, following Baxter. In Section 3, I shall consider the effects of removing the simplifying assumption in order to cover the more general case where the operation of an asset and the financial results of this operation may be strongly interconnected with the operation and results of other assets. In Section 4, I shall discuss how the deprival value concept might be used to improve the basis of financial accounting.

---

[1] I shall use the term "financial accounting" in this paper as a generic term for the preparation and presentation of formal annual accounts such as are required by the British Companies Acts 1948 to 1967, the enactments setting up the various state industries in Britain, the rules relating to publication of accounts of the Securities and Exchange Commission, and so on. "External accounting" (as opposed to "internal" management accounting) might be a better term, but "financial accounting" is so well established as a term that it seems best to stick to it.

[2] W. T. Baxter, *Depreciation*, London, 1971.

2

An asset can be regarded as a store of services. The financial effects of such services can be expressed as a set of expected future cash receipts and payments – a "cash flow."[3] The "receipts" may be actual cash realisations or may be savings of cash payments which, but for the asset, would have been made. Similarly, the "payments" are either actual cash outgoings or sacrifices of cash receipts caused by the asset. Typical receipts are the net revenues from the asset's services and the net sales proceeds when it is finally disposed of. Typical payments are the initial purchase price of the asset and payments for its operation, repair and maintenance. Receipts and payments may also be imputed if cost-benefit analysis calls for this.

Consider first the case of an asset that is not capable of replacement such that if it is lost or destroyed the service it provides must cease.

From the management point of view (and this must be presumed to reflect the point of view of those whom the management is there to serve, whether shareholders, government department, or some other group) the commercial value of the asset to the concern – the maximum amount that it would be worth their while to pay in order to acquire it in its present condition – cannot be greater than whatever present value is attributed to the best cash flow that its use or sale is expected to contribute to the concern (including in this, where necessary, the amount imputed to any non-financial benefits).[4] Any excess of past outlay over this present value is an expense or loss incurred or suffered by the management, to be written off.

Nor can the asset be worth less to the management than this amount, for if the concern were for some reason deprived of it – *e.g.* by a fire – it would be this present value and no less which, by definition, would just compensate for the loss: hence the term *deprival value*.

Good management calls for continuing knowledge of this value, that is, for periodic assessment of expected cash flows and their present values, in order to judge the current best use of the asset and the optimal date of its final disposal. So, perhaps less obviously, does the preparation and audit of financial accounts, even under the present rules, for no asset should, without note or comment, stand in the balance sheet at more than the value

---

[3] For purposes of exposition I shall ignore the fact that management are normally concerned not only with an "expected" outcome (in the probability sense) but also with the dispersion of possible outcomes about the expected quantity or set of quantities. This abstraction does not affect the central point under discussion here.

[4] The calculation of a present value requires, if discounting is to be used, the selection of an "appropriate" rate or rates of discount. The problems that arise in choosing such a rate or rates are outside the scope of this paper. It is evident, however, that any management must have some scheme for relating the financial benefits expected from an asset to its purchase price, or to its sales value, when they decide to buy, sell, or retain, the asset, and this implies some kind of assessment of the present value of the expected cash flow. The net cash proceeds of immediate sale of the asset can be regarded as a special case of a "one item" cash flow with a discounting factor of unity.

of the amount that it is expected eventually to bring in to the concern.[5] Where the possibility of replacement is excluded, deprival value, as defined above will, under present thinking, be a present value arrived at by discounting or by some other process. As Baxter points out, depreciation by reference to successive values calculated in this way at the end of each year will, in general, not be constant year by year. The net receipts created by an asset will vary from year to year with the incidence of cash outlays on running and upkeep, as well as with any variation in annual gross revenue earned. With constant revenue it is not depreciation, but the sum of depreciation, running cost, repairs and maintenance, and the adopted target return on investment (obtained by applying the selected discount rate to the written down value) that will – if all goes according to plan – be constant.[6]

If all does not go according to plan, the deprival value computed in the light of actual conditions will throw up a variance in the sum of these items as compared with the planned and budgeted deprival value: this is what one expects of management accounts.

Up to now it has been assumed that the asset is not capable of replacement. Suppose now that if it were lost or destroyed it could be replaced. This is the more likely situation. The present value of the best cash flow obtainable from use or sale of the asset will evidently remain an upper limit to value. The cost of replacement in case of hypothetical loss does, however, introduce an alternative upper limit, which may be lower than the one set by present value. If the asset were lost or destroyed, the financial loss would be limited to the outlay on replacement, that is, the outlay needed to put the owner back in his original position. (The "cost of replacement" here is assumed to include the amount of any loss of revenue and outlays caused by delay, where immediate replacement is not possible.) This upper limit set by replacement cost has clear economic and management significance. It is the maximum insurable loss. It is also the maximum amount any sensible purchaser with the same knowledge is likely to pay for the asset. Under competitive conditions the present value of the cash flow contributed by the asset is unlikely for long to exceed its replacement cost, for should it appear likely to do so, it will, by definition, be profitable for competitors to bring into use similar assets, the competition from which will drive down the contribution from the original asset until it reaches something approximating to a normal competitive return on investment (*i.e.* on replacement cost, allowance being made, as shown by Baxter, for any difference in cash contribution due to different age and physical characteristics of the hypothetical replacing asset.) In such

---

[5] ". . . it is obvious that capital lost must not appear in the accounts as still existing intact; the accounts must show the truth . . ." *per* Lindley L. J. in *Verner* v. *General Investment Trust Ltd.* [1894] 2 Ch. 239.

[6] The annuity method of depreciation is a special case of this where annual net cash receipts are assumed constant: in this case it is the sum of depreciation and target return on investment that is constant.

conditions it can be assumed that a management would wish to relate its pricing policy to the amount of a competitive return on the replacement cost of the assets concerned as a guide in judging the risk of over-pricing and losing sales or inviting more competition.

Calculation of the cost of hypothetical replacement can thus be regarded as part of the process of estimating the future cash flow and present value of the asset: in the end it is these, and these alone, that determine the usefulness of the asset, and therefore its financial worth, in the management's eyes.

Deprival value can therefore be defined more generally as the lower of: (*a*) the highest present value expected to be earned by use or sale of the asset, and (*b*) the current replacement cost of the asset, including in this replacement cost an addition for any loss that would be caused by delay in replacement and for other incidental outlays, and also an allowance for any amount by which the services of the replacing asset were expected to earn a higher (or lower) contribution because its age and physical characteristics differed from those of the original asset.

It may be objected that if competition were restricted, the net revenue contribution of an asset could remain above the normal competitive level and hence maintain its value to the concern above the replacement cost. However, this situation would imply that an additional asset had been introduced into the calculation, namely the property right, licence, reputation or other factor which enabled the competition to be excluded. The valuation would now relate to two assets instead of one, and replacement would have to be considered in relation to both together: replacement cost would have to include the cost of replacing the asset that gave the protection from competition. The introduction of a significant restriction on competition thus makes inapplicable the simple case of the single independent asset on which discussion has so far rested. The problem raised does not exclude the use of the deprival value approach, but it requires extension of the argument to cover a more general use. This is dealt with in Section 3.

3

On the simplifying assumption provisionally made in Section 2 (namely that an asset's contribution can be clearly distinguished from those of other assets of the concern) the deprival value concept provides a conceptually clear basis for the determination of asset value. Value determined in this way is necessarily based on estimate and opinion; but this is common to all value assessments except those based on some purely arbitrary rule that excludes all consideration of the future of the asset in question.[7]

---

[7] *e.g.* the written-down value of an asset for capital allowance purposes under corporation tax; but *not* the conventional balance sheet value, which requires at least consideration of the asset's future contribution, though this is normally only used in determining whether the asset should be written down.

Moreover, it can be argued with some force that the information and estimates used in arriving at the deprival value are in any case needed by an efficient management for planning and decisions, and can therefore be assumed to be available when the financial accounts are drafted and audited.

The next step is to consider the more complicated and general case of a complex of assets whose financial effects are closely interconnected. The cash flow contribution of a single taxi to a concern that owns a fleet of taxis which are hired out to drivers can be determined after the event without serious theoretical or practical difficulty.[8] The assessment of the expected future cash flow in such a case involves an estimation problem but not a conceptual one. What, on the other hand, is the cash-flow contribution of a railway bridge on a main railway line? If, for the moment, it is assumed that the bridge cannot be replaced (*e.g.* because of an earthquake) so that the line has to close, it can be said that its deprival value is measured by the whole net cash flow earned by the section of the line that it occupies less the net disposal value of the remaining railway assets, since this is the loss that the bridge's destruction would cause (the rest of the railway being assumed unharmed and intact). But this could be said of every bridge, tunnel, cutting, etc. on the line. Evidently cash-flow contributions, and their discounted values, calculated in this way for each asset in turn cannot be aggregated to give a meaningful total. This is an old economic conundrum.

A similar conceptual problem is likely to arise in many real-life situations when replacement cost of hypothetical replacement comes to be estimated. Replacement cost may have little significance if it is defined strictly in terms of a specific physical asset. It is true that, where exact replacement is possible, its cost (allowing for cost of delay) always provides an upper limit to value to the owner; but the limit may be so high as to be useless as a guide. It would probably seldom be sensible to replace an asset in exactly the same form. Sometimes this is obvious: one would not normally consider replacing a railway locomotive built in 1890 by another with the same physical specification. Nor can this point be met except in very simple cases (such as that of the taxis above) merely by stating the problem as that of costing the replacement of the asset's services. The difficulty arises because changes in consumer tastes or in technology since the asset was acquired may call for changes in a whole complex of jointly-operating asset services.

The output of an electricity generating undertaking, supplied at a given time by the services of a coal-fired plant, linked with similar plants by a network of interconnected transmission lines, may at a later time be more cheaply provided, say, by a single nuclear station supported by one or more

---

[8] It is assumed that the taxis cannot be identified as belonging to the same fleet for this could cause financial interaction between them, *e.g.* because the fleet acquired a reputation for reliability and comfort, so that the whole fleet earned more than taxis would if operated independently.

gas turbine generators, without a large-scale interconnected grid. How in such a case can the "services" of the original coal-fired station be defined in order to calculate the cost of their replacement, taken by themselves without the services of the rest of the network? It must not be forgotten that one of the aims of calculating replacement cost is to estimate the likely price that will be set upon output by a competitor coming into the industry; or, in a state industry, to estimate the current cost of the best method of supply, in order to test current pricing policy. The cost of replacing individual old machines in their existing form may have little relevance in this context.

In principle it would be possible to compute "replacement cost" of an existino asset in a complex situation of this kind by making two separate estimates: one of the present value of all the future costs of the whole complex with the station in question, and the second of the present value of all the future costs of the whole complex if the station alone, but no other part, had been destroyed and then replaced, including the outlay on replacement.[9] The difference between the two would be the "replacement cost" of the station. The replacement of one station would not allow the complete reconstruction of the system as a whole on the best basis available at the time of hypothetical replacement, but the new station would almost certainly be somewhat different in its technological characteristics from the old one, and would represent the best that could be done, given the rest of the existing system.

If all assets were to be valued separately on this basis, the sum of the "replacement costs" so obtained could in general be expected to exceed significantly the hypothetical replacement cost of the system as a whole. It follows that, apart from special cases (like the taxis) a replacement cost estimate based on taking individual assets one by one is not likely to be a useful figure in relation to such matters as the valuation of the concern as a whole or the assessment of the current most economical way available to a newly created concern of producing the enterprise's product or products – a question closely related to valuation.[10]

This does not invalidate the deprival value approach. It does indicate, however, that its proper use for valuation requires that the dual test of expected cash contribution and replacement cost be applied to the concern

---

[9] The costs here would be expressed as the flow of cash outlays in running, maintenance and future replacement into the indefinite future, receipts on disposition of assets being credited. The second flow would also include the immediate hypothetical outlay on the new station. If revenues were affected by the change, this too would have to be allowed for.

[10] This does not imply that the deprival value of an individual asset has no significance when that asset is a member of a closely co-operating set of complementary assets. It will be relevant in testing whether it is worthwhile actually replacing an individual asset. For this purpose the type of calculation described above is necessary – that is, the calculation of the two sets of cash flows into the indefinite future for the whole group of assets, with the old asset and with the replacing one. To test whether replacement is worthwhile the disposal value of the old asset must then be brought into comparison with the difference in present values of the two flows: if it is significantly more than the deprival value ın present use the asset should be replaced.

as a whole. The replacement cost so calculated for the concern as a whole gives an overriding maximum value, reflecting the cost to a hypothetical competitor of creating a similar organisation. This implies that the calculation should include an allowance for the cost of creating a working organisation – that is, for the creating of the intangible element commonly called "goodwill" as well as for the physical assets. This would include an allowance for return on investment forgone during the working up period.

The present value of the best expected cash-flow returns that can be earned for the owners of the concern may however be less than this replacement cost. It is then that present value which sets the overriding maximum. As in the case of individual assets, the net liquidation value, as a one-item cash flow, sets a lower limit.

The estimation of these values is difficult and the result is normally likely to be subject to a high degree of uncertainty. This, however, is due to the nature of the world, and it is no good complaining about it or arguing that the result is not "objective." It cannot legitimately be argued that making such estimates would place an undue burden on management: it is the job of management to form opinions on such matters as part of the normal process of running the concern and assessing its continuing economic efficiency.

It would also appear – and it is doubtful if this is fully appreciated – to be a duty of auditors to express an adverse opinion if, in their view, the balance sheet value of the net assets as a whole is in excess of their business value defined in this way.[11] It is difficult to see how such an opinion can be reasonably formed without evidence that the management have directed their mind to the above questions; in general this would seem to imply that there should be documentary evidence available to auditors in the form of planning studies and at least outline budgets.

The application of deprival value in the way suggested above amounts in effect to linking the valuation of the concern to its long-run planning. This link cannot be avoided in any approach to valuation that has reality for management decisions.

The application can take account of liabilities as well as assets. In estimating the long-run cash flows of the concern as a whole, receipts and payments from the creation or extinction of liabilities and for servicing these would be included.

If the valuation is for the information and benefit of the equity shareholders of a company, it should presumably be based on the expected cash flows to them. For this purpose preference shares would be treated as a liability. In state undertakings where in effect the whole investment including all loan capital bears an equity risk, whatever the formal nature of the finance, debt capital owned or guaranteed by Government would be treated as part of the equity.

[11] See footnote 5 above.

4

What has been said above suggests that to report the current financial position of a concern in a way that conveys to its owners a realistic view of the economic value of the resources invested in it requires a subjective assessment involving a look into the future, and involves consideration of the concern as a whole (including assessment of its value as a whole) as distinct from an assessment obtained merely by summing values set on individual assets.

So far as reported profit is to be a measure of the improvement in the concern's economic value in the same sense (allowing for payments in or withdrawals of ownership funds and withdrawal of dividends), it must be based on comparison of successive assessments, using the same approach.

Such an approach to annual accounting in effect implies a switch to reporting based on management assessments of the best cash flows that can be expected from the existing organisation and conversion of these in some way to a present value, coupled with a study of the cost of replacing the existing organisation as a whole in the best possible way. This is hardly likely to be acceptable immediately as a normal basis for financial accounts in practice.

On the other hand, as noted above, it can be argued that such an assessment is, in principle, required by orthodox accounting rules, since it is needed to test whether the balance sheet as a whole overstates "net realisable value" in the sense of its ability to produce future cash return for its owners that will amount in aggregate to not less than the present balance sheet net assets.[12]

One can, however, go further than this. In simple cases, where cash-flow contributions can be closely identified with particular assets, as in, say, a taxi business, or a shipping business, or a chain store, clear significance can be attached to deprival value assessments of individual assets – taxis, ships, freehold premises, etc. – and the method provides in these cases what is lacking in present-day financial accounting, a principle of general application, the use of which would lead to better balance sheet interpretation.

Even in such cases, however, the application of the assessment to the concern as a whole cannot be dispensed with if a full view is to be given. The economic worth of a concern to its owners will depend in part on the way in which it is operated as a whole. One can put this another way by saying that the deprival value of the asset "goodwill" cannot be assessed independently of the concern as a whole.

This has some bearing on what, for accountants, is the troublesome problem of accounting for goodwill. No method of dealing with this question is likely to be of much use in conveying information unless it is based on an overall assessment of the concern's value. Deprival value has a clear application in this context.

[12] Consider this in relation, say, to the balance sheet of Rolls-Royce before the débâcle.

Where individual assets are of specialised nature and their operation demands the co-operation of other assets, as in the case of the power station example above, it is doubtful if any method of "valuing" the individual assets for balance sheet purposes can have a great deal of significance in assessing the quality of the undertaking as a continuing concern. The deprival value concept can, however, supply a basis of principle to the balance sheet valuation process in the simpler cases. Given that there is a continuous spectrum of business types, the principle could well be extended generally to all concerns. As one moved from the simpler to the more complex, individual asset values would in general become more arbitrary and more reliance would need to be placed on any overall assessment that could be provided. This seems unavoidable.

The deprival value approach has the particular merit of drawing attention to the relevance of replacement cost (adjusted in the way described above for the effect of delay, and differences in age and other characteristics between the existing and the hypothetical replacing asset) as an absolute limit to the worth to the concern of any asset, and to the replacement cost of the concern as a whole as an absolute limit to its value to the owners.

This has special relevance to stock inventory. The application of the deprival value approach to this would mean that the familiar formula "cost or lower net realisable value" would be replaced by "cost, net realisable value or replacement cost, whichever is lower." That this formula has greater management significance in some contexts can hardly be doubted. A fall in the replacement value of purchased stock may be of considerable significance to a concern – *e.g.* a tailoring chain – that is competing with others that, by delaying their purchases, have avoided the fall. The fall is also evidence of an error in purchasing, attributable to the accounting period in which it occurs, and in which it would seem sensible to record the effect.

Deprival value may have particular significance for a nationalised industry, where it is particularly important that the financial accounts should reflect the economic and management realities. This is because under present circumstances it is likely that these accounts will be used as a basis for financial directives, on such matters as financial targets to be attained, without a full understanding of the limitations of this kind of statement. This in turn means that the level at which tariffs are fixed may well depend to a large degree upon the financial accounts. The estimation of a deprival value for sections of the undertaking, and for the undertaking as a whole, could provide an important check on the economic significance of the conventional accounts, and could, for example, highlight a situation where the past depreciation policy had been inadequate, either because the rate of cost reduction through technological advance had been underestimated in the past, or because errors in investment had occurred.

Authority

Accounting Standards in the British Isles

HAROLD C. EDEY

Professor of Accounting, London School of Economics

THE most compelling argument for accounting standards is that if they are good ones they speed up the process of communication. The definition of the standard provides, as it were, a dictionary reference which can be looked up if need be, and which becomes widely known. This avoids having to explain methods every time they are used.[1] Standards can only do this however to the extent that they are accepted and used. An important question therefore arises: should particular accounting standards achieve acceptance through individual choice or social and economic pressure, because they are found to be useful? Or should on the other hand adherence be imposed under the threat of legal or quasi-legal sanction? I shall suggest below that this question is closely related to the kind of standard under discussion.

The usefulness of a standard as a means of improving communication does not depend upon whether it is agreed to be the *best* way to do something. It is sufficient that it is an acceptable way. Spelling conventions in English are a form of standard. They might indeed be *better*, but we get along quite well by adhering to a spelling practice that is generally accepted. This does not mean that one should not strive for the better. But the business of life may be impeded if we cannot in the meantime agree on a working convention.

It has been accepted by the body that issues accounting standards in the British Isles—the Accounting Standards Committee[2]—that the exposure drafts and standards it emits, while intended to represent good practice, are certainly not claimed to be incapable of improvement over time. This must be the case if standards are to be issued on topics on which accounting opinion is sharply divided as to which of two or more methods is the best.

Writers of high reputation and distinction have suggested that the introduction of official recommendations or standards may inhibit experiment and the development and introduction of new ideas, either by creating a closed frame of mind or, if compulsion is applied, by forbidding innovation.[3]

This is a matter to be taken seriously. There is evidently a risk to be set against such advantages as are believed to accrue from having standards. My own impression is however that, far from quelling discussion, the formulation and issue of standards has brought about a great increase in the amount of open argument and controversy in British accountancy.

The most notable example has been the introduction of the provisional standard on inflation accounting, SSAP 7—the most controversial of all the standards so far. This not only brought the then British Government officially to acknowledge that a problem existed and to set up an official committee with wide terms of reference to consider and report on accounting methods[4]; it has, also, by bringing into the foreground the contradictions and anomalies that existed in historical accounting long before inflation corrections were envisaged by the practising profession, marvellously stirred up thought about basic objectives and conventions of income measurement and valuation in general.[5]

It is indeed true that many accountants are, and will continue to be, content to observe and follow. Accounting is not different from other human activities. Active thought and innovation is usually left to the few. So long, however, as the way is left open—as it is under the British standards—for those who disagree with a standard in a particular context to follow their own opinion and conscience—provided always that they say that they have done so and why, and, where it is reasonable to do so, specify the effect on the figures they are reporting—it is, I suggest, unlikely that innovation will be seriously blocked. The general climate of opinion in the community and the profession, and the responsiveness of the latter to debate and reasoned argument is, I suggest, likely to have a greater influence on innovation than the existence or absence of accounting standards. It is pertinent at this point to quote from the Explanatory Foreword to the series of British standards:

8 Accounting standards are not intended to be a comprehensive code of rigid rules. It would be impracticable to establish a code sufficiently elaborate to cater for all business situations and circumstances and every exceptional or marginal case. Nor could any code of rules provide in advance for innovations in business and financial practice.

9 Moreover it must be recognised that there may be situations in which for justifiable reasons accounting standards are not strictly applicable because they are impracticable or, exceptionally, having regard to the circumstances, would be inappropriate or give a misleading view.

10 In such cases modified or alternative treatments must be adopted and, as noted, departure from standard disclosed and explained. In judging exceptional or borderline cases it will be important to have regard to the spirit of accounting standards as well as to their precise terms, and to bear in mind the overriding requirement to give a true and fair view.

. . .

12 Methods of financial accounting evolve and alter in response to changing business and economic needs. From time to time new accounting standards will be drawn at progressive levels, and established standards will be reviewed with the object of improvement in the light of new needs and developments.

As Baxter has suggested, the strength of the case for a particular recommendation or standard requirement varies with its nature[6]. For this paper I divide requirements under standards into four main types, more than one of which may appear in a given standard.

Type 1 is unique: it simply says you must tell people what you are doing; you must disclose the methods and assumptions—"the accounting policies"—you have adopted. The case for this disclosure seems over-whelmingly strong. An accounting report is a kind of statistical statement and it is an elementary but fundamental rule of statistical presentation—as indeed of simple good sense, manners and respect for your audience—to make it clear how your figures have been compiled and, where it will be significant for interpretation of the figures, on what assumptions they rest.[7] This requirement is embodied in British Statement of Standard Accounting Practice (SSAP) No. 2. (This standard also provides a list of "fundamental accounting concepts" but these are not essential to the basic requirement and are discussed separately below.)

Type 2 requirements aim at achieving some uniformity of presentation of accounting statements. They are akin to standards of measure and description used in many branches of science and industry to improve communication and thought. In the British series of standards this type of requirement is rare, as the tendency has been to avoid specifying the precise form of presentation as a part of the formal standard. Where it has been thought useful, illustrative forms have been indicated in accompanying appendices that do not form part of the standard, so that deviation from the form indicated would not necessarily imply deviation from the standard. SSAP 6, *Extraordinary items and prior year adjustments,* takes a step towards a standard form of presentation by requiring that a statement of retained profits showing any prior year adjustments should immediately follow the profit and loss account for the year.

In this respect the British approach differs from that of some of the European continental countries. The E.E.C. Commission inclines towards the German and French practice of standardisation of the form of accounts, with numbered classificatory headings in income account and balance sheet[8] so that it is likely that British practice will move in this direction. (It is interesting that the model set of articles of association in the British Companies Act of 1856 included a balance sheet with numbered categories of assets and liabilities.[9])

Provided that there is reasonable possibility of development and amendment, and provided that departure from standard is permitted if clarity demands it and reasons are explained, there does seem to be considerable advantage in adhering to a fairly uniform presentation, and little to be lost. Interpretation is speeded up if one knows just where to look for each bit of information.

Type 3 requirements, like Type 1, relate to disclosure, but of specific matters as opposed to the general disclosure of methods and assumptions. It has long been recognised that where the amount of an item is subject to a particularly high degree of estimation, as with depreciation, it should if material be disclosed separately, so that users of the accounts are aware of this particular area of uncertainty. When dealing with such matters, standards are no doubt often anticipating requirements that will eventually enter into legal codes.

Somewhat similar reasons lead to requirements of disclosure where there is a recognised accounting treatment which, nevertheless, is based on convenience of uniformity or prudence rather than on finer grounds of theory. An example of this occurred in the original exposure draft on the treatment of research and development expenditure (ED 14). It was proposed—broadly on the basis of prudence and difficulty of estimation—that general expenditure of this type should be written off as incurred (itself a Type 4 requirement, to be discussed later), and as a corollary it was proposed that the annual amount of such expense should be separately disclosed.

It is difficult to see that either of these kinds of disclosure requirement are in themselves objectionable on the grounds mentioned above.

Another instance of specific disclosure requirement arises from the desire to identify in the income account what may be called the "standardised normal profit"—the amount of profit arising from "normal" activities—and to distinguish it from gains and losses due to causes outside "normal" activities. This gives rise to the concept of "extraordinary" items that are to be disclosed (Type 3 requirement) and also segregated in the income account so that they are added on or deducted after a profit or loss from "normal" activities has been struck.[10] These are to be distinguished from exceptional items that arise from "normal" activities and are included in the calculation of the profit or loss from these activities, but are nevertheless disclosed as separate items because they represent significant hiccups in the progress of the business which could give a false impression if not revealed.

The requirement for disclosure of extraordinary items due to non-normal activities does not in itself seem likely to give rise to rigidities and uniformity in accounting, or to reduce seriously the area of judgment of the auditor. On the contrary, it calls for what will often be extremely difficult decisions, since what is a "normal activity" and what is an "extraordinary" one, is often in a large degree a matter of personal judgment which cannot be solved by referring to any basic concept or postulate.

Indeed, the main criticism of this standard requirement is more fundamental and lies in the virtual impossibility of finding any satisfactory criterion of what comprises a "normal" activity in a changing and uncertain world. That there should be disclosure of items judged to be individually significant for assessment of the business progress does not require argument. But some may doubt the wisdom or usefulness of attempting in the published accounts to indicate how much of the profit is in some sense "normal" or "ordinary". The pressure for separating the results of "ordinary" from "extraordinary" activities seems closely connected with the present-day emphasis put upon the price-earnings ratio as an indicator of share value—an emphasis that it would be hard to justify on empirical grounds or on grounds of financial theory other than that, because it has gained wide acceptance, it has an influence on the stock market.

We might also include in Type 3 certain standard requirements that call for explicit disclosure of information already largely implicit in the income statement and balance sheet. Requirements for presentation of a flow of funds statement (SSAP 4) and of a statement of earnings per share (SSAP 3) fall into this category. Users of accounting statements could construct both for themselves provided that the accounts were carefully drafted with this aim in mind. To this extent these requirements could perhaps be regarded as concerned with presentation (Type 2) rather than disclosure. The flow of funds statement seems a useful addition to the set of accounts; and it no doubt saves many users trouble to provide an earnings per share calculation, whatever one's doubts may be about its economic significance under present conventions.

So far the standard requirements discussed have dealt with disclosure, either in general or in particular, and with forms of presentation. I have suggested that if present British practice with regard to non-observance is continued, the setting up of standards dealing with these matters need not produce unthinking uniformity in accounting, seriously inhibit innovation and change, or reduce the responsibility for independent judgment called for from reporting accountants and auditors. Where these kinds of requirements are most open to question—for example, where they attempt to distinguish between ordinary and extraordinary activities, so as to define a profit figure that results from the former—they are the less likely to do harm because the extraordinary items that are segregated will be fully disclosed, and users of the accounts can make their own judgments. Nevertheless, to the extent that an implicit or explicit attempt is made to define a "normal" profit, these requirements are subject to the reservations that apply to Type 4 requirements, now to be discussed.

Type 4 requirements involve implicit or explicit decisions on what shall be regarded as income, how income shall be allocated to periods, how assets shall be valued, how liabilities assessed, and therefore how net shareholders' equity determined. In this class are standards on such matters as stock valuation, depreciation, treatment of research and development, deferred tax, goodwill. All are highly controversial areas. All involve an implicit or explicit view of the basic economic criteria to be used in financial reporting, but so far have of necessity been drawn up without the benefit of agreement on this fundamental question. A cookbook approach is still necessary. If standards of this type are to be issued the authors are therefore placed in a quandary as Morison has pointed out.[11] Should they provide reasoned arguments for their choice of standard? If they give no reasons they will certainly be heavily criticised, no doubt rightly. But a logical basis for their argument is lacking. The most I think that would be generally agreed is that a company's accounting statements should contribute to a user's general understanding of its potential future, and that there should be some positive relationship between the balance of the annual income statement and the improvement or deterioration of the financial position as seen by a reasonable man with access to the information available to management. The level of agreement is so general that it can provide a logical basis only for very broad standards. For example, it is possible to derive from this, in the context of the general body of accounting methods, the inference that depreciation should be provided when the contribution that assets make to the business is falling over time. It is not however possible to deduce a method of depreciation that can be called "correct" or "better" than some other methods. Even this very broad conclusion is only possible if agreement can be reached on what is meant by a "contribution". Questions of this kind are economic questions. They can in the end only be decided by reference to a given set or personal scale of preferences or utilities—and people differ.

One solution is to admit boldly that there is no single answer and plump for the basis most commonly in use provided it does not seem to have some obvious and major defect. If the need is for a standard definition, does it matter which basis is chosen as standard? This approach, which Morison has called the "let's settle for one view argument" is, however, very far from satisfactory when it is applied to Type 4 requirements in order to secure uniformity of treatment. A standard treatment—say the writing off of all research and development—that fits one situation may fit another very badly, "fitness" being here the ability of the figure used to contribute to the kind of understanding of the company's financial potential referred to above. Only if the basic aim were uniformity for its own sake, irrespective of other considerations, would this approach be really satisfactory. The accounting statements would then be objective, but of very little use except in maintaining the income of accountants.

If therefore standards of this type are to be set up, it seems better openly to admit that in the nature of things it is often not possible to select a "best" method, or even give meaning to the term, otherwise one runs the risk of using bad logic to indicate that the "right" method has been chosen.

The impasse created by the absence of a sound basis of principle has been recognised by a fairly large number of those accountants who interest themselves in such matters, but there is far less recognition of what would constitute such a foundation. Morison has suggested[12] that it might be theoretically possible to develop a set of axioms and measurement rules such that only one accounting treatment could follow for each type of problem; the problem would be, as he agrees, to decide *which* set of axioms to select. He agrees that the search would be difficult and perhaps would fail, but suggests that it would at least clarify minds.

A prior set of axioms—if well chosen and defined—would no doubt lead to the same approach by every accountant. It would certainly not produce the same *answer*. This is because the problem is not one of physical phenomena as in the natural sciences, but of social behaviour, based on the perceptions of individual people. Suppose for example that accountants adopted the naive axiom: "an asset's balance sheet value is equal to the arithmetical difference between expected net cash inflow to the company (a) with, and (b) without, the asset, all other assets and liabilities being held constant". This would indeed tell us what accounting *treatment* should be used for depreciation and balance sheet valuation. But the actual figures would, and must, depend on assessments of the future by individual persons and on those persons' attitudes and temperaments. That this is so is realised by too few of the public at large, including politicians, financial journalists, lawyers and even financial "experts".

This supports Morison's view of the duty of the reporting accountant and auditor to exercise his professional judgment by posing to himself the question: "What figures will most fairly represent the underlying realities?"[13] However, although I am in agreement with Morison on this, I think some of his readers might not realise the full nature of the problem. First, these questions assume that the more fundamental question: "What aspect of reality, and on what criterion, are the accounts trying to represent?" has already been answered. If Morison's view of this is accepted—

namely that the object of the accounts is to present an estimate of "where the business now is" and "how a business is doing",[14] and if further agreement can be reached on the fundamental criteria for both these—a big question—it still remains essential to grasp the point already made above, that an economic assessment of the future—which is implied by the Morison aims—must be both uncertain and subjective. This applies as much to assessing a company's present position as assessing its future, for both are interlocked: the present position is a function of the future. That this is Morison's own view is indicated in his paper; but his use of the word "facts" in the sentence, "The object is simply to present a picture of the facts", suggests that there is to be found in any business situation an objectively determinable, ultimate truth to be detected if careful search is made; whereas business reality is a fuzzy and half-perceived wavering image that changes shape as one looks, is glimpsed through mists of uncertainty, and is highly personal in its interpretation. My conclusion is however similar to Morison's: standard requirements of Type 4 should never be mandatory: that is, there should always be a let-out where fairness of presentation demands it, and the latter should depend upon the judgment and good faith of the reporting accountant and the auditor.

Morison has pointed out that it is not possible to derive from existing practice, itself not uniform, postulates that will be generally applicable and lead to uniformity of treatment.[15] A leading Netherlands practitioner has recently reminded the profession that accountancy deals with the measurement of economic phenomena and that therefore in the development of accounting concepts or postulates greater weight should be given to economic reasoning than to experience, convention or accepted practice.[16] The difficulty of attempting to set up a basis of general principle without recourse to well-defined economic criteria relating to an agreed basic objective is apparent in the four "fundamental accounting concepts" formulated in SSAP 2, the British standard on disclosure of accounting policies, mentioned above: the "going concern concept"; the "accruals concept"; the "consistency concept"; and the "concept of prudence".[17] The standard requires that if accounts are prepared on the basis of assumptions which differ in material respects from any of these concepts, the facts should be explained. In the absence of a clear statement in such a case it is for the auditor to draw attention to the matter in his report to the shareholders.

The going concern concept is formulated as follows:

the enterprise will continue in operational existence for the foreseeable future. This means in particular that the profit and loss account and balance sheet assume no intention or necessity to liquidate or curtail significantly the scale of operation.

On the positive side it can be claimed that this concept reminds one that the income account and the balance sheet are not drawn up on a liquidation or break-up assumption and that some balance sheet "values" may be substantially lower than would be realised in an immediate sale. As however a full understanding of what is implied by the concept requires a knowledge of normal accounting procedures, it follows that it is not a basic postulate in the sense that the correct accounting treatment can be inferred from it. It can perhaps best be regarded as a reminder to the reporting accountant and to the auditor that if there is reason to believe that the business is heading for major financial crisis, or if the management have liquidation or partial liquidation or a major change in company activities in mind for some other reason, then the ordinary approach to balance sheet values and to the income account may not be appropriate; and that if these do not reflect the situation adequately, the audit report must be qualified. In short, the concept is a reminder that the current position of a business is a function of the specific management plans, and of the capacity of management to carry these plans out successfully. Insofar as the concept emphasises this, and underlines the importance of the auditor looking into the future and investigating the company's budget forecasts, it is evidently performing a useful and important function though it might be agreed that its usefulness would be enhanced if its aims were made more explicit by more detailed exposition.

The accruals concept is defined as follows:

revenue and costs are accrued (that is, recognised as they are earned or incurred, not as money is received or paid), matched with one another so far as their relationship can be established or justifiably assumed, and dealt with in the profit and loss account of the period to which they relate; provided that where the accruals concept is inconsistent with the "prudence" concept . . . the latter prevails. The accruals concept implies that the profit and loss account reflects changes in the amount of net assets that arise out of the transactions of the relevant period (other than distributions or subscriptions of capital and unrealised surpluses arising on revaluation of fixed assets). Revenue and profits dealt with in the profit and loss account are matched with associated costs and expenses by including in the same account the costs incurred in earning them (so far as these are material and identifiable).

This concept can be interpreted to mean that "receipts and payments" accounting is not acceptable; that on the contrary changes in non-cash assets, both in physical and in value terms (the interpretation of value being left undefined), must be included in the accounts; that shareholders should not be deceived or misled by reporting revenues and at the same time omitting costs that a reasonable person would regard as associated with those revenues, or—except where it is "prudent" to do so—by reporting costs related to revenues before the latter are reported, so that when they are reported an apparent improvement is indicated that a reasonable person would not regard as then justified; and that reserve accounting is not permitted except in relation to unrealised changes in the value of fixed assets.

The last of these requirements in effect says that all items treated as costs and revenues are to be brought to immediate attention in the income statement, not just those which the board of directors wish to emphasise. This is a "presentation" requirement which seems reasonable enough, though the exception for unrealised gains on fixed assets leads to anomalies.

The other requirements can only be given very broad interpretation and provide little or no help in deciding how to treat particular items, for this hangs upon the meaning of "earned", "incurred", "changes in the amount of net assets" and "associated", in the context of the statement. These terms are not defined, nor indeed could they be defined without some basic and workable definition of income, and criteria for determining it. It follows that an attempt to justify Type 4 standard requirements by referral to the accrual concept is likely to lead to circular argument. It has for example been argued that the accrual concept demands the operation of a deferred tax account and excludes the "flow-through" treatment of tax expense. This conclusion depends however upon the assertion that the conclusion itself is what accrual means. But as there are no basic criteria by which to determine what shall be accrued and by how much, the argument is circular.

Little need be said about the consistency concept. It has been reasonably enough said that there is little merit in being consistently wrong. However, making the figures useful is a separate question and the need to do so should not prevent adherence to the rules of good statistical presentation. The latter require that the bases of a given set of figures should not be changed in mid-stream without warning the user and doing one's best to reveal the effect of the change. This is therefore a Type 1 requirement and it is difficult to see why it should not be mandatory.

The prudence concept is defined as follows:

revenue and profits are not anticipated, but are recognised by inclusion in the profit and loss account only when realised in the form either of cash or of other assets the ultimate cash realisation of which can be assessed with reasonable certainty; provision is made for all known liabilities (expenses and losses) whether the amount of these is known with certainty or is a best estimate in the light of the information available.

This concept can be regarded as a rough and ready, pre-scientific way of dealing with the uncertainty that is unavoidable in financial reporting. It is understandable when it is looked at as a cautious way of ensuring that legal conditions for distributing profit under rules developed in Britain in the 19th and early 20th century have been met. It is less easy to justify if the aim is to provide as clear a picture as possible of the economic position of a company. Like the accrual concept, it has to be interpreted in the light of existing conventions. It is not a postulate from which the correct treatment of an item can be inferred by a logical process: it is rather a reminder of the existence of these conventions. Unlike the consistency concept, the prudence concept would be anathema to professional statisticians, whose aim is to present as unbiased a picture as possible of the phenomena they are dealing with.

I have suggested that the case for standard practices which impose requirements of Types 1 and 2 can be justified on canons of good statistical presentation. The case for Type 3, and especially Type 4, requirements is more open. There seem to be two main arguments in favour:

(a) There is a strong temptation for boards of directors, in deciding what information to disclose and on what basis to arrive at profits and at asset values, to apply the test of how the information will affect them and the company, rather than the test of what will give the fairest picture to outsiders. It is very easy to argue, without intention of dishonesty, that the non-disclosure of X or Y, or its presentation in such and such a way, or a change in the basis of its presentation, will in the end bring benefit to "the company" that will outweigh any temporary disadvantage to shareholders and others from the treatment in question—in short to regard accounting statements as tactical or strategic weapons of management instead of as intelligence reports for the world at large. It can be argued that the existence of well-chosen accounting standards is likely at least to reduce the manipulation of reported profits or balance sheet values. It may be said that it is the auditors' job to stop, or report upon, such action, and that they, highly-trained and highly-paid professionals, should not need the official formulation of standards to support them. However, we do not live in a perfect world. The education and training of accountants is not yet perfect. There is no agreement yet on basic aims of accounting. Present-day conditions have brought a rapid growth in what is required of the accountant. Accountants, being human, vary in ability, and some need help more than others in judging what is the appropriate treatment in particular cases, and in persuading boards of directors that the auditors' views are not due to the auditors' personal and unreasonable whims.

(b) Politicians, financiers, financial analysts and financial journalists, not to mention the general public (and, it may be added, many accountants and economists) can be well-versed in the legal and day-to-day technical detail of finance and still be remarkably innocent of deeper understanding of the more fundamental questions involved in profit measurement and of its relation to financial theory. Deeper study of these matters on a wide scale is a relatively recent development. There is therefore what may be called a general educational problem. The issue of standards certainly cannot be regarded as completely solving it: for reasons given above, the logical basis for many of the standards is still weak, to put it mildly. But their issue itself acts to increase interest (sometimes it must be feared by causing irritation) and tends to encourage study of these matters in a way that has been remarkably effective in bringing to the surface fundamental issues that have hitherto been glossed over in practice.

At its most fundamental, the question that has to be answered before satisfactory ground rules for accounting statements can be set up, is this: should statements of income and financial position be based on economic values as seen by a defined class of individuals, or should they merely indicate events by means of classified reports of past cash flows—that is, of past receipts and payments—perhaps combined with inventories of the physical resources owned by the company and of the claims against it? If the former, the figures must in the nature of things depend in part upon subjective judgment coupled with conventions for the use of workable approximation methods. If the latter, the figures can be completely factual

and objective, so that the subjective element enters only into the classification and form of presentation adopted; and, once these questions have
been settled, the degree of accounting skill needed is little above the book-
keeping level.

The present procedures and forms fall somewhere between these two
conflicting notions. Accountants, by allotting money figures under asset
headings, and appearing to show a figure for the net worth of the stockholders' interest (whether expressly so described or not—"the figure is
there so it must mean something", reasons the layman) confuse, and at
worst mislead, the outsider. Worse, accountants confuse themselves, for
while they are at great pains to refute the suggestion that the "amount"
they allot to asset headings in the balance sheet is an economic "value",
they are in fact constantly and unavoidably forced into considering and
reporting upon valuations and references to value. It is impossible to make
economic sense of a figure which is described as "profit for the year" or
"net earnings for year" unless that figure rests on a comparison of values
determined in some generally specified way at successive points of time.
Nor does "cost" make economic sense except as a sacrifice of money or
money's worth, i.e. of value in some sense.

Much talk is now heard of "current value" and "fair value", as the
appropriate bases for accounting statements, though these are less often
defined in a way that would make them usable. Perhaps the most promising
candidate for a reformed accrual accounting method is one based on the
notion of *deprival value*, developed by Baxter,[18] and traceable in its essence
back at least to Bonbright's seminal *Valuation of Property*[19]. In its simplest
and crudest approximation this notion would mean valuing assets at the
estimated replacement cost of the same asset in the same condition (making
use for example of selected index numbers of asset prices), but subject to
an upper limit set by the higher of the net realisable value of the asset or the
estimated present worth of the asset's contribution to the business in its
best use (which for assets soon to be sold would be their net realisation
value). Put shortly, the rule for all asset valuation would read "replacement cost or lower economic value to the business". Each asset or asset
class would be assessed separately, making the assumption that other
assets remained unchanged. Liabilities would be assessed on the basis of
the present money outlay that would be needed to eliminate them.

If users of the accounts were not to be misled it would be necessary,
however, because assets often complement one another so that the arithmetical addition of values thus determined can exceed the economic value
of the whole, to add a second requirement, namely that a similar assessment should be made for the business as a whole. This would set a maximum overall value for the statement of financial position.[20] Provided that
reserve accounting was excluded, the income account balance would then
be automatically determined through the ordinary accounting procedures.
Corrections for general inflation would require no more than the application of general price index adjustments to the current values derived
on the above basis in order to express them in the same purchasing power.
The adoption of the deprival value approach would not avoid the need to
settle *whose* economic utility the accounts were reporting upon, for this

can affect the interpretation of the "contribution to the business" of an asset; the usual assumption is that the annual accounting statements relate to the financial and economic interests of the owners: shareholders in a company or nation at large in a state industry. Given a decision on this question, the approach could bring a basic principle to bear on a whole series of debates which have arisen in the context of standard practice on such matters as the treatment of deferred taxation, research and development expenditure, goodwill, depreciation and stock valuation. It would also go a long way towards assimilating the criteria for the preparation of financial accounting statements to those for satisfactory management accounts, and would direct attention more specifically to the role of the fundamental instruments of financial control, the long-term finance forecasts and budgets and the cash flow reports of actuals that control these—an outcome much to be desired.

NOTES

[1] See, for example, Peter Bird, "Standard Accounting Practice" in H. C. Edey and B. S. Yamey (eds.), *Debits, Credits, Finance and Profits*, London, 1974.

[2] The bodies represented on the Standards Committee at present (June 1977) are: the three Institutes of Chartered Accountants in England and Wales, Scotland and Ireland; the Association of Certified Accountants; the Institute of Cost and Management Accountants; and the Chartered Institute of Public Finance and Accountancy. References here to British practice should be understood to apply also to Ireland and Irish practice.

[3] See William T. Baxter, "Recommendations on Accounting Theory", in W. T. Baxter and S. Davidson (eds.), *Studies in Accounting Theory*, London, 1962, reprinted in S. A. Zeff and T. F. Keller (eds.), *Financial Accounting Theory I*, 2nd ed., New York etc., 1973; and A. M. C. Morison, "The Role of the Reporting Accountant Today", *The Accountant's Magazine*, 74 (1970), reprinted in this volume and also in Zeff and Keller.

[4] The Sandilands Committee.

[5] Some 40 years after such questions were being discussed by accounting theorists such as R. S. Edwards—see "The Nature and Measurement of Income", which first appeared in *The Accountant*, July to October 1938, and is reprinted in a shortened version in this volume.

[6] Baxter, *op. cit.*

[7] Morison, *op. cit.*

[8] See, for example, Appendix to *Survey of Published Accounts 1973–1974*, Institute of Chartered Accountants in England and Wales, London, 1975.

[9] See Edey and Panitpakdi, "British Company Accounting and the Law 1844–1900" in A. C. Littleton and B. S. Yamey, *Studies in the History of Accounting*, London, 1956.

[10] See British SSAP 6.

[11] Morison, *op. cit.*

[12] *Ibid.*

[13] *Ibid.*

[14] *Ibid.*

[15] *Ibid.*

[16] A. F. Tempelaar, "Standards have their dangers", *The Accountant*, 22 May 1975.

[17] It will be noted that the British "concepts" have followed earlier American examples which have been strongly criticised, e.g. by David Solomons, in *Divisional Performance: Measurement and Control*, Homewood, 1965, chapter II.

[18] W. T. Baxter, *Depreciation* (London, 1971) and *Accounting Values and Inflation* (London, New York, etc. 1975).

[19] J. C. Bonbright, *Valuation of Property* (original edition New York, 1937, reprinted Charlottesville, 1965).

[20] See H. C. Edey, "Deprival Value and Financial Accounting", in *Debits, Credits, Finance and Profits*.

Why all-purpose accounts will not do

Accounting is justified only if it serves a need. Setting up an accounting theory involves (a) identifying a need and (b) selecting and defining a set of accounting procedures (which one may call a 'model') to satisfy the need. The theory is the assumption that the selected model is appropriate for the particular need.

If a theory is to be useful, the model must be operational, that is, it must be capable of being handled effectively by all those who have to use it. This means that either the procedural rules are specified in some detail, or that general principles are laid down which enable practitioners to deduce the procedures appropriate in particular cases without undue doubt or difficulty.

The procedural rules and any general principles must be within the range of knowledge, education and general understanding of those who will have to operate them, and must be acceptable to them. This limits the speed at which new ideas can be introduced.

In setting up a model for use, eg as a standard, it is necessary to make judgements about the needs to be met, and the probable effectiveness of the model in meeting them. So judgement has to be based on past experience and such writings on the subject as are available. It is necessarily a speculative exercise, for it will seldom be possible to envisage all the consequences.

The effectiveness and usefulness of a model can be judged in the end only by the systematic study of results over time. If this is to be done, a programme of monitoring and assessment is called for.

Why financial statements? Financial statements are needed for various purposes. To consider the role of theory in setting standards, these purposes can be divided into two distinct categories which may be described as (a) legally-oriented needs and (b) decision-oriented needs. This division is necessary because the two categories call for models that are not wholly compatible, a fact which gives rise to difficulties in the search for the best workable standards.

Before 1948, legally-oriented needs largely prevailed, so far as published accounts were concerned. Historical cost profit measurement rules developed largely in the latter part of the 19th century, against a background of case law relating particularly to the legality of dividend payments and to fraud. By the middle of the present century, the rules had become well defined within certain limits, so much so that perhaps they were beginning to be regarded by some people as leading to the reporting of 'facts' instead of a convenient set of rules to produce information that was thought to be useful, but needed interpretation.

Before 1929 there was no legal obligation to publish a profit and loss account and before 1948 there were no legal rules as to what it should contain. Up to then, the general idea underlying reporting of profit was that the money amount of the capital value of the undertaking at the beginning of the accounting year should be maintained, capital value being defined as the amount shown in the books for the net assets. The emphasis had been on prudence and the importance of the underlying financial position being at least as good as was shown by the accounts. Secret contingency reserves were regarded as quite acceptable.

In 1948 there was a turning point and thereafter emphasis was to be on 'accuracy' rather than excessive prudence. Profit was to be disclosed in full, and secret reserves created by reducing that profit were no longer legal. This change was undoubtedly due in large part to the considerable influence of The Royal Mail case in 1931 and the misuse of secret reserves revealed by it. But profit was still defined by the legally-based 'normal' accounting rules.

Another trend was also developing in the second half of the present century. The profit and loss report and the accounts generally were increasingly being regarded as a guide towards the assessment of the value of quoted shares, and were being used more and more by investment analysts. This, coupled with inflation, led to increasing emphasis being laid on the inadequacy of historical cost accounting to produce useful information for decisions, and led to increasingly critical consideration of the underlying theory.

Legally-oriented needs. When the accounting figures presented may have legal consequences from statute or case law, or from contractual arrangements, legally-oriented needs arise. They cover such matters as tax assessment, legality of dividend distribution, remuneration by share of profit, pooling of profit and restriction of borrowing by reference to profit or asset valuations. Most of these matters relate to the 'sharing' of the results of business among different parties.

Legally-oriented needs demand that there should be reasonable certainty in the figures that will be used. Where there is a risk of legal action or prosecution, or where taxation is involved, a high degree of subjectivity is undesirable. Figures derived for these purposes must be calculable without undue difficulty by large numbers of accountants who have no time to indulge in a deep consideration of fundamentals at each stage of the calculation. They must be susceptible of verification by audit.

In particular, the accounting procedures should lead to a single set of figures that satisfy the legal requirements. In practice this means that a single figure of profit is wanted and that it will be based on conventional procedures which reflect a rough, but workable, approximation to an accepted conception of profit in the abstract. Similar considerations apply to the asset valuations adopted for balance sheet purposes.

The preparation of legally-oriented figures demands, therefore, fairly standardised rules, judgement of what lies in the future being reduced to a minimum. The traditional historical cost approach, coupled with well-defined accepted procedures, satisfied these criteria until inflation caused it to depart too far from reality.

Decision-oriented needs. Matters calling for decision-oriented figures include investment analysis (judgement of share values of listed companies); judgements on lending, wage negotiations (if they are carried out sensibly) and price control (again if carried out sensibly). They are also relevant in judging the performance of management. Decision-oriented accounts are needed for this purpose because the quality of management of a business up to a certain date cannot be judged effectively without summing-up the quality of the financial legacy bequeathed to future years. This summing-up involves looking into the future and is, therefore, in a large degree judgemental.

Where the financial statements are used for decisions, it must be assumed that the users will have their own view of the kind of information that is relevant and how they will use it (ie they will have their own 'decision models'). This suggests that the information supplied by the financial statements should be related to the performance criteria needed to control the company and to judge its past success and future potential.

Decision-oriented needs call for an approach akin to that of management accounting. Judgements or guesses about the future become important. Estimates of the value of intangibles, considerations of the life and earning potential of assets, future realisations and so on, become important.

In broad terms, the need is for information that can help in forming judgements of the future cash flows of the company, and the risks thereof, on various assumptions of what may happen. Balance sheet break-up values may be relevant as additional data. Values of properties in alternative use may be relevant.

Clearly, there are limits to the information of this kind that can be put into the accounts. It is impossible to capture all intangibles. The equity as stated in the balance sheet cannot, for example, be an estimate of the actual value which the shares in aggregate should have in the market. Something must be left to the interpretation of the user if the accountant is not to become a straightforward valuer.

Conclusion. There is no doubt that legally-oriented data must be provided and that no radical and rapid move towards accounts prepared on a very judgemental basis is likely to be acceptable. This suggests that if the basic accounts are to be all-purpose, they must be based on an acceptable model, the rules for which are understood widely, which is susceptible of interpretation and audit, and which gives the legal-type data required.

Such a model is unlikely to be ideal for decision-oriented purposes. In particular, because of the high degree of approximation and use of arbitrary rules that it demands, the figure of profit it produces cannot be related by a precise formula to the economic state of the business, however this may be conceived. The theory on which the financial statements rest can be specified at only a very general level. So far as decision needs are concerned, the emphasis must be not so much on a theory in the sense stated above, but on the usefulness of the figures as a whole.

This suggests that if decision-oriented needs are to be reasonably satisfied, information supplementary to the basic accounts should be recognised as playing an important part. It is particularly important to get across the idea that it is impossible to encapsulate the whole financial state of an undertaking and its future potential into a single figure. Decisions need multiple data. This view carries more weight in that there is no uniformity of opinion, or strong empirical evidence, on what kind of theory would be best for decision-oriented purposes.

Clearly, however, the basic model should be as good as possible for decisions without running it into difficulties for legally-oriented purposes. How can this be achieved?

Management accounts are designed to improve decisions. Management decisions must also be assumed to have the aim of satisfying those for whom management are working, so data that is better for management should on the whole tend to help other users in their interpretation of the results.

It follows that reference to accepted management-oriented accounting procedures may well provide the best basis for deciding what are the best measures and standards for use in financial accounting within, of course, the limits of what can reasonably be disclosed to the world at large.

It would be consistent with this approach to place emphasis on the education of users by appropriate releases on the use and interpretation of financial statements. This is particularly important in view of the readiness of the lay public at large, including politicians and financial journalists, to assume that legally-oriented, or indeed any figures, produce definitive answers to business and economic problems. It would also help in spreading recognition of the fact that the limitation of the range for use of subjective judgements necessarily imposes some degree of arbitrariness in laying down standards.

A programme for systematic monitoring of the use made of financial statements, and of the effect of the particular system adopted, so far as this is possible, would also be in keeping with this approach. This would imply a systematic research programme of some sophistication.

Sandilands and the Logic of Current Cost

Harold C. Edey

The Sandilands philosophy

At an early paragraph in its Report the Sandilands Committee defines a company's profit by adapting the well-known Hicks definition of an individual's income [Hicks, 1946, p. 172]. The adaptation reads: 'A company's profit for the year is the maximum value which the company can distribute during the year, and still expect to be as well off at the end of the year as it was at the beginning' [Inflation Accounting, 1975, paragraph 98]. For a company, continues the Report, the same degree of well-offness means maintaining its capital intact. If we were granted perfect knowledge of the future, the quantification of this capital would be fairly clear. It would be the discounted net present value of all future net cash flows arising for the company [paragraph 100]. The Report gives examples that indicate that cash flows here mean cash flows distributable to the shareholders [paragraphs 101 and 102].

Surprisingly, the Report does not quote Hicks' alternative definition of maintenance of well-offness, which for companies would be the maintenance of the level of cash flow distributable to shareholders. This is not the same concept as the first unless the discounting rate is held constant and it can be argued with some plausibility that it is a better model of the commercial view of profit than the first. However, as the procedures recommended by the Report do not, as I shall argue, fit into either definition, the point is perhaps an academic one.

Hicks, it will be remembered, also notes that if the monetary unit were not stable it would be necessary in measuring income to deflate the changing monetary values by using a suitable price index related to the consumer's spending pattern: translated into company terms this would presumably be the average shareholders' spending pattern. However, this idea is firmly rejected by the Report [paragraph 129].

After referring to the Hicks concept, the Report says that as it is impossible accurately to forecast future cash flows, the concept cannot be used directly. Other concepts must be considered which approximate to it and which are capable of practical application' [paragraph 103]. It then examines what it describes as five alternative concepts of profit, each associated with a corresponding concept of capital maintenance, and selects, as the most useful method of accounting for inflation in the longer term, one based on the use of the monetary unit as the unit of measurement, under which profit is 'gains arising during the year which may be distributed after charging the 'value to the business' of the company's assets consumed during the year' [paragraphs 128 and 143]. (Here it speaks of profit; elsewhere it uses the term 'operating profit', and in paragraph 201 'operating profit' is equated with 'profit for the year'.)

The 'value to the business' of an asset is identified with the concept of deprival value, used by J. C. Bonbright [Bonbright, 1937]. This is the amount which would just compensate the company if it were suddenly to be deprived of the asset. The method of estimation of deprival value specified in the Report [paragraph 219] can be summarised in the formula: 'the lower of current replacement cost (depreciated replacement cost in the case of fixed assets) and the best discounted recoverable value by sale or use'.

The Report makes clear that liabilities should, in principle, be dealt with similarly, i.e. treated as negative assets. but accepts that practical difficulties may limit the application of the principle [paragraph 593].

A valuation on the basis of deprival value does not, as we know, imply that the asset in question is to be replaced: only that the owner of the asset could be fully compensated for its loss if paid this amount. Bonbright's definition requires that consequential side effects, such as loss of earnings during replacement, be taken into account. The Report does not, however, deal with these niceties.

The measurement of capital maintenance is thus specified indirectly by laying down a procedure for calculation of profit. The Report believes that this procedure produces the most useful figure for the majority of users of the accounts [paragraph 522].

So, despite the earlier reference to the Hicks definition, the interpretation of capital maintenance as the maintenance of the shareholders' investment in the company, whether in terms of the currency unit or of general purchasing power, is abandoned. Instead, the Sandilands approach becomes the practical one of choosing what seems to be the most useful set of figures for those interested in the financial state of the company.

The procedures developed in the report for the calculation of operating profit require 'value to the business' to be assessed at the time of consumption of the asset, in principle at the time that the sales revenue accrues, though the Report suggests. the use in practice of an averaging method for stocks consumed, and an end-year figure for depreciation [paragraphs 594 and 606]. The adjustments to bring the book values of assets to current deprival value produce 'holding' gains or losses, to be credited or debited to reserve accounts—the 'revaluation reserves'—which I shall hereafter refer to as 'reserves for capital maintenance'.

(It is worth noting that as the amount recoverable by sale or use of an asset must be estimated in order to determine whether its value to the business is below its written-down replacement cost, the assumptions and estimates needed are similar in kind to those needed for investment decisions, including decisions relating to the retention of the asset.)

The Report says expressly that the concept of profit which it has chosen does not imply the maintenance of the physical assets which the company happens to have, or the purchasing power invested in these assets [paragraph 129]. This rejection by the Report of any correction for the change in the value of money in measuring profit means that monetary assets and liabilities—cash and claims fixed in money amount—cannot therefore give rise to reported gains or losses [paragraph 537]. On the other hand, as noted below, a consideration of the recommendations shows that in effect the procedures will generally lead to a calculation based on the maintenance of the existing physical assets or of their potential physical output.

Consequences of the Sandilands procedures

I think it is generally accepted that deprival value gives a better assessment of the current economic cost of using fixed assets and stocks than does historical cost, whether under conditions of inflation or not. It is therefore a significantly better guide for management and government on the use of resources. It is true that the measurement is far from perfect. The existence of intangibles, and of complementarity among groups of assets, prevent the sum of the deprival values of the separate recorded assets from being in general a satisfactory indicator of the deprival value of the undertaking as a whole [Edey, 1974]. Nevertheless, provided these limitations are understood, deprival value seems to be as good a basis of valuation as is at present available for use in annual financial statements as we know them. In the end this can only be settled on the basis of experience.

However, if one is to assess the full significance of the Sandilands procedures, one must bear in mind that, as already noted, the debits and credits to profit and loss account for cost of sales and depreciation are based on the deprival value costs *at the time of consumption*, not at the beginning of the year of account. The Sandilands measure of capital to be maintained is based, in effect, on the amount of money value needed to replace the 'bits used up' of the particular mix of assets which happens to be held when the revenue arises, and on the basis of the deprival value at that time. As the mix of assets changes through time, the 'capital' or 'substance of the business' changes with it, so that the capital to be maintained becomes the sum of the changing deprival values of a changing collection of assets.

The Sandilands operating profit cannot therefore be regarded as the surplus remaining after maintenance of capital as it was at the beginning of each year, whether that capital is defined in physical or in value terms.

Furthermore, the procedure to be followed in practice for the assessment of deprival value is likely to vary sufficiently to cause variations in the implied capital maintenance concept unless the latter is defined broadly. If deprival value is given its strict meaning, it is measured by the amount of money which would just compensate the company for the loss of the asset concerned. In principle the deprival value of an asset is the capitalised value of the forecast loss in future cash flow caused by the hypothetical deprival, all other existing assets of the company being assumed retained. In practice, however, the measurement will usually be cruder. In many instances the 'replacement cost' will be interpreted simply as the cost, based on a price list, index number or estimate, of replacing the same asset in the same condition. Or the estimate may reflect the cost of replacing the physical output capacity, with or without an allowance for different operating costs where the new asset differs from the old. (In this context it may be noted that, in general, official index numbers of asset prices do not allow for changes in the operating cost of the assets to which they refer.) Maintenance of the 'replacement cost' could therefore imply in practice maintenance of the same physical asset, maintenance of the same physical output, maintenance of the same cash flow or maintenance of the present value of that cash flow, according to the actual method of calculation selected. Where calculation is based on the recoverable amount from use or sale of the asset (because this is less than the calculated net replacement cost) the maintenance of the asset's deprival value will imply the maintenance of the present value of the asset's expected future cash contribution.

Under the Sandilands system a company could continue to report profit in a year in which a significant fall occurred in the replacement cost and money earning power of its assets when the price level of most other goods and services was constant or rising. Indeed, if operating revenue kept up in the short run, reported profit might even increase because of the fall in depreciation or cost of sales. Only when operating revenue began to fall would the deterioration in earning capacity be signalled in the profit and loss account. It does not indeed follow that users of the financial statements would be deceived: movements on the reserve for capital maintenance would tell the story when interpreted along with the profit and loss account, as the Report recommends. The point does, however, illustrate one of the effects of tying the quantum of capital to be maintained to movements in the price level of the assets the company happens to have from time to time, as distinct from the general purchasing power of its asset values at the beginning of the period, and emphasises the departure of the Sandilands recommendations from the basic Hicks model.

'Distributable profit'

The Report considers that operating profit, as it defines it, is a better guide than historical cost profit to the amount available for dividend appropriation [paragraph 544], but it also makes it clear that there are circumstances when it would be right for less or more to be regarded as avail-

able. Thus [paragraph 540] 'holding gains which accrue outside the profit and loss account will be of importance to the reader of the financial statement' (and presumably to the directors in considering dividend policy); and the Report states that where a company's purpose is to generate holding gains these may reasonably be described, when realised, as 'profits' (though not as 'operating profits') [paragraph 718].

The conclusion must be that the Sandilands Committee did not intend operating profit to be used as an iron measure of distributable profit in either a business or a legal sense; its use was rather to act only as a 'first approximation' indicator of the amount which could be distributed without 'weakening' the business [paragraph 96]. The concept of maintenance of 'capital' or of the 'substance of the business' underlying the Sandilands procedures can thus only be defined in very general and rather subjective terms. The final decision on what is 'distributable' is left to the directors.

Exposure Draft 18

The Inflation Accounting Steering Group (IASG) was set up to implement the Sandilands proposals and was required to base its recommendations on the Report. It is, therefore, not surprising that the proposals of the Accounting Standards Committee, set out in Exposure Draft 18 (ED 18) and based on the work of the IASG, followed the Sandilands philosophy. The profit and loss account, showing the operating profit calculated in the Sandilands way, was to be accompanied by an appropriation account. The latter was to show the extent to which the operating profit needed to be modified, upward or downward, in order to indicate the directors' views of the amount which could reasonably be regarded as attributable to the shareholders' interest in the company. Attached to this there was to be an explanation by the directors of the way in which they had arrived at this amount. [Accounting Standards Committee, 1976, paragraphs 22–24]. This approach left the final results for the year defined only in the broadest of terms and the interpretation of these to the directors.

This has led to much criticism. Superficially, it might appear to be a sharp departure from existing practice, which has, since 1948 at least, taken the view that the 'profit available for distribution' is to be determined on the basis of accepted accounting rules, though it is known that an element of subjective judgement cannot be excluded, for example on questions such as stock valuation, depreciation and treatment of intangibles. It can, however, be argued that the unavoidable element of subjectivity in assessing the reality of a company's financial state is so great—particularly in relation to the value of intangibles and changes in these—that no reasonably objective profit measurement is compatible with a close approximation to economic or business reality. It is certainly a delusion to believe that profit measurement as we have known it in the past is, or can be, both 'factual' and 'objective' [Edey, 1973). The Sandilands Report itself says: ' "Profit for the year" is a practical business concept used as a guide for prudent decision making by companies. It may usefully be defined as the amount of the total gains arising in the year that may prudently be regarded as distributable. It is thus a subjective concept...' [paragraph 95].

It should also be pointed out that the concept of operating profit defined by the Report, and in ED 18, represents no giant departure from the existing long-recognised and accepted practice of some companies. A company which made use of the base stock method of valuation of stocks, or of LIFO, and which annually revalued its fixed assets and depreciation on a replacement cost basis, would report a profit which would often be no bad approximation to a Sandilands operating profit. LIFO it is true is not at present a standard method of stock valuation in the British Isles (though not illegal for company reporting), but it is respectable elsewhere; and there is nothing very new in the base stock method. Recalculation of depreciation on a current cost basis, with or without revaluation of the assets in the balance sheet, is quite respectable in the British Isles.

Why then the fuss about the appropriation account and the leaving to the directors—with a requirement of full explanation—of the final assessment of what is potentially distributable without damaging the company's future? How does this differ from the approach under historical cost accounting, where everyone should know that the 'profit' balance is highly conventional and certainly not a definitive statement of economic or business reality, and where the directors make the dividend decision, though without the requirement of an explanation of its rationale?

One explanation may be that many people still do not appreciate that all practical profit reports must be conventional, though the conventions may differ and some may be better than others. The Sandilands Committee in issuing its Report,

and the IASG and the Accounting Standards Committee (ASC) in preparing and issuing ED 18, took the view that the current cost operating profit convention is better than the historical cost one.

Strong exception was taken by some auditors to the subjectivity of the appropriation account and the 'leaving to the directors' of the final determination of what is 'distributable', even though auditors have been satisfied for many years to state their view on the historical cost profit balance, and to leave to the directors the decisions on dividends and appropriations to reserves provided the law is not violated. Under ED 18 the directors would be required to state the basis of their assessment of the final results reported by them, and it would be possible for auditors to test whether their statement was consistent with the way in which the actual amount disclosed had been calculated, in the same way that auditors test the consistency of profit forecasts against the stated assumptions on which they are based.

However, it must be admitted that legal difficulties could arise in the absence of a single figure clearly denominated as 'profit'; these could arise from existing contractual arrangements, and also if the dividend law were more tightly defined than it is at present in Britain, so that an annual 'profit' figure was required to interpret it.

The Sandilands philosophy seems to have been more acceptable to some business managements than others. Some have joined with many accountants, auditors, financial analysts and academics, in pointing out that full distribution of the Sandilands profit would in some cases—notably banks—lead to erosion of the shareholders' capital, whether measured in terms of maintaining the shareholders' interest in the existing physical entity, or in a more general sense of preserving the investment in real terms having regard to the depreciation of the currency; and that in other cases full distribution would still leave the shareholders' interest enhanced in some real sense. These points can be met by leaving the matter to the discretion of the directors, but it is clear that for many people these objections reflect a desire that financial reporting should be based on a well-defined model of capital maintenance to which the practical measurements can approximate. At the more extreme end of the spectrum of opinion is the naive view that the whole financial reality of a year's operations of a company can be expressed adequately in a single figure.

The prevailing philosophy of the Sandilands

Report seems to be that the central aim of the financial statements should be to provide a useful set of information and that the figure of profit is not unique. Under this view, whether one particular figure or another is called 'profit' is of lesser importance than the usefulness of the statements as a whole. Indeed, such has been the confusion and misunderstanding in the debate on this question that there is much to be said for abandoning the use of the word 'profit' altogether. The Report does however seem to have difficulty in making up its mind. In some places 'usefulness' is put in the forefront, with emphasis on the conventional nature of any profit figure and the arbitrariness of any choice between concepts. Elsewhere the Report seems to elevate its 'operating profit' to a position where it begins to acquire unique validity. For example, in paragraph 739 the Report claims that its operating profit is the profit that could be maintained (and presumably distributed) in the future if all conditions surrounding the company's operations remained the same. But, as noted already, and demonstrated early in the discussion which followed the issue of the Report, the exclusion of any adjustment for the effect of changing price levels on monetary assets and liabilities would mean that some companies which distributed the full Sandilands profit would find themselves short of working capital; and others would have a surplus [see e.g. Inflation Accounting Steering Group, 1976, Paper 18].

Alternative models

There is certainly a strong and fairly widespread desire for a single figure of profit which, if not perfect, is at least a reasonable approximation to some well-defined model, and from which among other things an earnings per share figure can be calculated. Unfortunately there is no general agreement on a precise concept or model. In what follows I shall examine some of the problems that arise when an attempt is made to graft procedures on to the Sandilands model in order to produce the unique figure of profit desired.

One problem arises because the Sandilands proposals, systematically applied, exclude from the profit and loss account gains or losses that arise from trading operations in the same market. For example, a successful purchasing policy may enable a company to record a holding gain on stocks, but under Sandilands principles this is excluded from operating profit. A company whose business it is to deal in a commodity market will show virtually all its gains in the reserve account;

its expenses will appear in the profit and loss account. Under the philosophy of 'looking at all the figures' to assess results there is perhaps no problem. However, this does not satisfy people who want the relevant results concentrated in a single figure of profit or in a single earnings per share figure. Nor is a profit that excludes this amount likely to be accepted by the Inland Revenue for tax assessment. There is indeed no reason to suppose that skilful purchasing is necessarily less productive, nationally or for individual businesses, than skilful selling or manufacturing. But no acceptable test has yet been found—or is likely to be found—for deciding how much of such gains should be transferred to profit and loss account while adhering to the general Sandilands approach. It is difficult to see any effective solution that does not involve the separation of real from fictitious or inflationary gains by the application of a general price index.

This demonstrates a particular problem that arises from the physical concept of capital maintenance implied by the Sandilands operating profit. Much more attention however has been directed to the question of the so-called 'monetary items'.

There have been two quite different conceptual lines of approach to this question, both outlined briefly in the IASG's *Background Papers* [Inflation Accounting Steering Group, 1976, Paper 18]. Both are departures from the spirit of the Sandilands philosophy, in that each aims at producing 'the profit' rather than 'a profit'.

No empirical tests yet exist to tell us whether either of these, or the more pragmatic approach of Sandilands and ED 18, produce the 'best'—which is presumably the most 'useful'—results. Nor indeed are the supporters of either alternative agreed on the test of usefulness, and in particular whether this should be the ability of the user to improve prediction of the company's future and judgement of its past (both essentially the same so far as information needs are concerned [Edey, 1970]) or some other purpose requiring less subjectivity, such as tax assessment.

Each of the two lines of approach has variants, but it will be convenient to describe each by reference to one of its specific variants, using the initials of writers who have been closely associated with each. I shall call one the Baxter or *B* system, the other the Gynther or *G* system, after academic exponents of the two basic ideas [Baxter, 1975, and Gynther, 1966]. It is a fortunate coincidence that *G* also stands for Gibbs and for Godley, the names of contemporary contributors to the debate whose views are an extension of the main Gynther line [see Inflation Accounting Steering Group, 1976, Paper 18]. As however they advocate an extension of practice into an area rejected, as I understand it, by Gynther, I shall refer to their variant by the letters GG.

The B system (called the 'Ideal' system, in the IASG paper already mentioned) could equally be called the 'CCA/CPP' system, as it is in effect a combination of the Sandilands/ED 18 CCA system of deprival valuation with a constant purchasing power system of the type specified in the provisional accounting standard of 1974 [Accounting Standards Committee, 1974]. Under this system the capital to be maintained is defined as the value of the shareholders' equity at the beginning of the year, uplifted by the percentage increase in a suitable index of the rise in the general price level during the year of account. Only part of the holding gains are real—the part which reflects a percentage rise in value greater than the general inflation. This 'real' part is fed back to profit and loss account immediately or as it is realised over the life of the asset; the 'fictitious' part attributable to inflation is retained in the reserve for capital maintenance. When there is no inflation, the fictitious part is of course zero, and all gains or losses are fed into profit and loss account as they are realised (or immediately if no realisation criterion is imposed). The system operates in reverse when the general price level is falling.

In its most developed form the transactions during the year are translated, by application of the general price index, to currency of the same date; for example, a transaction of £100 that occurred midway through a financial year, say on 30 June, would be re-stated using the number of pounds that had the same purchasing power at 31 December as did £100 on 30 June. In this way the accounts are 'stabilised'—expressed throughout in money of the same purchasing power—so that the results are all measured in a constant unit that is the same for all companies whose accounts end on a given date.

Under this system, whether or not the final step of stabilisation is taken, monetary assets held during a period of inflation will, by definition, throw up a loss, to be charged to profit. Similarly the financial statements will show a gain from holding monetary liabilities which is the counterpart of the lender's loss: where this gain is not realised at once, as in the case of longer-term liabilities, it can be retained in a reserve and fed into profit and loss account over the life of the liability.

Naturally, such gains will be cancelled out by real losses to the extent that the assets have failed to rise in value in proportion to the inflation, but the accounts will split the overall effect into its constituent parts (a point misunderstood by some in assessing the practical application of the CPP method when it was introduced in the British Isles in the form of a supplementary statement).

If there is some long-term debt, distribution of the full B profit will, in general, in conditions of inflation, necessitate some increase in such debt in money terms if assets are not to be reduced or additional equity capital raised; this reflects the fall in capital gearing that will already have occurred through a rise in money value of the proportion of physical assets financed by debt.

The system thus deals automatically with the problems of monetary items and dealing profits. It is a shareholder-oriented system, in the sense that its rationale of profit measurement is that of showing the results as they affect the equity shareholder's interest insofar as these can be indicated by the use of current costs based on deprival values and removal of the effect of the depreciation of the currency. It is the only system of those I am discussing that applies a general inflation adjustment to the measuring unit, and it is the only one that can be described as 'inflation accounting' in the strict and full sense.

In a period of zero inflation the B system would in general report a profit equal to the Sandilands operating profit: the G system would do so only by chance. The latter extends the basic Sandilands system by adding, to the physical entity whose maintenance determines the zero level of reported profit, the monetary working capital associated with it. This involves applying to the net monetary working capital, positive or negative, an index adjustment the size of which is determined by the change in value of the varying mix of physical working capital (stocks) held. Insofar as the current liabilities exceed the current monetary assets, an increase in the cost of stock is automatically financed (assuming the credit terms are unchanged) and, it is argued, can be reported as profit; so that to this extent holding gains on stock can be brought into the profit and loss account instead of being retained in a reserve for capital maintenance. If, on the other hand, the current monetary assets exceed the current liabilities, additional provision is made by debiting profit and crediting the reserve for capital maintenance in order to provide for the extra finance associated with the stock holding. These adjustments are in principle, like the stock revaluations, made continuously through the financial year, but in practice may be based on some kind of averaging. The system is not directly linked to inflation or deflation and can produce monetary adjustments when the general price level is stable.

The G system described by Gynther is not shareholder-oriented. The capital to be maintained is that of the business entity, whether financed by share capital or by loan capital. If 'profit' calculated on this G system was distributed in full in circumstances where the company had some loan capital, and when asset prices were rising, there would be an annual decrease in capital gearing as measured in terms of current values. The GG system takes account of this by regarding the holding of non-current monetary liabilities as reducing the need for a full retention of holding gains: in effect, this amends the G concept of capital maintenance to a shareholder-oriented one. As originally put forward, the system would bring into the final balance of reported profit all holding gains, whether realised or unrealised, insofar as they could be regarded as attributable to finance which was provided by net creditors and loans; the system as sketched out by Gibbs would however show the G profit separately in order to indicate the amount of profit which was 'automatically' financed by the extension of net trade credit as stocks rose in value or the additional retention needed in respect of net monetary assets in working capital. Under inflation, and where there was some long-term debt, the distribution of the full GG profit would in general necessitate some increase in debt finance if assets were not to be reduced, reflecting as in the B method the previous fall in effective gearing as physical assets rose in value. Adjustments of this type are now sometimes known as 'gearing adjustments' [Accounting Standards Committee, 1977].

As put forward by Gibbs therefore, the distinction between the operating profit after the working capital adjustment, and final profit for shareholders after allowing for the effect of long-term debt, is seen in terms of the availability of cash flows, so that the conceptual basis begins to approach that of cash flow reporting and move away from that of direct measurement of the amount needed to maintain capital value. Gynther, if I understand him, would regard the calculation of the operating profit of the entity—the net assets financed by capital, reserves and long-term debt—as the final step, and the calculation of any benefit derived by the shareholders from the existence of long-term debt as something

for the individual shareholders to figure out for themselves [Gynther, 1966, p. 151].

B and G type systems provide rules for dealing, each in its own way, with the 'problem' of monetary assets. Unlike the B system, but like Sandilands, the G type systems in effect base the uplift needed to maintain what they regard as the business entity on an implied index of the changing deprival values (or on some interpretations, replacement costs) of the varying mix of physical assets; adjustment is not directly linked to general inflation.

Acceptability and problems

The B concept does not seem to be acceptable to business men and practitioners, at any rate at present. This is perhaps because it has received relatively little attention and has not been widely studied, but also because of what I consider to be a mistaken view that indexation in *measuring* will lead to indexation of *transactions*. Some of those who have examined it have misunderstood it, sometimes because of a failure to comprehend fully the mechanism of inflation, and sometimes through not appreciating that a general price index can be useful even if not technically or theoretically perfect. The system undoubtedly appears at first glance rather complicated and this in itself is unlikely to commend it to practitioners and business men; though initial difficulty of comprehension is sometimes a price worth paying if it enables subsequent difficulties to be met on grounds of principle. For those who do not accept the pure Sandilands philosophy and wish for a unique figure of profit, it avoids some of the problems that arise when a G type solution is pursued. Some of these I shall now discuss.

One of these problems has already been discussed in connection with the Sandilands operating profit: insofar as the business or part of it is that of dealing in a well-defined commodity, in a single market, the G system provides no usable principle for separating dealing profits from retentions in reserve for capital maintenance. Any standard or established set of procedures must fall back on an arbitrary rule.

A major problem arises in deciding which assets are to be treated as 'monetary'. At first it seems right to define monetary assets as those fixed in terms of currency—e.g. pounds sterling. However, on further consideration the question is more puzzling. For example, assets with a face value fixed in currency, can nevertheless fluctuate in value: short-term government stocks are an example where such fluctuations are visible because there is a good market. Is indexation to be reduced (or increased) to the extent that such assets have risen or fallen in value by amounts that may have no. close relation to the changes in the prices of the physical assets? Are gold bullion, or overseas money balances, 'monetary assets'? In the *B* system these questions may affect the classifications in the profit and loss account, but do not affect the size of the profit balance. In the *G* system they can affect the amount of profit reported.

Banks and other financial institutions raise particular problems of principle for the *G* method because of the operational vagueness of the concept of the business 'entity'. What index is to be applied to the monetary items? The entity to be preserved cannot be seen as a collection of fixed assets and physical stocks. If we define the entity in terms of its money value we are driven back to historical cost or, if we wish to measure in units of constant value, to the *B* system. If we wish to define the 'entity' physically we can only do so in some such terms as the 'ability to continue to provide the same level of banking services', whatever that may mean. In practice therefore we have to revert to the use of a general price index, carefully avoiding the suggestion that we are using *B* concepts.

Another question arises where such fixed assets as government stocks are held, e.g. by financial institutions, as long-term investments. Are these to be regarded as part of the corporate entity, and an indexed adjustment applied? This is a particularly knotty question for those who support the *G* but not the *GG* system; if the company's borrowing is increased substantially and the funds made available are invested in securities, has the 'entity' changed? And if so, why should provision not be made for losses to the extent that the securities fail to keep up with the rate of inflation?

This is a special case of a type of problem which arises generally from the attempt to define and measure the profit of the entity as distinct from that earned for the shareholders. The definition of the entity not only runs into the difficulty that the same funds can finance a mix of assets that varies through time and hence is not even a physical constant; it also requires the separation of long-term debt finance from finance which is part of the working capital and therefore of the entity. In real life—and in theory—these things are not sharply separated, for one type of finance shades gradually into another, and business is not static. Is a bank overdraft a (negative) part of the

entity? Does a company that switches from finance from creditors to overdraft finance change the size of its entity?

I can see no answer to these problems within the framework of the *G* or *GG* system that does not involve the application of arbitrary rules (the consequences of which in all circumstances cannot be foreseen). The concept or concepts of capital maintenance which these procedures may be said to apply can, I think, only be stated in some such terms as, so far as operating (*G*) profit is concerned, 'maintenance of the average physical entity broadly defined, together with the finance needed to support this entity at its current level'. The profit after adjustment for the contribution of the long-term debt (the final *GG* profit) can then perhaps be stated as the surplus available for shareholders after allowing for maintenance of their interest in the same entity.

Conclusion

The *B* system is I suspect about as near an approximation as one could get to a practical measurement based on the Hicks model. Its major practical and theoretical defects (shared with the historical cost and the *G* systems) are firstly its inability to deal adequately with intangibles and with the problems that arise from aggregating the deprival values of complementary assets, and secondly its adherence to a conventional realisation test in recognising profit (which, however, is probably a practical necessity in view of the other defects, and certainly a legal one).

I find it more difficult to relate the *G* and *GG* systems to any precise economic model. However, I wonder whether it is necessary to do so. In the end no practical *ex post facto* measure of profit can be perfect or 'right' in an absolute sense as there is no obvious way of bringing all the intangibles into the accounting measurement. All accounting procedures are conventional and all have to be interpreted. It is perhaps enough that if there is good understanding of the methods used, conclusions—or at least conjectures leading to further enquiry or consideration—can be drawn in the knowledge of their limitations, and that judgement of the best method must be left to experience and empirical research. This, however, is a conclusion unlikely to satisfy those who wish to find the answer in a single specified and objectively verified set of general purpose rules of profit calculation.

References

[1] Accounting Standards Committee, *Accounting for changes in the purchasing power of money* (SSAP 7) (London, 1974).

[2] Accounting Standards Committee, *Current cost accounting* (ED 18) (London, 1976).

[3] Accounting Standards Committee, *Inflation accounting, an interim recommendation* .... (London, 1977).

[4] Baxter, W. T., *Accounting values and inflation* (London, 1975).

[5] Bonbright, J. C., *The valuation of property* (New York, 1937).

[6] Edey, H. C., 'The nature of profit', *Accounting and Business Research*, No. 1, Winter 1970, reprinted in Parker, R. H., *Readings in Accounting and Business Research 1970–1977* (London, 1978).

[7] Edey, H. C., 'The public company and the shareholders', in Institute of Economic Affairs, *Mergers, takeovers and the structure of industry* (London, 1973).

[8] Edey, H. C., 'Deprival value and financial accounting', in Edey, H. C. and Yamey, B. S., *Debits, credits, finance and profits* (London, 1974).

[9] Gynther, R. S., *Accounting for price-level changes: theory and procedures* (Oxford, 1966).

[10] Hicks, J. R., *Value and capital* (Oxford, 1946).

[11] *Inflation Accounting: Report of the Inflation Accounting Committee* (Sandilands Report), Cmnd. 6225 (London, 1975).

[12] Inflation Accounting Steering Group, *Background papers to the exposure draft on current cost accounting* (London, 1976).

The
Logic of
Financial Accounting

Harold C. Edey

PROFESSOR OF ACCOUNTING
LONDON SCHOOL OF ECONOMICS AND
POLITICAL SCIENCE

The Deloitte, Haskins and Sells Lecture
given on 28th February 1980
at University College, Cardiff

University College Cardiff Press

First published 1980 in Great Britain by University College Cardiff Press, P.O. Box 78, Cardiff, CF1 1XL, Wales.

ISBN 0 906449 21 9

Printed in Great Britain by University College Cardiff

By 1914 the foundations of historical cost accounting (HCA) had been largely established. As Professor Kitchen has recently pointed out,[1] leading accountants and teachers of accounting at that time could justify the use of historical cost figures in the balance sheet by assuming they were reasonable approximations to going-concern values. This assumption, stated or implied, was no doubt related to the experience of a period when the price level might fluctuate but was not subject to a persistent change in one direction.

By 1945, when the Cohen Report on Company Law Amendment[2] came out, the original justification had ceased to hold. There were two possibilities. The use of historical cost could be reviewed. Or it could be adhered to and the suggestion of a link with going-concern value (or as it can now be called, 'value to the business') abandoned. The second path was followed. The Cohen Report explicitly states that a balance sheet is an historical document and that reference to 'values' of assets is inappropriate.[3] So the substance was now firmly seen to be the recording of past expenditures or the residues of past expenditures. 'Amounts' was to be preferred to 'values' in referring to balance sheet items, though complete consistency in this respect has never been attained.

As the profit and loss account and the balance sheet were, and are, articulated by the double-entry system, and this articulation is maintained in the financial accounts, the decision to adhere to the historical cost basis in the balance sheet necessarily had implications for profit reporting.

The historical cost ideas had by now become so deeply embedded in the training of accountants that, for some, financial accounts based on the convention acquired the quality of factual truth.

It is not, I suspect, wholly a coincidence that the professional education of chartered accountants in England and Wales has, until quite recently, paid little attention to the simpler established doctrines of economics relating to demand, supply, value and price, which tell us, among other things, that we must think in terms of sacrificed values if we wish to assess costs in a way that is significant for management action. Economics, even as an optional subject, was dropped from the syllabus of the English and Welsh Institute after the 1920s and has only been restored to Foundation status in the official syllabus in the last decade. Omitting the basics of this subject from the education of accountants is, in my view, like leaving physics out of the curriculum for engineers. I think that its neglect has had serious effects on fundamental thought in the profession. It has long been recognised as a foundation discipline in university departments concerned with accounting. I must admit, however, that even there the concentration is sometimes on the less relevant aspects of the subject.

In the 1950s the procedures of financial accounting seemed well-established, buttressed by the legal requirements of the Companies Acts of 1947 and 1948. Some questioning about the solidity of the foundations was to be heard, but a glance through the professional literature of the time suggests that few doubts were held by the leaders of the profession.

But by the late 1960s unease was growing, fostered by a number of factors. Institutional investors and investment analysts were playing an increasing role as users of accounting information. The rate of inflation was growing. A rising tendency to divergence in the accounting treatment of similar transactions was noticeable. Voices were heard questioning the view that the annual financial statements of companies should be drawn up only or mainly for the benefit of shareholders and creditors.

II

Today, some ten years after the issue of accounting standards was initiated in the British Isles, there are insistent calls for the clarification of the objectives of financial reporting and for the specification of the conceptual framework by means of which the objectives are sought to be reached.

We can perhaps sum up the substance of these calls by saying that the production of accounts is only justified if they are useful; and being useful implies that they are intended to lead to potential action by someone. Few people other than accountants derive active pleasure from the mere contemplation of accounting documents. So the questions are: useful for what, for whom, and how?

We can distinguish between two kinds of action in this context. One is action directed to the achievement of some economic target, internal or external to the business; for example, a decision to invest or to censure management with the aim of improving the results. The other arises from some obligation imposed by public law or by

4

contract, which depends for its fulfilment upon the accounting information provided; for example, the settlement of a tax liability or of an amount due under a profit-sharing agreement. We can call accounting information of the first kind 'economics-oriented' and the second 'law-oriented'.

Where due thought has been given to the legislation, we might indeed expect many law-oriented decisions to call for accounting measurements or assessments that are equally appropriate to economic decisions. For example, an aim of the taxing authority may be to avoid upsetting what would otherwise be rational economic behaviour of the taxpayer. Similarly an authority responsible for some aspect of price control, or price-setting in a state industry, would be acting foolishly if the accounting regulations prescribed or used for the purpose led to the approval of prices adverse to the economic future of the enterprise and of the economy at large.

Other legal requirements may be intended to supplement or interfere with the market mechanism. In such cases the logic of the accounting measurement is imposed by the political aim of the legislature, and discussion about it falls into the field of discourse of national economic policy. There is then no problem of accounting theory, for the rules are given to the accountant by Parliament and the judiciary, and the resulting accounting statements are recognised as providing special-purpose data.

A problem for accountants does arise where an accounting measurement will be used both for legal purposes and for economic purposes, internal or external to the organisation. When legal rights and duties are themselves affected by accounting data there is seen to be a need for a high degree of certainty, and for as low a level of personal judgment and opinion as possible in the assessment of the relevant magnitudes. Here there is a real possibility of conflict between objectives. In the process of settling workable and acceptable accounting rules for the production of general purpose accounting reports, legal needs may impose constraints that make the results less than satisfactory for business needs.

Moreover, where the legislature is inclined to accept current standards set by the profession, accepted standards of accounting may react on legal requirements, especially in the longer run. Methods worked out to meet most commercial requirements are bound to involve an arbitrary element, based on some degree of compromise, so they are likely to disappoint some of those to whom they apply. Agreed accounting standards that are thought likely to affect a particular industry's tax position adversely will not be welcomed by companies in that industry. Such questions can seriously affect the search for workable and generally acceptable accounting procedures.

III

Having noted these matters, I now turn to the question of settling the logical framework of accounting reports that are intended to aid economic decisions, whether externally of shareholders and others, or internally of management.

We cannot expect to get the logic of an economic decision right unless we are clear in whose interest it is made. On the face of it, this might suggest that a single form of financial accounts is not likely to satisfy the needs, or assumed needs, of such varied groups as shareholders, employees, the Government, the public at large, and management.

The Sandilands Report[4] and the Corporate Report[5] took a broad view of the audience to be served. But both concluded that general purpose accounts, drawn up with the interests of investors particularly in mind, are likely also to serve the other interests named, given that additional information of interest to special groups can always be provided separately or as an adjunct to the main accounts.

The Financial Accounting Standards Board in the United States has expressed a similar view, while putting emphasis on the function of the financial statements in serving the smooth working of the capital market — that is, in providing information to guide the market in allocating investment funds in the economy.[6]

So all three reached the same practical conclusion about the central objective to be assumed so far as external reporting is concerned. How is this objective related to the needs of management?

If the management objectives are oriented — as presumably they should be — to the interests of those whom management serve, it is difficult to see why the information needs of either should differ in substance, though management needs may call for more detail. The future of the enterprise is dependent upon management's opinions,

6

intentions and decisions. When these are expressed in the accounting figures of assets, liabilities and provisions which the management record and use for their own guidance, the data are on the face of it likely to be of equal relevance to external users. It seems reasonable to assume that the thought patterns of shareholders, creditors, employees and others who are concerned with the economic future of the company, or at least those of their financial advisers, will, if informed and rational, tend to run on much the same lines as those of internal management.

The distinction which has grown up in recent years and is expressed in the use of the terms 'financial accounts' and 'management accounts' has its practical uses, but in some ways has misleading implications. So-called stewardship accounts have always had a management element. A medieval steward presenting accounts to his lord could be surcharged with shortfalls in the standard crop or stock yield.[7] Accounts of ancient Sumerian city temples — among the earliest written records — embodied standard allowances of thread for textile workers.[8]

I conclude that in looking for help in settling the best forms, assumptions and procedures for so-called financial accounting, the path to success is to consider *management* needs. One can then decide how far data and methods satisfying these require to be condensed for a wider range of users. This view is reinforced by the fact that for many companies the management and the shareholders are the same people, as well as by the *prima facie* absurdity of reporting the results of activities on bases that are substantially different from those used in directing the same activities. What, however, are the latter?

IV

The theory and practice of financial management suggest that the key figures for financial planning and control are those of the flow of cash receipts and payments and the various elements of which the flow is composed: the central financial tools are the cash forecasts short and long term, and the cash reports.

The financial history of a single-period business venture would, in general, be adequately summarised by an analysed statement of its cash receipts and payments for the period in question. For the normal business, however, the corresponding cash data have to cover a string of periods, running well into the future for planning, and reaching back into the past for control. The business cannot be run properly by considering only one year's cash flows. There are inter-temporal connections because investment in plant, equipment, development and so on produces services spread over a number of years, and because almost every action in one year interacts with, and affects, what is financially possible in others. This is commonplace, but needs to be said because a view is sometimes expressed, or implied, that the financial results of a business can be adequately summarised by reporting the current year's cash flows alone.

The key relevance of cash flows in the representation of the financial aspect of a business can be summed up by the following three expressions of functional relationships:

1. The potential of a business to develop positive cash surpluses in future (or limit its cash deficits) depends in part upon the assets it can acquire or create.
2. The assets it can acquire or create depend upon its ability to dispose of cash made available by owners or lenders.
3. The readiness of owners or lenders, or those acting for them, to provide cash to the business, or to allow it to retain cash it could distribute, depends upon the positive cash surpluses the business is expected to generate in future (or, where subsidy is contemplated, on its ability to limit to specified amounts its needs for future cash injections).

These three statements link together the different kinds of cash flow of the business and express in summary form the financial conditions of successful operation. In the longer run these conditions cannot be broken without economic disaster.

In stating these relationships, no difficult or obscure point of accounting jargon was needed. The financial magnitudes were all amounts of cash — of spendable money. There was no need to mention 'profit' — a word with many meanings — or to speak of balance sheet values or amounts. The conditions need little explanation to the layman. Everyone knows what cash is.

I do not, of course, imply that other aspects of the business — equipment, personnel, technology — do not matter. Far from it. The flow of finance is linked with these and interacts with them, reflecting the economic constraints under which any enterprise must

8

operate. It is precisely from this interaction that accounting derives its importance.

V

If the central financial management of the business is based on the planning and control of cash receipts and payments, what is the role of profit?

'Profit' in the economic sense — for example, as a factor motivating management — is the return on investment that is implicit in the relation of the stream of cash receipts to the stream of cash outlays. It is a characteristic of this economic return that its assessment, while the business continues, always involves taking a view of the future.

If, for some reason, we wish to note how well the business has done in a given calendar year, we compare its position as we saw it on January 1 with its position as we see it on the following December 31. In making these assessments of financial position it is not sufficient just to take into account the actual cash flows of the year. We have to consider also the future flows. So if, for example, we wish to compare the budgeted results of the year with the outcome at the end of the year we have to compare the stream of expected flows for the whole future, as forecast at the beginning of the year, with the actual flows for the year *plus* the flows expected thereafter, as re-estimated at the end of the year. The financial legacy passed on at the end of each year to the next year is a crucial element in the judgment of the year just ending, as anyone experienced in business valuation well knows. Cash surpluses created this year can mask deficiencies in later years.

So in principle we cannot derive a figure of profit in an economic sense for any given period until we have made our strategic decisions for the succession of later periods. We then use, in the process of the profit calculation, the financial forecasts implied by those decisions. There is no circular reasoning here. What the approach tells us is that an economic measure of profit — that is, one that has relevance to behaviour in the use of resources — must in principle embrace the financial future of the business as expressed by expected future cash flows. Only then is the present state of the business taken fully into account.

9

As the Sandilands Committee noted,[9] such a procedure is not a practical basis for preparation of financial accounts as we now know them. So far as management is concerned this does not matter. For a management which considers it can run the business successfully on a cash-flow planning and reporting basis, a calculation of economic profit in the sense just described, if it is required at all is merely a by-product, the figures for which emerge *after* the decisions are made and the resultant cash flows estimated.

There is, I think, no reason in principle (excluding for the moment the impact of legal requirements and the needs of parties external to the company) why a business cannot be successfully run without a profit and loss account and a balance sheet ever being prepared. We know from historical studies that businessmen in earlier centuries might not trouble to balance their books for years, unless perhaps a new ledger was to be opened.[10] If they wrote up a profit and loss account it might be merely a means of disposing of unwanted balances cluttering up the ledger. Business is often more complex now. But with present-day computing facilities I see no insuperable difficulty in using rolling cash forecasts or budgets, with corresponding cash reports, as the central accounting control. Indeed, such systems must exist, though no doubt in parallel with, or as adjuncts to, more traditional reporting systems.

The present-day data-collection system is not affected. The recording and classification of cash, debtors, creditors, stocks, fixed assets, and so on through the double-entry system, with the accompanying internal control, remains essential. The systematic monitoring of sales achievements, current overhead expenditure, liquidity ratios and the like remain necessary. Such records and analyses continue to provide data for the day-to-day running of the business, and are essential supports to the building-up of the cash flow forecasts and to the control of these.

But when the planning and control is centred on the short and longer term cash flows, we can in principle forget such matters as capital-revenue allocations, depreciation calculations, capitalisation or non-capitalisation of development expenditure, whether stock should be valued on FIFO or LIFO, how overseas currency transactions are to be translated and the like. In short, a large number of the questions that now raise controversy and require arbitrary compromise solutions simply disappear together with the traditional profit report. With these disappear also many of the issues of accounting for inflation.

The logic of the cash-flow approach to accounting is on the face of it very attractive. This has led me to reconsider the case for our present form of annual accrual accounting, whether this is based on historical or current cost, or some other convention.[11]

VI

Whatever may be possible in principle, few managements would, I suspect, wish to abandon completely the present form of financial statement, including the profit report, even for internal management purposes, and quite apart from such external objectives as giving information to the stock market and satisfying obligations imposed by company and revenue law. One obvious reason is that few people in business are yet ready for such a major change. One does not lightly abandon tried and trusted methods for new ones, and certainly not before very full consideration has been given to what might be lost. Even a management that was convinced of the usefulness of a switch to pure cash-flow accounting for management purposes would have to take account of the degree of understanding and conviction of its own staff — or, for that matter, of its Chairman.

It may seem at first that we are forced into our present system of discrete annual reporting, using accrual accounts, by the management need to think for many purposes in terms of annual periods. Production plans, sales campaigns, price fixing, and many other matters are subject to the annual cycle, and the financial data that relate to them need to be formulated on the same pattern. However, these matters can be accommodated within a system where the accounting budgets and reports are in the form of a series of annual cash statements covering a range of years. One can picture the financial planning process as the study of a set of such budgets stretching over a number of years into the future. For each decision relating to a given year, one then needs to identify the expected effect on the receipts and payments of that and of each other year. This is exactly what has to be done in those situations where multi-period mathematical programming is to be used. The cash-flow approach will necessarily then be followed: a fact which suggests that a similar accounting approach is not likely to be wrong for the

11

cruder trial and error methods that most businesses have to use in arriving at what they judge to be their optimal plan of action.

It is a major merit of the cash-flow method that it focusses attention on inter-period reactions. We have not yet perfected techniques for this kind of exercise, but in the longer run, as experience is gained, these will no doubt be developed and will find their way into the general body of accounting knowledge.

A greater problem is the effect of uncertainty. It is one thing to formulate the strategic plans of the business as estimated and partly conjectural forecasts of cash flows, expressing the financial logic of present-day decisions, and based of necessity on assumptions, hopes, fears, and assessments of probabilities. It may be quite another thing to accept the numerical quantities written into such a plan as a firm base for the annual financial control of the concern. Even one year ahead the future is dim. In planning for five years there is likely to be a major element of hope, coupled with sensitivity to developments that may invalidate existing assumptions. Further ahead it is hazier still, even though the business may be committed to investments that will only recover their cost, if at all, over a substantially longer period.

It is easy to understand that a management may prefer, for day-to-day purposes, to substitute a set of balance sheet figures for the numbers that, if known with certainty, would be the future cash flows of the business after the end of the current year. These balance sheet figures can then be described as 'unrecovered costs' expected to be eventually recovered, and as liabilities and provisions that will need to be met out of the recoveries. An economist might prefer to regard to such figures as conservative, rule-of-thumb proxies for the present values of future cash contributions and outgoings.

By, as it were, collapsing the whole cash future of the business into a set of balance sheet figures at a given date, we can specify with arithmetical precision the costs we need to identify with *this* year's operations. We thus put to the back of our mind the complications that arise from the inter-relations of this year's doings with future costs and revenues. Seen in this light, depreciation estimates and other capital-revenue distinctions from which balance sheet figures emerge are by-products of the long-term forecasts — that is, they are expressions of targets to be reached in the current year on certain assumptions about minimum achievements in future. The depreciation provision this year on a particular piece of equipment assumes that the asset concerned will in later periods contribute an amount at least equal to the end-year balance of the asset. It is true that our accounting procedures often make it appear that it is the balance sheet figures that are the residue; but the economic logic is, I think, the other way round. It is the economic logic that should guide us in our thinking.

So if uncertainty is too great for us to express the future potential of our existing business assets in the precise form of future cash flows, we fall back on conventional procedures for expressing this potential in balance sheet form. In doing this, however, we still need to keep an eye on the basic purpose of the operation, remembering that in the end it is the long-run out-turn of the cash flow that matters. So we should try to design our accrual accounts accordingly, bearing in mind that, under the accrual concept, what we put into the balance sheet affects what our profit report tells us, and therefore what both tell us about the relation of return to resources invested.

We must be clear about this if we are not to mislead ourselves and others. The use of accounting statements that purport to deal with a single year's results do not remove the difficulties and uncertainties of cash-flow forecasting. And the latter is an essential element in running the business and, ideally, in assessing its current economic state. Accrual accounting merely covers up these difficulties and uncertainties with a façade of apparent precision and arithmetical accuracy. This at present misleads many members of the lay public, and even some accountants, into a belief in its factual accuracy in some fundamental economic sense or, worse, in the possibility of an accuracy which is not achieved because of the incompetence of accountants. Factual accuracy in economic matters that involve the future is a meaningless conception.

VII

We can, I think, assume that most managements will want, for their own purposes, accounts which are consistent with, though no doubt in substantially more detail than, the legal financial accounts. Probably most managements will wish to use those accounts and corresponding budgets for budgetary planning and control. Those who regard cash flow budgets and statements as their central tools of financial control will still wish to relate these to the financial accounts which will be published and on which stock market and other public reactions will be based.

This reinforces the view that the basic accounting procedures should be the same for both financial and management accounts, and that those which best serve management are likely best to serve external users too. Good management accounting practice should be a guide in settling financial accounting standards.

This brings me to current cost accounting (CCA) as now proposed, and its relation to some of the ideas that I have been discussing.[12]

Evidently CCA is not perfect. It will have to stand the test of experience and in the process will no doubt be changed. Nevertheless, for the reasons I will give, I think it is a major step in the right direction. In particular, its acceptance will recognise the final abandonment of the implicit assumption, appropriate perhaps to 19th century accounting, of a reasonably stable price level. CCA is not inflation accounting in the sense of using, as current purchasing power accounting (CPP)[13] does in effect, a specified bundle of consumers' goods and services as the unit of account, and translating historical figures so expressed into pounds that will currently buy that bundle: CCA takes the more radical step of accounting in terms of current values and costs, cutting completely the link with original cost, and replacing it by the basic idea of replacement cost.

The replacement cost of a resource is an indicator of the economic cost of using that resource, to a business or to the community, where economic cost has its fundamental meaning of the sacrifice from loss of alternative uses. Certainly it is likely to be a much better indicator than some bygone historical amount, even when the latter is adjusted for a general price index change, as under CPP. Note however that the ideal figure in this context is not the replacement cost of an identical asset in the same condition but rather that of an asset capable of providing the same economic service, measured in current pounds — that is, of providing the same contribution as the asset whose current value to the business is being assessed.

The present CCA proposals for assessing the current cost of sales and depreciation probably go as near to this ideal as is possible at present in a workable system. The degree of roughness and approximation which will be unavoidable in the calculations can be attributed on the whole to the imprecision inherent in all economic

14

measurement and hence to the nature of the world rather than, as can be said of historical cost accounting, to bad economic logic.

This is of major importance in the public as in the private sector. If in our accounting we fail to show the amounts currently needed to replace the resources being consumed, for example of natural gas or oil, we are encouraging the dissipation of the nation's standard of life.

The current public controversy about gas and electricity pricing, in which it is being suggested that the corporations concerned are using replacement costs in order to conceal 'true' profits and justify higher prices, shows the importance of putting financial accounts generally on to a satisfactory basis, consistent with the economic logic of the operations whose financial effect they report. This is a good example of the way in which accounts not ostensibly designed for the management can create pressure on the management by the media, politicians, and others external to the undertaking who do not understand the basic problems.

It needs to be said that the estimates and assumptions that a business uses in order to calculate its CCA data for depreciation and cost of sales — the commercial lives of assets, their direct or indirect contribution to cash flow, their current and future realisable values — are precisely those which are in any case needed for proper management decisions with respect to acquisition, retention and use of the assets in question, and which enter into the process of estimating the future cash flows of the enterprise.

A management which says it cannot make these calculations, even on an approximate basis, may be coming close to saying that it cannot run its business effectively. It is true that assessments of relevant current values often, of necessity, span a wide range, and may be of the nature of 'not less than' or 'not more than', rather than 'equal to'. They will usually be matters of opinion and judgment since they involve looking into the future. This is the nature of business. The roughness and lack of precision may be a nuisance for auditors, and may puzzle or annoy some politicians and journalists who prefer sharp shadows to fuzzy realities. As accountants we have to accept the world as it is. Part of our job is to explain it to the public at large.

The essence of the CCA proposals is to classify those changes in accounting values which are due to price movements separately from those due to operations, leaving operating profit as the excess

15

of revenues over the current replacement costs of the economic resources consumed. Insofar as rises in prices are due to inflation, this has the effect of removing what may be called 'illusory profits' from the profit and loss account. Unfortunately the method removes more (or sometimes less). Unlike CPP it contains (as yet) no apparatus for distinguishing the result of general inflation from relative changes in prices. So the results of successful dealing in commodities, perhaps owing nothing to inflation *per se*, may be removed from the profit report. This need not upset management reporting, as internal accounts can be organised to make the distinction. But the distinction will often be so much a matter of opinion and judgment that the treatment in published accounts designed to leave such dealing profits in the profit and loss account may raise auditing difficulties with respect to consistency of treatment. Experience will be needed in dealing with this problem. My own view is that, for the time being, it will need to be dealt with by a full and careful explanation of whatever treatment is adopted.

The method of CCA now proposed, as distinct from that recommended by the Sandilands Committee, includes so-called monetary adjustments: the monetary working capital adjustment (MWCA) and the gearing adjustment.

The MWCA is intended to measure the amount of net additional finance needed for monetary working capital as the result of price changes, e.g. where debtors exceed creditors; or the amount of net finance made available for monetary working capital through the increase in short-term credit from the same reason, e.g. where creditors exceed debtors. In both cases the effect of volume increases in activity is excluded. The net result is credited or debited, as the case requires, in the calculation of operating profit.

This seems likely to be useful in that it brings directly to notice the effect of price changes on the financing of operations. This may be particularly important for less sophisticated managements that do not go in for systematic cash budgetary control. Perhaps it will bring home more sharply the importance of the latter. I am bound to add that from the point of view of economic profit measurement the adjustment is a somewhat uneasy compromise. The economic cost of increased finance is not the amount of the finance, but the cost of the additional capital, in loan or equity form, needed to service the finance. The MWCA can be regarded as a surrogate for this.

It can be argued with some strength that, where the business is partly financed by borrowing, the absence of a 'gearing adjustment' would lead to an underestimate of the current economic return to shareholders, though the precise quantification of this is impossible. If future sales revenues rise as the replacement cost of the fixed assets and stocks rises, as it is reasonable to suppose will tend to happen, and if full provision is made in the accounts, as CCA requires, for the replacement of the fixed assets and stocks consumed, then, unless allowance is made for any gearing effect, a full distribution of the reported current cost profit will (where prices have risen) tend to reduce the gearing ratio year by year, i.e. the costs reported will include an element of provision for debt repayment. This arises because borrowing, which partially finances the assets concerned, is fixed in monetary terms. The gearing adjustment takes the form of an abatement of the CCA adjustments for additional depreciation, cost of sales and the MWCA, reducing these in the proportion that borrowing bears to the total long-term finance. The formula for this adjustment has been inevitably a matter of compromise, and no doubt discussion will continue.

There are clearly circumstances where a gearing adjustment is not relevant, as where the loan capital is provided by a 100 per cent parent company and is in essence equity capital. The capital structure of the nationalised industries is in large degree the result of political accident and bears no clear relation to market forces. Their debt capital is either legally guaranteed by the Government or carries by its nature a *de facto* implication that there will be no default. In their case the economic test of success is better judged by relating their operating profit before interest to a financial target which reflects an economic return on the total investment.

It can be claimed for CCA that its balance sheet figures contain a much better representation of the reality — a better financial representation of the potential future of the business — than historical cost figures. This is the opposite face of the better representation of economic costs in the profit and loss account. Return on invested resources is likely to be at least a less unreliable indicator of achievement when calculated with CCA figures than in those of HCA.

Absolute economic reality cannot be achieved. In some degree economic reality is always in the eye of the beholder — or of the appraiser. While broad or even close agreement may be possible on

17

many items, the replacement cost of the resources represented by some intangibles and specialised tangible assets, and such assets as mineral deposits, are subject to great uncertainty.

On such matters the accounting profession will have to decide whether a high degree of judgment aiming at economic realism, with supplementary explanation where necessary, is to be preferred to an approach by formula which will produce a standard answer with less practical relevance.

One must not ask too much too quickly. The best is the enemy of the better. If the economic logic of CCA is better than that of HCA, the CCA figures will be of more use to management than those of HCA, and therefore also to other users.

REFERENCES

[1] J. Kitchen, 'Fixed asset values and depreciation: ideas on depreciation 1892–1914', *Accounting and Business Research*, No. 36, Autumn 1979.

[2] Cmnd.6659, 1945.

[3] Paras. 98 and 99. The reference is to fixed assets, but the context makes it clear that the Committee did not recommend the revaluation of current assets except where realisable value had fallen below cost.

[4] Report of the Inflation Accounting Committee. Cmnd.6225, 1975.

[5] The Corporate Report, Accounting Standards Steering Committee, London 1975.

[6] *Statement of Financial Accounting Concepts No. 1*, Financial Accounting Standards Board, Stamford, Connecticut, 1978.

[7] See for example J.S. Drew, 'Manorial accounts of St. Swithun's Priory, Winchester', *English Historical Review*, LXII, 1947.

[8] See Sir Leonard Woolley, *Excavations at Ur*, Benn, London, 1955.

[9] Paragraph 103.

[10] See B.S. Yamey, 'The development of company accounting conventions', *The Three Banks Review*, September 1960, reprinted in B.S. Yamey, *Essays on the History of Accounting*, Arno Press, New York, 1978.

[11] The idea of cash-flow accounting is not new. I owe my own introduction to it to my former colleague, the late Sir Ronald Edwards. It is implicit in his series of seminal articles, 'The nature and measurement of income' first published in *The Accountant* of 1938. They are reprinted in shortened form in W.T. Baxter and S. Davidson (Eds.), *Studies in Accounting*, Institute of Chartered Accountants in England and Wales, London, 1977.

[12] See *Statement of Standard Accounting Practice 16* Accounting Standards Committee, London, 1980.

[13] See *Statement of Standard Accounting Practice 7*, Accounting Standards Committee, London, 1974.